Jacquieline Davis is one of the few females in the male-dominated world of close protection, surveillance, commercial espionage and security (the 'Circuit'). Specialising in counter-industrial espionage, close protection (body-guarding) and latterly hostage rescue, she has travelled widely, working and living in Holland, Germany and the USA.

As well as writing for trade magazines on the role of women in the security industry, Jacquieline Davis devised her course 'Anti-Rape' and then conducted lectures and workshops on the subject around the UK. Her hobbies include shooting and scuba diving. She lives in Berkshire.

The Circuit

Jacquieline Davis

PENGUIN BOOKS

PENGUIN BOOKS

Published by the Penguin Group
Penguin Books Ltd, 27 Wrights Lane, London w8 5tz, England
Penguin Putnam Inc., 375 Hudson Street, New York, New York 10014, USA
Penguin Books Australia Ltd, Ringwood, Victoria, Australia
Penguin Books Canada Ltd, 10 Alcorn Avenue, Toronto, Ontario, Canada m4v 3b2
Penguin Books (NZ) Ltd, 182–190 Wairau Road, Auckland 10, New Zealand

Penguin Books Ltd, Registered Offices: Harmondsworth, Middlesex, England

First published 1998
1 3 5 7 9 10 8 6 4 2

Set in 10/13½pt Monotype Minion
Typeset by Rowland Phototypesetting Ltd,
Bury St Edmunds, Suffolk
Printed in England by Clays Ltd, St Ives plc

It has been necessary to change the names of some of the people mentioned in this
book in order to protect their identities.

For Sarah, who gave her life for her children

Acknowledgements

I would like to thank Liz Halsall and Hannah Renier for making this all happen, my agent Christopher Little for his advice and help, Steve and Chellie Burns for believing in me and Peter for all his support.

1

I was nineteen, all shiny and new with glossy hair neatly cut and my uniform pressed by my mum, and I was talking to the sergeant in the police canteen when the chair opposite me scraped away from the table and a man with a leather jacket and a smirk sat down. He spoke across me to the sarge as if I wasn't there.

'All right, mate?'

'All right.'

The sergeant went on munching his beans and chips. I was eating spaghetti bolognese, the finest that the canteen ladies could produce. I glared at this bloke, finished what I had been saying and went on eating it. He leaned back in his chair with his thumbs in his jeans pockets and stared. He really fancied himself. God, I hate that. The long slow burn, and me with a mouthful of spaghetti.

Mr Wonderful said, 'That looks nice.'

'It's OK.'

'Who are you, then?'

'Who are you?' I retorted.

He didn't answer. He got half out of his chair and reached over to the steel cans where the clean forks were and took one. He sat down again, hunched over the table, and picked with his fork at my food. Then he started talking to the sergeant.

'You want my dinner?' I said.

I gave it a shove that sent it spinning. 'You can have it.'

It landed splat on his lap as I got up and left.

He was cursing and people were turning round and sniggering, as they well might, because he had a steaming pile of pasta in his crotch.

'Jacquie!'

The uniformed sergeant caught up with me down the corridor.

'You know that's the new DS, don't you? You'd better go back and apologize.'

'Apologize nothing,' I said. 'He can apologize to me. Big-mouthed creep, he is.'

I had always had attitude. I probably got it from my dad, who was a charge nurse at a vast red-brick crenellated Victorian institution for the mentally ill called Friern Barnet. For years he was in charge of a closed ward which held the overflow from Broadmoor, a hospital for the criminally insane. Dad had learned defensive living. You react first and ponder the ethics later. Having picked that up, I should have done well in the police. I was quick-minded, fit, assertive, and stood no messing.

It was 1977, and I was going to be the first woman police commissioner. Not that my ambition knew no bounds; I prided myself on being realistic. I'd set my sights on chief superintendent first. At that time, no woman had ever been a chief super.

I had been born and brought up in Barnet, within a few miles of Hendon Police College. I had done all the right things and, in theory, give or take a plate of spaghetti tipped over a detective sergeant, there was nothing to stop me climbing the ladder the way it said in the recruitment literature.

But after eighteen months in the job I was beginning to suspect that there was a lot more to this than they told you at Police College. First there was the whole issue of who you had to know to be noticed. You needed to be in a squad – Flying Squad, Serious Crime Squad, Drug Squad, C11 (which dealt with active criminal networks). There were others, too. And I was just dimly aware of MI5 and MI6, Special Branch and the Special Patrol Group.

None of them operated out of Barnet nick.

The other thing was that, as a woman, for most of the officers who could get you promoted you ranked somewhere between wimpy kid at the back of the class and sex symbol. This major disadvantage had not yet struck me as forcibly as it should have.

I was on duty in Barnet High Street at two in the morning. This meant strolling along past the greengrocer's and the off licence, downhill past the magistrates' court, and walking round the bend in the road where it swooped down off the high ridge that Barnet stood on and rolled, thick with traffic, eleven miles to Charing Cross. London came up this far, crowded, baying and needy. Behind me was Hertfordshire, detached houses set in woods interspersed with riding schools. Here at the top of the hill stood Barnet, neat, three-storey and red-brick, upright as a banner, advertising a way of life for the common herd down there in the Smoke to aspire to.

We were all Conservatives, in Barnet. We did not have a problem with crime. What we had was a 'criminal element'.

This consisted of a couple of dim, violent and persistently offending families on what we called the Alcatraz Estate, and the diddicoys – tinkers who came every year to the Horse Fair and stole ponies from the riding schools. If it rained on a fair day, dye matted the coats of the horses for sale and came off on your hands.

So the high street was looking as sedately pleased with itself as usual, on this particular morning, when the station called over my radio to tell me CID wanted a word. I was pretty sure it wasn't about crime. Fidgeting from foot to foot in the cold I scanned my recent past for some gaffe and could think of only one.

An unmarked car rolled up. A GPV: general purpose vehicle. The detective sergeant told me to get in, so I left the high street unattended and we drove about a bit, talking. When we had exhausted the topic of crime in Barnet, it got more personal.

Then we parked up, so that the DS could enlighten me as to the full potential of a GPV.

His name was Steve, he was thirty and divorced and living in a section house near his old posting on the other side of London. He was an attentive boyfriend. I mean, he was interested in spending time with me personally, not socializing with me and a bunch of other officers. Until now I had spent a lot of my free time at the Police Club out at Bushey, but once I met Steve I never went there. He always wanted to be alone with me, or if not alone then round my mum's.

My mum's house was already known as the sub-station, because we all used to drop in for cups of tea when we were on duty, and my mum and dad thought the world of Steve.

He was respectful, never swaggered or seemed less than a dutiful copper when he was around them, and was obviously devoted to me. I had just broken off an engagement to a rich young man who cringed when I told his friends I was in the police force. Now along came Steve, who was friendly, understood the work I did, and was obviously in love with me. My parents were much relieved.

We went out together for months. There was an exciting unpredictability to the affair because of the job we were both doing. We were on different shifts, and if you arrest somebody just before you go off shift you have to stay late, so there was no knowing when we would finish. And in his case, because he was a detective, he never even knew what part of London he might be in; he might have to cancel a date at the last minute or he might suddenly find himself free to take me somewhere interesting. It all added spice and I was happy. Also, he was giving me ideas about getting into the CID and making my way towards promotion.

One day I climbed the stairs to his office to see him and we talked for a while before he went to the washroom. I hoisted myself idly on to his desk and peered down through the window at a police van manoeuvring its way into the yard below. The phone rang.

'Hello. DS Adams' phone.'

'Is DS Adams there?' a woman asked.

'Sorry, he's away from his desk at the moment. Can I take a message?'

'Yeah. Could you ask him to get a brown loaf and two pints of milk on the way home, please?'

There was a pause.

'Fine.' I said. 'Who shall I say rang?'

'His wife,' she said.

He came back into the office a minute later. A rapid economical slide around the desk and into his chair, smiling up at me.

'Your wife rang,' I said, and hit him accurately and hard with the fire extinguisher.

I had wanted to move on anyway. All I had needed was a really good reason to ask for a transfer. Now I had one.

They sent me to Peckham. To say that I was unprepared would be an understatement. I had done police work in the north London suburbs and this was South London, Inner.

There are a lot of ways to explain what this means but they are all too complicated. The short cut is to say that when you stopped a driver in Barnet you said, 'Excuse me, sir, would you mind stepping out of your Mercedes/Jaguar/Rover?' In Peckham you dragged him out of his Mark II Cortina and threw him across the bonnet before he stabbed you.

The visible difference was skin colour. I had literally never seen so many black people. Barnet was white. Not white with Ugandan Asian newsagents and a Chinese chip shop, but white as in Pony Club and Garden Centre. White. In fact my mum was a racist, bigoted in the way only people who don't know what they are talking about can be. I was not racially prejudiced, at least not then. After I had had knives pulled on me a few times in Peckham, I adopted some of the well-known police attitudes with a sense of grim revenge, but when I went there, I had an open mind about who might be responsible for crime. Down there the police themselves seemed prime candidates for the kind of criminal profile I'd come to recognize in Barnet. They were all white with hair cut to a meaningfully short clip and they all taw'lie'tha', nowarramean? This was sarf Lunnun, aw'ri?

They were all right, as it happened. Somebody must have told them I was interested in detective work, because within weeks of arrival I was put on to the shoplifting squad.

Peckham is a huge huddle of Edwardian streets and Sixties council houses strung along a mile or so of the main road to Dover out of the West End. To the west it bumbles into Camberwell, which is the same only smarter, and to the east it shades into Lewisham and New Cross, which are the same only duller. If you live in Blackheath or Greenwich, Peckham is where the daily woman lives. It is a cheap place to live and shop because it hasn't got a tube station and the main street is constantly clogged with traffic.

It was my job to go out every morning and circulate in the mill of people going to work, returning from work, buying and selling. Pickpockets operated mainly at the more crowded bus stops and gangs of kids nicked stuff out of the Asian shops. Steaming was in fashion at the time: three or four louts would swarm through a shop in a posse, taking exactly what they wanted, and get out while the staff wobbled with terror. Thieving housewives, and professionals, generally stole from the bigger stores.

I found I was good at this work. There were generally four of us in plain clothes out on the street at once, linked by radio. I learned how to spot a gang of pickpockets at a bus stop. If you watched for half an hour, the dippers were the ones who queued and then when the bus left were still there. They never got on a bus. Number one would nick a purse and pass it to number two, who would pass it to number

7

three, who would then nip round the corner, take out the cards and money and dump the purse. If number one was grabbed by an indignant victim, he would be empty-handed. It was the late seventies, before the credit card boom. A lot of people in Peckham and places like it didn't even have bank accounts. They kept cash in bulging purses. So when a bag got dipped it meant rich pickings for one set of poor people and misery and the Christmas Club money gone for another.

I also caught a lot of shoplifters. You look at the eyes first. When they walk into the store the eyes are everywhere. There were no security cameras in those days and even the clothes shops didn't tag their garments, so all the thieves had to look out for were floorwalkers, strategically arranged mirrors and casual nosey parkers. As soon as you saw those busy eyes you knew you were on to one. You stopped looking at the eyes then and watched the hands. The hands of a shoplifter seem to have a life of their own. While the thief is watching a huddle of gossiping sales girls, her hands are busy sliding something expensive into an inner pocket or bag.

I loved the work, but it didn't give me a lot of overtime. It was a regular nine to five job, unless you got a body shortly before five, in which case statements and other paperwork kept you at the station until ten. I was supposed to be living in a station house in Peckham, but I didn't. I stayed at home in Barnet and drove down every day. The petrol was expensive, so was car repair, and police pay was crap. (Also, thanks to my parents, I had learned to like travelling abroad; now I couldn't even afford a decent holiday.) We all complained about it. There were articles in *The Job* about low morale in the force and people muttered about getting a rise after the General Election. But it would be at least six months before the election, nobody knew for sure that the Conservatives would get in, and I was impatient.

Somebody at the station knew a sergeant at another south London nick who recruited bodyguards. Not minders, all brawn and no brain, but trained men, ex-SAS or moonlighting police. He had happened to mention that one of the security companies was interested in hiring a woman for a special assignment. I rang this sergeant, was interviewed by a couple of men who ran Special Operations out of the fourth floor of the company's office block somewhere on the South Circular, and was taken on. I would work for them whenever I was free – vacations, evenings and weekends. Moonlighting was a sackable offence, but I needed the money and this promised to be a whole lot more interesting than driving a minicab.

I took fifteen days' annual leave and began work on a Monday morning. I didn't know it at the time, but I was one of very few women who had ever worked on the Circuit.

2

The lift carried me to the top floor of the Intercontinental hotel, where its doors slid open to reveal a tall man in a suit. I was expected.

'Morning,' he said. 'Down there, door on your left at the end.'

The Gulf royals occupied an entire floor. Their suite was quiet, the carpets thick, all the doors shut. I heard a television somewhere, a childish shout from inside a room, and a dim ambient hum. Luxury has a warm smell and a gentle soporific buzz.

In the security office, converted from a bedroom, with a desk, phones and a big fridge, a grey-haired man ran through the brief as if he'd said it all before. The royal family came from one of the Gulf states and had taken up residence along Park Lane for the next three or four months. The Sheikh was living in the Dorchester and each of his three wives in another hotel. Here at the Intercontinental, at Hyde Park Corner, eight of us were guarding the Sheikha (the number one wife) and her four children, daughters aged ten, eight and seven, and a son of five. I would be her personal bodyguard. The only son was of course heir to the throne, so at five years old he also merited round-the-clock protection from a personal guard. Kidnapping was the main threat.

'You will be invisible until required,' concluded the grey

man drily. 'In other words, don't speak unless you're spoken to.'

It was going to be a claustrophobic couple of weeks, I thought, as I sat outside the royal suite that first morning staring at one of the Intercontinental's immaculate walls. You were a flunkey on call and, short of any threat, you were expected to hang about in a kind of watchful coma unless told to do something by one of the royal family. As far as they were concerned, we were like the wooden figures on a Swiss clock, who exist only when visible and have no life when they are out of sight.

In each of the hotels the entourage occupied an entire floor. I wanted to know who everyone was, so one of the bodyguards came and stood by my chair keeping up a rapid-fire commentary out of the side of his mouth as short women swathed in yards of cloth scuttled past.

'– servant. Another servant –'

People emerged from the lift.

'That's the boy's tutor. Turns up every morning, poor bugger.'

And half an hour later, 'Hairdresser. Comes Mondays and Thursdays.'

Hours passed; chambermaids hoovered and left; room service trudged past with laden trolleys; berobed women flitted in and out of the suites; some Arab women visited with a small boy. Two little girls appeared. My companion had mooched off somewhere and one of the girls was frowning at me, so I nodded and murmured, Good morning.

'Good morning.'

They might be the princesses, and if so I should know them.

'Are you sisters?' I ventured.

One girl scowled and raised her hand. Without warning, she smacked her companion hard around the head.

'I am Princess,' she announced.

They walked on together, the second child with her eyes firmly fixed on the carpet.

Besides the bodyguard team the Sheikha was served by ten or twelve women and girls from some of the poorest countries in the world. These Eritreans, Filipinas, Sudanese and Tamils were personal nannies to the children, maids to the Sheikha and general gofers. They never left the building except as part of the royal entourage.

Neither did we. Some of the team were perfectly happy with the arrangement, especially those whose day jobs were based at West End Central, because they could have been spotted by senior officers at any time. We were all a bit cagey about being Job, but coming from Peckham I felt there was no chance of being seen up here. In any case, all risk was outweighed by the relief of a change of scene. By the end of a morning in the corridor I would have done anything to get out of the hotel. In fact I did. Placing myself between the Sheikha and an assassin's bullet, should the occasion arise, was the non-negotiable aspect of the job.

When the Sheikha's door opened on that first morning and she emerged, in full going-to-Harrods *shabbah*, to see me standing opposite, her eyes widened above the yashmak. She stopped in shock on the threshold. The women behind her, clustered like crows, fell silent. I could see nobody had told her a woman would be guarding her.

'Good morning, Your Highness,' I said quietly.

She nodded and swept onwards as I took up my position behind her. That was the worst part over with.

Some deferential person always asked the Sheikha what her plans were for the day, so in theory we knew when we would have to move. In practice we didn't because she changed her mind. The cars might be wanted an hour before or after the time she had said, so we always had to be fired up and ready to go. Usually we left the building at about twelve to go shopping somewhere expensive like Knightsbridge or Bond Street. Our convoy of three limousines linked by radio consisted of a SAP (security advance party) team of four men in the first car, the Sheikha's limousine and a back-up vehicle. The Sheikha's limo contained whichever nannies, servants and children were going out that day, plus the lady herself, me and a driver in front.

The other wives travelled the same way, and all the bodyguard teams kept in touch by radio. The Sheikha used to listen idly to discover where the other wives planned to go, and if number two wife was on her way to Selfridge's or Harvey Nichols we would suddenly find that our Sheikha had changed her mind and wanted to go there instead. Since she took priority, number two wife would have to eat dust and make do with Debenhams. I got the impression that this game was the most fun our Sheikha had had in years.

I soon got used to the routine. When we swept up to the front of the shop, three of the SAP team were already out on the pavement. The back-up team came to a halt behind us, I got out and one of the SAP team opened the limo door to let the Sheikha step out. I strode quickly with her and her entourage into the store. With two guards behind us and two ahead, we clove a path through the tourists and headed like an Exocet for the Designer Room, hoping that nothing would catch her eye on the way. Not that anything much could; we moved as fast as possible and since most of her body including her head was swathed in black cotton there was little opportunity to swivel and dither.

I loved all this. It was glamorous, there was no doubt of that, arriving with an exotic image of mysteriously acquired wealth at shops like Harrods and Liberty's when police pay in those days barely got you past the door of Kwiksave; but there was also a heightened sense of awareness. You were with people so rich and so politically sensitive that there was a genuine risk of an attempted kidnap. I got an adrenalin rush from these shopping trips. They were a lot more fun than having eggs thrown at you on the North Peckham Estate.

So when the Conservatives got in at the General Election, Maggie hopped into Number 10 after her St Francis of Assisi speech and we humble and grateful guardians of the law were awarded a huge pay rise, I didn't stop close protection work. I kept on doing it, evenings and weekends. By now I had discovered that the men I worked with who were not police officers were freelancers working through a word-of-mouth network called the Circuit. They reckoned there were about two thousand men constantly in work. They seemed to do a lot of surveillance as well as close protection and undercover work and most of them had worked all over the world. This was exactly what I had been looking for, only I couldn't put a name to it until I saw it.

I asked the directors of the firm I worked for if there might be regular work for a woman on the Circuit. They said there would be plenty, but only if she was properly trained. Most of the men had been trained by the SAS or the Paras or one of the security services, and had done a special one-week course in Herefordshire. No women had yet come forward who had the remotest chance of getting on to this course. You did unarmed combat, outdoor survival skills, firearms training, defensive driving and surveillance and detection techniques.

It sounded exactly what I had been unconsciously preparing myself for all my life. As a schoolgirl I had got AAA certificates for running and shotput; when I was about sixteen Dad had set up a target so that I could practise with an air rifle in the back garden; when I joined the police I had joined a gun club; and I had already completed a police driver's course. I hadn't been sewing a fine seam in my spare time. I had been getting ready for this.

On the other hand, I had to look at my chances of promotion through the Force. The picture wasn't too rosy. If I stayed with the shoplifting squad I might get into the CID, where I could plod along for years. They wouldn't let me into a proper squad since I didn't have a funny handshake. (A penis might have helped as well.) And the security services were as remote as they'd ever been. Two years after joining the police, I was disillusioned. If anybody was going to become the first woman commissioner it would probably be some fast-track pen-pusher with a degree.

While I thought about all this I kept on doing the day job.

*

One Saturday afternoon in November 1979 I arrested a kid of about fourteen nicking a pair of trainers from a department store in Peckham High Street. I had just collared him and radioed for assistance when the little bastard head-butted me. I kept hold of him but there was blood everywhere and we were struggling and effing and blinding and people stepped into the traffic in alarm, which was a good thing because it made a panda car stop. Out of it stepped a big blond policeman with an honest face, who grabbed the little toerag and held him while I mopped my bloody nose with a handkerchief.

He took me to hospital and hung about while I got the thief (who turned out to be nineteen) sorted, by which time it was early evening.

'You're in no state to go home,' he said. 'Let me drive your car, I'll get you there.'

This was all a lie of course. Really he was brandishing a sword and riding a dashing white charger.

We had a long way to go, to Barnet, and all of it through the Christmas traffic. We got well into north London and stopped at a pub for a drink. I was looking terrific: the full Saturday night drop-dead two inches of plaster over the nose, blood-encrusted hair and scruffy jeans. He didn't seem to mind. We talked. We had hardly stopped talking since he drove me to the hospital. I told him I was thinking of leaving the force and after an hour or two I told him why. He turned out to have done some work for the same security company. We had a lot in common: he was a member of a gun club, he played squash. In general it was all this that attracted me more than his looks; he just seemed so straight and friendly, and he even made me laugh. I liked him more than anyone I had met for a long time. Well, ever.

At about eight o'clock he said, 'Will you marry me?'

I said I'd think about it.

'Well, don't think about it for too long.'

'Umm . . . I wouldn't be breaking anything up, then?'

'Not a thing.'

He finished his pint and we left. Twenty minutes later he pulled up outside my mum's house, which was a modern red-brick semi set well back from a quiet road. At regular intervals around our lawn there were severely clipped cohorts of rosebushes, now leafless in the cold. On a Saturday night up here, everybody was in, watching telly. Tim took the key out of the ignition and gave it to me.

'Have you thought about it?'

Drizzle was slanting through the ice-white glare of a street light, and one side of his face was in shadow. He kissed me.

'Yes.'

'And?'

'I will.'

'Good. I'll be round to meet your mum and dad in the morning.'

We got out of the car. He was putting an overcoat on ready to walk to the station.

'Where are you going now?' I asked.

'Home to tell the wife,' he grinned.

My face must have gone as white as the street lamp because he said, 'Come here.'

He hugged me and spoke softly.

17

'I haven't slept with her for a year,' he said. 'And yes, before you ask, we have got a baby. But the marriage is finished. The whole thing's kaput.'

I said nothing.

'Jacquie, I've never fallen in love before.'

I hadn't either.

3

My mum and dad had me when she was forty-six and he was forty-eight. They had already brought up a family of three girls. The youngest was nine when I came along. These three, who were not far apart in age, had a much tougher upbringing than I did. We lived then in an ancient low-ceilinged house just off Barnet High Street, and before I was born there was not a lot of money; Mum couldn't work when they were small, so there was only one wage coming in.

By the time I was old enough to appreciate nice things, the three eldest had left home and both Mum and Dad were working, so I got five-week holidays in Europe every year in their Winnebago with a friend brought along to keep me company, and riding lessons on Sundays, and ice skating with my own boots, and anything else I wanted.

For my sisters, I was the squealing brat who spoiled their teenage years. When I was five, Mum went back to work and my sisters had to drag me around with them just when they were starting to get interested in boys and clothes. I was made to feel their resentment and I vowed then that when I grew up I would never be dependent on anybody. I never have been. They went on resenting me, though, after they left home, because I also escaped the usual Take that muck off your face! and You treat this house like a hotel!

and What time d'you call this then? of growing up. By the time I was of an age to worry about, Mum and Dad had relaxed.

Dad never said he wished I'd been a boy but he always treated me like the boy he'd never had. I was a tall, athletic girl, a natural tomboy, and Dad got me out on a Saturday morning tinkering with the car, helping change the oil and clean the sparkplugs. Both my parents were kind to me but Dad was a friend I could confide in. He was a big man, six foot four and eighteen stone, dark, as he was of French and Spanish blood. I shared his true blue Tory opinions and no-nonsense attitude to life; I had no self-doubt. By the time I was thirteen, I was subconsciously grooming myself to be a female combination of John Thaw and Dennis Waterman in *The Sweeney*. I wanted to leap out of a police car as it skidded to a halt. I wanted to slam doors and growl, 'Right lads, let's get a ticket and spin this drum.'

Given all this, when Tim walked in cocky as only he could be, grasped Dad's hand and said, 'How d'you feel about me as a son-in-law?' it is no wonder that Dad said, 'Fine. But you should find out what it's like to live with her first. Set up house for a year or so and then get married.'

That was the Sunday. On the Monday, forty-eight hours after we had met, we found a flat in Mill Hill and moved in together.

Tim was gentle and good-natured. He shared the same go-get'em attitude to police work I had; in fact, he wanted to join the Special Patrol Group, which even down the nick was called Smash Plant and Grab, but he didn't bring all that home. He changed as soon as he was off duty and became considerate, teasing, a charmer; he had a persuasive way with him and I adored him more with every day we spent together. He made me feel desirable. Yvonne, the estranged wife, had already run to fat, he told me, and the fatter she got the less she appealed to him, so he had no regrets. I hardly spoke to her. She wasn't keen to let him have their son very often. She was always saying we could collect him at the weekend, and then she'd change her mind.

What I had not been prepared for, though, was money worries. I had been doing quite well since the police pay rise, my agency work at the Intercontinental brought in a bit extra and I had lived at home, paying my mum a reasonable rent, so I was able to run my own car. Tim didn't have a car. He got a lift down to Peckham from me, or he used public transport. I found myself volunteering as a ferry service. Dad, seeing this, got Tim a car of his own. He wasn't just being generous, although he liked Tim and thought he'd make a good husband; he was indirectly looking after me.

I was getting a bit ground down by the general financial situation all the same. Every month Tim had trouble meeting his share of expenses; every month, his debts got bigger. You had to feel sorry for him. He was living with one woman while another one could charge expenses to their joint account. Yvonne was an unemployed lone parent occupying their police flat in Peckham; her £250 monthly maintenance came all too often out of my salary.

I needed to earn more money. Promotion comes slowly in the police, unless you are a highflyer with a degree. I knew pretty much all there was to know about catching the shoplifters of Peckham by now and it was time to move on. I wanted to do undercover work, but there was no chance of that unless I got into one of the squads run out of Scotland Yard. Even the CID didn't work undercover. At this rate I'd be chasing toerags through south London's traffic for years before I got anywhere in the police. And there was never enough money.

I went to see my employers at the agency again.

We sat down over a drink in a pub in Sutton. They were both in their thirties, knew the Circuit well and, more importantly, understood the police and squad and services hierarchies. Over a beer-stained table set on a swirly brown and orange carpet, deafened by a nearby pinball machine and occasionally cowering as the door opened to let in a great gust of wintry air from the street, I heard my future laid out for me.

'You've got three options,' they said. 'One: stay in the job. You ain't got a hope in hell of getting into a squad. So you make DS in your forties, collect your pension. Two: go for MI5 or 6. It'd be the same story for you, you got the wrong connections and you're the wrong sex. Three: come on the Circuit full time. You've got to be ready to drop everything at a moment's notice, go anywhere in the world, risk your life. You've got to have the bottle to kill people in self-defence. You'll make a bloody good living and we'll train you.' I didn't hesitate. I drove home rehearsing what I would say to Tim. Have a good day, dear? Yes, my sweetiepie. I have chosen to make a career shift. From now on I shall drop everything at a moment's notice, go anywhere in the world, risk my life, and kill people in self-defence.

Hmm. It might work.

It went down quite well, actually. The money on the Circuit

was good, and it dawned on me that that went a long way with Tim.

I did a deal with the agency. I would do one major undercover job they had lined up, and they would send me on a course before I returned to guarding the Gulf Sheikha full-time during this year's visit to London.

The undercover job meant living away from Tim for as long as it took – six weeks, maybe – in a bedsit in a safe house in another part of north London. My day job would be at Liberty's.

Liberty's is a rambling multi-level mock-Tudor department store in the busiest part of the West End, at the junction of Great Marlborough Street and Regent Street. Arthur Liberty, the founder, made his fortune catering to the Arts and Crafts taste of fashionable late-Victorian ladies. He sold a range of textiles influenced by Indian and Chinese designs, intricate florals and sinuous paisleys in cotton lawn and other natural fabrics. These same designs are the foundation of Liberty's fame today, reproduced on expensive scarves in hand-blocked silk and fine wool.

Even so, the scarf department had been losing money for months. It looked like an obvious target for shoplifters. The main entrance on the Great Marlborough Street side, a dark oak neo-Tudor lobby with glowing display cabinets inside, admits customers directly into the scarf department. They come in out of low light, low ceilings and carved black oak into a soaring hall resplendent with colour. Orange and viridian and ultramarine silks slither from every surface, and great swags of luxurious fabric hang from above. Idle shoppers can stare down on this opulence from panelled galleries on the upper floors. There is a temptation to steal. The scarves are folded and laid in overlapping rows, dainty as cucumber sandwiches at a garden party, and easily slipped into a bag.

However, with up to three thousand pounds' worth of scarves disappearing every week, the security department were sure it must be an inside job. I became a sales assistant.

Monday mornings were the only quiet time and even then, customers emerged endlessly from the lobby. A Sloane in an old Liberty headscarf, an American couple in Burberries, young office girls, a party of Japanese tourists, some German pensioners, a couple of preening black homosexuals, a group of chattering French housewives, a businessman, an African in magnificent green and white robes and a head-dress, a well-preserved grandmother with two whining children, an old rock chick, on and on they came, most of them looking as if they knew where they were going and then, bedazzled by the scarves, hesitating, gazing. May I help you, madam? The pink silk is forty-nine pounds. That will do nicely, madam. Otherwise, discreet, hovering behind the counter. Don't make them feel pressurized.

You were discouraged from talking much while you were out on the floor, but as you trailed up the grubby back stairs at coffee time past walls thick with dusty cream and green gloss paint and an inch of black fluff on the pipes, you got chatting.

'Don't even ask,' I would sigh. 'I've got a room in Archway. I went up to Birmingham as soon as I left school and it was a big mistake. I feel I've got to start all over again.'

I had a false surname, a false P45. The other women were friendly enough. The first time I told a glib lie, I held my

24

breath; something irrational inside me was convinced that a voice would say, 'No you're not. You're Jacquie Courroyer. What are you doing here?'

They took the story at face value. It was so easy. I was careful to stick as close to the truth as I could, and not to volunteer information I couldn't substantiate. They had no suspicions. I met about twenty saleswomen in the first few weeks and got to know others by sight. The core of the scarf department, who were always there, were five women in their twenties and thirties, and the buyer, a nervy blonde of about forty-five. I figured if anyone was at it it must be these six.

'Archway's OK for now. When I've got a bit of money saved I'll move. Where do you live?'

The surveillance team began to follow them from work. We swapped information in the course of long telephone calls most evenings.

'That one Paula, her old man picks her up from Bromley station. Find out what he does, will you? They've got a nice house.'

One lunchtime I walked down to Boots in Piccadilly with one of the girls. As we dodged delivery vans in the narrow gulf of Kingly Street I wondered aloud if they needed evening staff in one of the bars we passed.

'You're not that broke, are you, Jacquie?'

'You must be kidding. By the time I've paid tube fares and rent, there's about enough left over for a pair of tights. It's all right for you, you've got a husband working.'

'My husband's not working. I make every penny that comes in. You want to talk to Trish.'

Trish was the buyer.

'She'll get me a rise after two and a half weeks? I don't think so.'

'There are other ways.'

'What? . . . Go on.'

'Some of the scarves go out the back door. You can get a tenner each for them down East Street. It's easy money.'

'What, you mean carry them out? Don't they ever do spot checks?'

'No, none of us does that. Trish's got some guys in the stock department. You should see her spare room at home, she's got boxes of stuff round there. It turns over ever so fast.'

Nothing more was said.

The surveillance team was following the six women and digging into their backgrounds. One woman's husband was collecting heavy brown cardboard boxes from the buyer's house on a Friday night and the husband and wife were flogging forty-pound scarves for a tenner the next day in East Street market, that much was confirmed by observation. The others seemed to be in on it, too, and all six of the women had much more money than they should have. All the same, we were getting bogged down in the confusion of keeping so many of them under observation at once. Although there were indications of a conspiracy to steal, it was hard to work out who was doing what or to get pictures of them together.

I knew honest staff at the store who weren't in on the racket and worked hard for their commission. It annoyed me that these women thought they could get away with this.

The one member of the surveillance team I knew well was a bloke called Tommy, ex-SAS and recently split from his girlfriend. We all teased him because he fancied his target, and maybe it was the frustration of sleeping alone that drove him to have a brainwave.

One of the guys said, 'We've got to get to know this lot better.'

'We can,' Tommy said slyly. 'Jacquie's birthday, innit. Why doesn't she have a party?'

The birthday party was going like a train. The whole top floor of the safe house had been taken over. It was Saturday night, with blaring music and plenty of booze. The crucial guests were half a dozen policemen pretending to be lodgers or old school friends of mine, and all the targets, who were there without their husbands. A bemused fireman was sprawled over my sofa and another one was propping up the sink unit. The Scarf Department, faces glossy from alcohol, had had their pictures taken in a group, in hilarity, in a long-lost-friends embrace with the policemen. A constable from Barnet was even now snogging quietly on the landing with the woman who had walked down Kingly Street with me. As I repaired my lipstick in the bathroom mirror down the hall I thought the worst thing that could happen would be a complaint about the noise followed by a visit from a panda car.

I knew now that I loved this work. I liked the edge that being watchful gives to life. I liked knowing that what I was doing was key to the whole investigation. I thanked my stars that I was on the Circuit now.

Next week I left Liberty's. We handed over a thick folder: six weeks of reported conversations, incriminating photographs of the suspects selling scarves, and observations of comings and goings. The buyer had been thieving from Liberty's for years. I don't know what happened to the guilty parties; Liberty's probably brought in the police. It wasn't my concern, because after a weekend with Tim I left home again, this time for the seven-day intensive training course.

The week in Herefordshire changed my life. It was a sort of postgraduate course in policing. It was the foundation my career would be built on. I went back to the Circuit confident that I could handle anything that was thrown at me, quite literally.

Eight of us were on the course and I was the only woman. We lived in Nissen huts in an old army camp. We were up and out running at five every morning. A few hours of the army PTI (physical training instructor) course followed after breakfast; in the afternoon and evening we were in a classroom or out getting practical experience. We learned reconnaissance, surveillance, map reading, first aid, firearms drill, protocol – everything from how to address a head of state to which knife and fork to use at dinner. I found out how to embus and debus a principal (which is a bit like formation dancing) and defensive and evasive driving techniques: how to spin a car through 360 degrees and block a suspect vehicle when travelling in convoy. Every one of us felt confident enough to run a team or to be part of one.

At the end of the week we acted out a mock scenario. Our imaginary situation was outlined on a piece of paper: 'An Englishwoman wants to buy a stud farm in Wales. The Sons of Glendowr see it as their business to prevent her. Your job is to protect her.' The instructors would be playing the terrorists.

28

We were introduced to our principal, got her into the car and set off down Welsh lanes to the address we had been given. We were in correct formation, the SAP team scouting well ahead of us, and close to the top of the lane where the stud farm was when we were flour-bombed by an ambush party. All eight of us and our VIP raced through to the stable yard, where she announced that she would like to have a look round. We surrounded her as we had been taught, and had started moving through the buildings when we heard an explosion.

We knew what to do: get out. The drivers were gunning the cars towards us, I grabbed the woman and threw her into the back of the car and hurled myself on top of her. Sniper fire was flying as the three cars skidded across the gravel and roared down the lane with a team of balaclava'd 'terrorists' in pursuit.

It was hard to follow that.

A few weeks later, still on an adrenalin high, I had my big wedding: hundreds of guests, yards of tulle, the whole bit. Our white-ribboned limousine was held up in a jam in the Edgware Road on our way to the Hilton. I was staring dreamily through my veil at the Christmas shoppers – not looking for shoplifters at the time – when one of my sisters said reverently, 'This is the most exciting day of your life, Jacquie.'

'Like hell it is,' I murmured.

4

Soon after the wedding, at Christmas 1980, we moved into a police flat, one of a block of three in Chelsea. Our married life was exactly what I had been brought up to expect: I did the cooking and shopping and cleaning, and he checked the tyre pressures and put the bins out. I liked it this way. I'd have had Tim out mowing the lawn if we'd had a lawn. The idea of a man washing up or making a bed shook me to the bone. Besides, my mum in her way was just as much of a perfectionist as Dad and as I wiped the work surfaces to a gleaming finish I was mentally rehearsing her nod of approval.

In our time off we played squash or went to the gun club, or socialized with other couples who were in the police force. That spring, Tim was moved from Peckham to Notting Hill. By now I was back working at the Intercontinental with the Gulf royal family.

I had taken close protection work seriously before the week in Herefordshire, but with hindsight I think in a real emergency I might not have had the hair-trigger timing that comes only with training and commitment. Since the course, there was no doubt about it: the Sheikha and her children were getting the best protection money could buy.

Money entered into every aspect of their lives without exception. Most people spend in order to save labour or impress their friends or amuse themselves, but all these ordinary things were so easily attainable that they were meaningless to the Gulf royals. Their buying decisions were on another level altogether. Money was a psychological weapon. When they handed it over they expected power, fear and love in return.

One day I took the eldest girl, who was eleven, downstairs in the hotel to buy some sweets. She stood in front of the display, choosing packets and bars and piling them on the counter by the till. An untidy heap of shiny paper packages was accumulating and the kiosk woman, busily counting out change to a man for a box of cigars, said, 'That's a lot of goodies. Can you afford all those?'

The child stared.

'I can afford anything,' she said icily. 'I can buy all the candy in this store if I want to.'

'Yes, dear,' said the woman indulgently, and looked quizzically at me as I handed over the money. I remained stony-faced. Carrying the sweets in a striped carrier bag, I escorted the silent princess back to the penthouse floor. As soon as we got out of the lift she snatched the bag and ran into the suite, shutting the door behind her. Five minutes later she came out, flushed, carrying the same striped bag.

'You take me downstairs to the shop,' she commanded.

The kiosk woman didn't see us coming. She was sipping a cup of coffee and she nearly choked on it when a small brown hand once again began stacking chocolate on the counter. She looked at me.

'Her Royal Highness will pay,' I said.

Mars bars, Twix bars, fruit gums, nougat, Bendicks mints, she made the woman put all of them into carrier bags.

31

Boxes of chocolate pralines, Walnut Whips, marshmallows, humbugs, acid drops, chewing gum. She didn't stop collecting until the woman had piled every last item of confectionery into a bag and climbed on to a set of steps to retrieve a couple of dusty boxes of crystallized fruit from the display behind her. Silently the woman rang up everything at the correct retail price. The child handed me her striped paper carrier and I counted out over £2,000 in crisp twenties. As she handed me the change I caught a look pass between her and the Princess. The child cut her eyes at the woman in utter disgust.

Carrier bags became quite a little feature of life with the Gulf royals after that. Money was just a meaningless token; they had no idea of the price of anything. One morning I had just arrived and had barely sat down in my usual chair in the corridor when I was summoned into the suite by the Sheikha, who was lying on the sofa in a baggy pink garment while the hotel's manicurist painted her toenails.

'Good morning, Jacquie. My son is not well today. In five minutes a slave will give you some money. Go to Harrods toy department. He wishes a train set and war things. Soldiers. You will find them.'

I would. A skinny Eritrean woman all in white, her eyes downcast, scuttled out shortly afterwards and handed me a shiny sage green and gold Harrods bag with £9,000 in it. I did my best, and like to think I got the sheikhlet quite a nice train set. Maybe when he grew up he would reproduce it full-size across the desert for the benefit of his people.

The girls had to be kept amused too. To get them out of their mother's hair I took two of them to Hamley's one morning. They spent £5,000 in an hour, on Barbies and

Sindys and wooden Pinocchio puppets; I had been handed the money in a Waitrose bag, and remember wondering who on earth had slipped out to Waitrose and why. There was certainly no need for extra groceries. Room service was called six or seven times a day, the waiters mincing out of the suite with a ten per cent tip every time, having left a trolley laden with Lapsang and whole gâteaux which would remain untouched, except for the sticky depression left by a child's thumb, until half a day later when they mysteriously reappeared in the fridge in the security room.

The royal wife and children were bored witless. Inner resources were not in their repertoire. The Sheikha spent tens of thousands on trunkloads of dresses that were shipped home, and some gaudy new toy or riotous action must be provided every day for the kids. The children soon tired of Hyde Park and throwing bread for the ducks on the Serpentine. For a short time they took to charging gleefully along the length of the corridor behind the food service trolley and ramming it into the bodyguards' shins. My legs were black and blue and I had to buy a new pair of tights every day, but I put up with the little bastards in silence. Even that game got boring after a few days – maybe I should have winced more; they would have enjoyed that.

They were distracted when the princesses saw a funfair on television. The Sheikha immediately commanded me to take them to one. It was late January, and phone calls all over London winkled out only one travelling fair, on Hampstead Heath. Its rides were locked up for the winter but another carrier bag with a couple of thousand pounds in it worked a treat. That grey London afternoon, eight bodyguards positioned themselves watchfully around four children shrieking past on a merry-go-round and waltzer, and peered into the dripping trees for potential kidnappers.

At least two of the girls usually accompanied their mother on her daily shopping trips. We would sweep into some toffee-nosed emporium in Bond Street, the advance body-guard followed by the Sheikha and myself, a couple of nannies and a couple of slaves and the two little girls, with two more guys from the close protection squad on watch outside and the drivers waiting in the limos on double yellow lines. Then the Sheikha would point a scarlet-nailed finger out of her all-enveloping *shabbah* and demand and order while her daughters trampled about in calfskin stilettos or squealed and chucked hand-made patent pumps at each other. The saleswomen couldn't have been more obsequious. The man-ageress rushed out from behind a pillar, nose a-quiver like a nervous rabbit, as soon as our entourage arrived. She could smell commission.

'What delightful children you have, madam.' A tiny flinch of the neck as a riding boot hurtled past her immaculate cheekbones. Christ, I thought, you crawler, you must be desperate. She had said the right thing, though, for the Sheikha was a proud mama.

'Yes. My children speak three languages fluently.'

As the girls were by now screaming like the kindergarten from hell in all of them, you could hardly hear what she was saying. Disciplining these brats was evidently not in the nannies' job description. They smiled timidly as the girls wrecked the joint and the saleswomen gritted their teeth and the slaves made themselves invisible and the bodyguards, as ever, looked outwards for a threat.

Meanwhile, back on a sky-level floor of the Intercontinental, the remaining prince and princess would be getting bored again. They might amuse themselves by painting on the wallpaper or carefully scoring their names into a leather desktop. When they finally returned to the Gulf, the resulting bill for damages amounting to twenty-five or thirty thousand pounds would be settled without question.

Their father, a petulant and chubby fifty-year-old in snowy dishdash and Arab head-dress, visited their mother for about twenty minutes at six each evening. He might occasionally see the boy. The girls were rarely brought to him. I do not of course know what he talked about with his number one wife during these interludes, but they can't have covered much ground. As far as I could see, they had nothing in common at all.

Though the team guarding the Sheikh in his own hotel were mostly off-duty policemen, they had to turn a blind eye to a lot of things. The conciergerie of these places provided connections to anything that was asked for; they saw it as part of the job. Girls would be taken up to the suite, and cocaine delivered and snorted in the rooms, with open doors, allowing an unimpeded view. The management, who wanted their establishments to maintain at least the impression of a classy joint, looked the other way when it came to Arabs spending on this scale. As to the close protection team, they enjoyed the casino outings and ignored the rest.

Tim and I still needed all the work we could get, so I did close protection for the Sheikha from eight until six and then crossed the road from the Intercontinental to the Hilton, where I had taken up an offer to work from six until two in the morning on a tom squad.

All the big London hotels have a prostitute problem,

especially the ones on Park Lane because they get a lot of wealthy, single male visitors on business. Tree-lined Park Lane with its empty pavements is a mecca for kerb-crawlers and the huddled shops and cafés of Shepherd Market are only a few hundred yards away, on the Mayfair side away from Hyde Park. There have been toms in Shepherd Market since Mayfair was where they held the May Fair and, presumably, sheep ran through the back alleys. The Shepherd Market girls did not look bad – not at any rate as bad as the rough old dogs from King's Cross – but they looked enough like hookers to lower a hotel's reputation. The police had a tom squad to contain the problem on the streets but they couldn't be everywhere, and if a hotel started to get notorious the police would warn its security department that they might oppose renewal of its licence.

Security at the Hilton called in five of us: me and four men from the Circuit. Connected by radio, we hung about in the foyer or moved from floor to floor. Girls slipped in through staff entrances and up back stairs and went on the knock from room to room looking for punters. When we got one, we would take her to the security office and see if there was a warrant out for her; if there wasn't she'd get cautioned. Her photo would be added to the book if it wasn't there already. Most of them were. *The Big Book of Toms* was compendious, and new snaps were added and circulated around the hotels all the time, but the girls were not easily deterred. They could make a good living: one I got to know had two children at a fee-paying school, and the Williams sisters, who had both been on the game for years, had set up a carpet shop in Leeds out of their earnings.

If the duty manager in the foyer saw a likely prostitute

come in and go to the lift with a hotel guest, he would radio up to us and we'd be on that floor to see which room they went into. If he told us it was a single room, we'd get her out. Under an old law called the Hotel Act, a hotel manager can be done for keeping a brothel if he lets two people share a room when he's got any suspicion that they might not be married.

One night, one of us saw a girl go into a single room with a Japanese man. I arrived and put my ear to the door. She said she was leaving to buy some cigarettes, so two of us waited round the corner and nabbed her as she got to the lift. We were on our way down to Security when she remembered she'd left her coat behind. I said I'd go back for it, and as they disappeared into the lift I set off down the corridor.

When I knocked on the door it opened a tiny fraction, then a bit more, then wide.

'Ah, herro!' said a delighted voice. 'Come in!'

I looked down. There stood the Japanese man, his head level with my chest, naked as a baby except for a thin gold thong thrust forward by the most enormous stonker.

'Hotel security,' I said crisply. His equipment flopped sideways like a deflated balloon.

I got some laughs one way or another, but by March I was working such long hours to pay the bills, and Tim was doing so many broken shifts at Notting Hill, that I did not see much more of my husband than the Sheikha did of the Sheikh.

I had been getting pains every month and knew what the matter was; ovarian cysts had formed inside me before. I first went into hospital to have them removed when I was about twelve. In March 1981, not four months after our wedding, I was taken in a state of collapse by ambulance from the Hilton to St Stephen's hospital in the Fulham Road. I was told an immediate operation was necessary, so I signed the release form and went under.

I woke up staring at a white ceiling and thinking about Tim. It must be morning by now; he would be on duty. Failing Tim, I would have liked my dad to talk to, but he wasn't in great shape himself these days. He had had several heart attacks. He had been a diabetic since before I was born, and lately he always seemed short of breath and walking had become painful. I promised myself I would go and see him before I went back to work. I raised my head and realized I was feeling rotten. A nurse saw me.

'Jacquieline? Mr Dundas will be in to see you in a moment.' She disappeared to return within a few minutes with Mr Dundas, an elderly Scot in a white coat.

'Good evening, Jacquieline. Feeling a wee bit drowsy still? Well, I am glad to say you will have no further trouble . . . You are twenty-two, I see, Jacquieline. Is that correct?'

'Yes.'

'However, I am sorry to have to tell you that it hasn't all been plain sailing. It's always difficult – I'm afraid we found the trouble had progressed much further than we had expected. We considered what course of action to take and I'm afraid there was nothing we could do except a complete hysterectomy.'

I was still a bit slow-witted from the anaesthetic and did not understand properly.

'Is that what you want to do?'

'No, Jacquieline. That's what we have had to do. We had no option.'

'Oh. You've done a hysterectomy.'

'Yes.'

Something drastic had happened but I could not quite take it in. I would never be able to have children now. Well, I had never consciously wanted to. I had vaguely expected that would come later. My parents had been old so none of their friends had babies and I'd never really seen the attraction of pregnancy and prams and all that.

The surgeon went away and I lay in bed trying to decide how I felt. Nice not to have to worry, in a way. But not thinking about having children and not physically being able to have them are two different things. I wondered how Tim would take the news.

5

I did not cry. There was no point. I was my usual matter-of-fact self when I told Tim. He held my hand for a minute and then he muttered something about how I didn't seem very upset. So that was that. Visiting time left me feeling as if there was nothing to discuss.

An ambulance took me back to the Chelsea flat, but I wasn't well enough to go to work right away. I fretted, I loved my work and was lost without it, but I had to lie down most of the time. I watched TV, Tim went to Notting Hill nick.

After a few days of this we had not got a lot to say to each other. We usually talked about work or the things we did together. Squash is not recommended after a hysterectomy, so we couldn't talk about that, or the gun club. We didn't see any of the other couples we went out with. Tim said he was too tired and I certainly was, even after three weeks. Then one night Tim came home looking more cheerful than usual, and said we should get away before I went back to work. Why didn't we, he said, go down to Devon with my mum and dad? That way, if anything went wrong he would know there were a couple of nurses around.

Off we went, all of us in Tim's car, on the Sunday morning. Tim had taken annual leave and I thought that was nice of him. On the Tuesday morning he had a call from work.

'Shit. I've got to go back. I'm due in court.'

'What d'you mean? You're on leave.'

'Yeah, but there was a case due up before, I told you they deferred it, and now it's on tomorrow because one of the witnesses has got to go abroad next week and he won't be back.'

'How long will you be?'

'Couple of days. It should be over by Thursday.'

I was disappointed but there was not much I could do about it. I pottered around Taunton with Mum and Dad for a couple of days, admiring the sea view and eating restorative cream teas. I felt like a geriatric. The case dragged on and Tim didn't come back on Thursday. He finally turned up late on Friday night. I felt sorry for him, having had to work all week and now spending most of Saturday driving us all the way back to London.

We dropped Mum and Dad in Barnet and it was three o'clock by the time Tim left me at the police flats in Chelsea. He went over to Notting Hill to catch up with some paperwork and I started to put washing in the machine and unpack. I was taking some laundry downstairs to the line when I met my upstairs neighbour on her way up, laden with shopping. She was a red-haired woman married to a DC from Chelsea.

'Hi, Jacquie! How you doing?'

'Fine. Much better.'

'You had company anyway.'

We knew each other to pass the time of day, but I didn't know she knew I'd been down to Devon.

'My mum and dad, you mean? Yes.'

'No, I meant that dark girl, is she your sister?'

'Sorry?'

'The girl who came over your place with Tim in the week.'

'What day was that?'

'Wednesday.'

'A dark girl with curly hair in a leather jacket?'

'Yes.'

'Oh, I know who you mean. No, she's not my sister.'

I went on my way to the washing line but my knees felt like jelly.

Tim had met Janine here.

I had known it would be her. She was one half of a couple we knew. You register signs subconsciously, a look between two people or how they hand things to each other or the way they pointedly sit apart. It's like recognizing a smell of gas; you smell it, but it's a while before you notice it. When you do, everything changes.

The colour had drained out of everything. My life was spoiled. Tim had brought Janine here. Just the two of them. The flat had never felt so empty. I walked into the bedroom and saw, now, that he had changed the sheets. I felt sick. My chest hurt with the pain of not crying. I started blindly cleaning floors. I was still polishing and cleaning when Tim came home in the middle of the Saturday evening. He flung his jacket over the back of the settee and sat down to take his shoes off in the living-room. It was quiet in the flat. He looked surprised by the silence.

'Nothing on telly? What's to eat?'

'You've had Janine here.'

'What d'you mean?'

'Janine was here.'

'So?'

'You never said a word. You got me down to Devon so you could get her over here.'

'That's crap. You're going out of your mind. Pull yourself together, Jacquie, for Christ's sake. The sooner you get back to work the better. I drove you all the way down there –'

'Well, what the fuck was she doing here then?'

Tim swore that Janine had only been at the flat because she and her husband were thinking of divorcing and she wanted somebody to talk to. He became furious with me for questioning him and slammed into the bedroom. I needed to believe Tim so badly that I never brought up the subject again and we soon settled back into our routine of work, eat, sleep. It was at work that I needed to mistrust people automatically. Not at home.

The Sheikha had gone home, and to make up for the lost daytime earnings I worked six or seven nights a week on the tom squad. The long light days were here now, and one warm evening I went for a walk outside just to get out of the bar. I was in a cocktail frock and high heels, wandering down a quiet street behind the hotel hunting in my bag for a cigarette when I saw a man coming towards me in half blues. He had a suit jacket on, but you can tell a police shirt and trousers and shoes anywhere. I was getting a sardonic appraising stare. It feels great, being looked at like a prize horse.

'Want a light?' he said.

'Thanks.'

He took out a lighter.

'You doing business?'

I put my cigarettes back in my bag. Then I took out my radio. All his facial muscles sagged.

I smiled sweetly at him.

'Fuck.'

He turned and ran. I sprinted after him right through Mayfair to Marble Arch and he was still dodging desperately between cars and down alleyways when I let him go. Served the bugger right. If I hadn't had heels on I'd probably have got him.

I was becoming a bit disillusioned with policemen. Not that Tim was like the rest, of course; I had been letting this job make me paranoid.

I finally got the holiday I needed, although it was a working holiday. A highly paid executive had been injured at work, and had claimed against his employer for loss of earnings. It seemed he could barely walk since the accident and would be in constant pain. His employer's insurance company wanted him followed to the South of France. I jumped at the chance and spent five or six days at an expensive hotel with a glorious private beach. Wearing dark glasses against the hot sun, I shot several reels of photographs of the target as he learned to water-ski and improved his diving skills at the hotel's pool. I had to admire him. For a man who could barely walk he was a bloody good water-skier.

Not long after I returned, a couple of the agency's directors dropped by our flat one afternoon to talk about a special project. The Ayatollah and his supporters had forced the Pahlavi dynasty to escape Iran in a hurry, and European capitals at that time were teeming with rich Iranians. The Shah's sister was in Geneva, though she was finding it difficult to leave because of some alleged illegal activities. For whatever reason, the Swiss did not want to let her go and quite a few other countries were not keen to have her as a visitor.

It would be my job to get her out of Switzerland. It was exactly the sort of challenge I wanted. It was risky and important and would use all the skills in undercover and close protection work that I had learned so far. It would be my blooding; it would make my name on the Circuit. After this I would never want for work. I was quietly exultant that they had chosen me to do the job.

We were working out how to do it without either her or me getting shot at when Tim walked in, still in uniform.

One of the guys was just saying,

'Good thing it's a woman that's going –'

'Going where?' asked Tim.

'Geneva.' They told him about the job.

'Dream on, mate. She's not doing that,' Tim said.

'What d'you mean?' I said. 'I bloody am. Butt out, Tim, it's got nothing to do with you.'

'Oh, right. Who d'you think you are, Modesty Blaise? You must be out of your mind if you think I'd let you go out there and do that.'

'Jacquie's good, Tim,' said one of the guys. 'She'll handle it fine. You don't need to worry.'

'She's going nowhere.'

'You mind your own business. It's me who's on the Circuit, Tim, not you. It's nothing to do with you –'

'Just go and make us a nice cup of tea, will you? Let me have a word with the lads here.'

I was speechless.

'Go on, run along.'

I was not willing to play out this scene in front of these guys. I just sat there, furious. Tim turned to them.

'Come on, lads. Would you let your wife go?'

'My wife's not Jacquie,' said one. 'Jacquie's trained. She knows what she's doing. If we thought anybody else could do it we'd ask them. We want Jacquie.'

It was three of us, against him, and I knew I'd won. Tim turned to me, his face thunderous.

'I want to talk to you in the kitchen.'

We squeezed into the kitchen together and I leaned on the back of the door and got my word in first.

'You're being a total dickhead. It's my job.'

'It's illegal. A lot of what you do is illegal.'

'That's got nothing to do with you. I'm going, Tim, you're going to have to live with it.'

Tim had gone red in the face.

'You stupid fat cow. I'll get you stopped. You'll never work again. All it'll take is a phone call.'

I wasn't fat. He had never called me that before and neither had anybody else. He must have seen the twitch of anxiety in my eyes.

'What are you saying?' I stammered.

'If Special Branch think you've got some idea of getting the Shah's sister into this country, you won't have a fucking prayer, you stupid bitch. Not a fucking prayer. You want me to call them? Those guys in there won't know what's hit them.'

I was silent. He knew he'd won. He looked triumphant.

'You'll thank me for this one day,' he said, and pushed past me to pull open the door. 'Come on. You're going to tell your friends.'

We went back into the living-room and he looked on while I wiped out my career.

I could see it in their faces as they left: That's the trouble with women . . .

The more I saw of Tim these days, the less he seemed like the man I had married.

He had been so nice to me, last year in Mill Hill. Even his family were bearable if you didn't see too much of them. His father was henpecked, a company secretary who commuted from Essex to the City every day and did the housework when he got in. His mother ran the show. She was one of those judgemental types, like Tim: a headmistress. Everybody had to fit in with her view of the world and preferably follow the life script she had written for them. Tim, the elder of two sons, was Mummy's Little Soldier. He knew he would be all right if he kept on the right side of her, and cast into outer darkness if he didn't. The daughters and daughter-in-law had also got the message and toed the line.

The way I led my life didn't quite fit in with her plans, so this woman disliked me and took no pains to hide it. The feeling was mutual; I thought she was two-faced. She was knitting something that summer and, to make conversation, I asked her what it was.

'Well, it won't be anything for a baby of yours, will it?' she said.

I was badly disheartened after Tim made me turn down the Geneva job. I knew word would get around and I would never again be offered the work I wanted on the Circuit. I could have felt embittered but there would have been no point; as I saw it (and I saw it the way I had been brought up to), marriage was for life, and if I had married a man who stood between me and my work I'd have to change his mind. So I put my career on hold and convinced myself he would come round, given time. In the meantime I would stay on the tom squad in the evenings and look for a day job that I would do so outstandingly well that Tim would begin to trust me. I thought that must be the problem; he must think I couldn't cope. A few more years with me and he would understand. He would let me get back on to the Circuit in the end.

I was working all the hours I could at the hotel and hardly stopping to eat. Leering men in the Hilton bar always said I looked like Princess Diana, because we were both tall and thin with short hair. After an evening of approaches as original as this it was a relief to get up and patrol the corridors. There was one middle-aged man I had seen at least three times with different women, but none of them looked like prostitutes. They were older, usually well-preserved American blondes in their fifties, dripping with diamonds; and when we checked up, the rooms were always in their names.

One day one of the guys on the team pulled this man as he sat in the foyer. After a lot of probing he reluctantly admitted that he was a professional gigolo. A nice dinner, and then straight to the suite, ignoring her bedtime phone call to the old man safely back home, running the First National Bank of Poughkeepsie.

He had been happily employed two or three nights a week for years. He charged £400 a time. He had a day job, too; he was a police sergeant. He's an inspector now.

*

On the twenty-third floor, where several suites had been taken by the hangers-on around some Middle Eastern potentate, I heard a terrible scream. It sounded like an animal in distress, but when it happened again and again I could hear it was a child. I radioed a couple of the team from downstairs and we quickly decided to go right in using a pass key. In a bedroom we found a tear-stained blond boy naked on a bed. Five half-dressed Arab men were either on the bed or standing around watching. We hustled the boy out and down to the office. He was from the meat-rack in Piccadilly Circus. One of them had pulled him, but when he got to the room he found it was a gang-bang. He was fourteen.

This sort of thing really annoyed me. I got tense. I needed somebody to talk to when I got home but Tim was always out if I came back early. He was on all sorts of odd shifts.

One night we had a particularly long and tearful argument and I demanded to know once and for all whether he had had an affair with Janine. He said yes, of course. It was all over now, she'd been posted to Orpington to split them up. He spoke casually. They had started going to bed together in March, he said, when I was in hospital.

'When I was in *hospital*? Having a *hysterectomy*?'

'Look, men are different, Jacquie. You were away, she came on to me, what was I gonna do?'

'You could have told her to piss off.'

'I hadn't had sex for weeks. You were in hospital. And to cap it all you'd just told me you couldn't have kids.'

'So it was my fault, then.'

'You couldn't help it.'

'If you want a divorce because I can't have children then say so.'

'No. You're my wife, Jacquie. For better or for worse.'

I was actually grateful. I felt so worthless that I was glad of the chance to be his punchbag.

Dad was ill again. He had had at least four heart attacks and this time, what with the diabetes, when he went into hospital in August both his legs were gangrenous and would have to be amputated. The horror of this was too much to think about. He was taken into hospital on Thursday and the surgery took place on Friday. I went to see him on Sunday.

There is really nothing you can say to anyone in that situation. There is none of the usual Get Well Soon, because he won't. It's final. From now on, he would be dependent, and Mum would be looking after him. He wouldn't be able to perform even routine bodily functions without assistance. Dad was somebody who had always made his own way. He ran things, he didn't sit around waiting for something to happen. Now, white as the hospital sheets, he was literally half a person. I could see he couldn't cope. There were long silences after everything we said to each other.

In the end, he said, 'I can't live like this, Jacquie.'

'I can understand that, Dad.' I took his hand. 'I really can.'

'I gotta do something. I can't go on like this.'

'You do what you've got to do.'

Because he had been a charge nurse, the nurses on the ward used to let him administer his own insulin injections twice a day. On the Monday, I got a telephone call to say he had gone into a coma overnight and I was needed at the hospital.

When I arrived he was dead. My mother and sisters were

weeping and snivelling but I remained dry-eyed. I rang the funeral director and organized what had to be done.

The medical verdict was that Dad had died of natural causes: a combination of diabetes and heart problems. I believe he deliberately forgot to administer an injection.

Tim said he was very sorry. He came to the funeral. On the way home I had nothing to say. Dad had been my best friend, so I felt particularly lonely.

6

Tim and I faced a bleak future together, but we couldn't admit it so we did what most people in the same situation would have done: averted our eyes and aimed for a new goal. We began to save up for the deposit on a house. As he was still spending everything he earned and more, while my money went on the debts, and I wasn't going to get good assignments on the Circuit for a while, I still needed a proper job. I went for one I had seen advertised in the *Police Review*, and got it. A small family-owned chain of department stores in west London was losing five per cent of its profits through shoplifting, and they had decided to take on a head of security with a brief to build up a small team. I knew a couple of policewomen who wanted to get out of the force; I advertised for more, and soon had a team of four floorwalkers.

Ealing, about six miles out of the West End and linked to it by tube, was a fashionable suburb in the early years of this century and still has a lot of trees, parks and big detached Victorian houses. Some of these are occupied by wealthy families, but most have been converted into language schools, retirement homes or flats. Ealing sees itself as not quite London, somehow; as a staging post on the way to lush Virginia Water or Weybridge. It definitely turns its back on slatternly Acton, with its seething polluted high street snaking from Ealing to London, and has nothing at all to do with Southall where the Indian shops are. Ealing is supposed to have a touch of class.

The shop in West Ealing was an old-fashioned department store. It had creaked its way into the 1980s somehow, but many of the staff were elderly unmarried women who had been recruited so long ago that in their day single salesgirls were expected to live in staff accommodation. There was another store in High Wycombe that trundled along and would shortly be sold off. But the flagship, where I was based, was Fields, in Ealing Broadway. The Broadway Centre, a new shopping mall, had just been built and a new extension to Fields store was inside it. So were Safeways and Fields' main rival, Bentalls department store.

Fields was a well-organized store that specialized in upmarket women's clothing. The labels were there: Versace, Ralph Lauren, Armani, Donna Karan. They sold furs, too. At that time the Knightsbridge and Oxford Street department stores were reconsidering their position on the ethics of the fur trade. Some finally decided that they were losing more by alienating customers than they were by stocking expensive furs for those few women who still wanted to buy them. Out in Ealing, Fields still sold everything. My job, besides running the team of floorwalkers, included checking stock levels, and over the months it became pretty obvious to me that designer clothes and furs were disappearing fast. Profits were right down. It had to be an inside job, again. I put a couple of people on to it and waited.

In the meantime, I did the job I had learned so well in Peckham: I got out there and nicked thieves. We caught hundreds in the first year. One of the directors of the company was a magistrate, and he told me I was a talking point in the courts. He couldn't sit on our cases, since he had an interest, but he heard what the other magistrates were saying and they were amazed by the constant stream of shoplifters.

I quickly realized most of the thieves were professionals. We even got Australian gangs. Luckily, all the women I had trained were as committed to thieftaking as these people were to getting away with it, so we scored some spectacular arrests. We didn't let go. They tend to move from store to store in a shopping mall, and sometimes we would follow a suspect out of Fields and into Bentalls or one of the other shops where they had CCTV. Their security staff would spot us on the monitors and one of their floorwalkers would sidle up, murmuring, 'What you got?'

We did the same for them. We co-operated very well and set up regular meetings between the security departments of all the stores, and the local crime prevention officer, to pool information. Our detection rates improved still more. We had no closed-circuit TV at Fields, but we were linked by radio to each other through the switchboard and if a chase started, which it often did, the radio would switch directly to the local nick so that they got a live broadcast of what was going on and where.

I might just as well still have been in the police, because I was down Ealing nick almost every day. A lot of the officers there knew Tim slightly; he was stationed only a few miles away, at Notting Hill, and their paths crossed, but we never discussed him. Maybe some of them only knew him by reputation. I couldn't have spoken about my marriage in any case. It was as if it was lived by some other woman. At work, I was strong and decisive; with Tim, I was a limp doormat. My idea of showing him how well I could handle a rough job didn't seem to be working. He drove over one evening at the end of his shift to collect me from Ealing Hospital after I had had my thumb broken by a shoplifter, and as he walked out of Casualty with me he said disgustedly, 'God, another injury. This is ridiculous.'

I felt guilty. He always made me feel guilty. He got into the car with me and by the time we pulled out of the car park he had relented a bit.

'I'll stop for a takeaway. Save you cooking.'

He was being so magnanimous, and here I was letting him down, not providing piping hot food on the table. Not being at home with a pinny on.

I wanted him to tell me he loved me, but he never did any more. I thought it was no wonder.

I felt a complete failure with Tim, but I was exactly the opposite at work. I was in the canteen one day when Mick, my best friend at Ealing, came and sat down with us and said, 'Your fame's spread, Jacquie.'

'What d'you mean?'

'We turned over some houses last night, it was a bunch of kids, we got one of them doing a burglary. Well, we were looking through their houses and one of them was full of electrical stuff from Bentalls, with the tickets still on, and John said to this kid, D'you ever nick stuff from Fields? And he said, Not on your life, not since that bitch has been there.'

I was really pleased with myself. I behaved at work like a lean mean fighting machine. Lean, especially. I hardly ever had time to eat because I was knocking off work at five, driving over to the Cumberland or the Hilton to work on the tom squad or occasionally do some close protection work for a visiting pop star, getting home about two in the morning and driving out to Ealing by nine o'clock. I kept going through the day on coffee and cigarettes and sometimes a sandwich, but in the evenings there was usually no time to eat at the hotel. But men kept telling me I looked like Princess Diana, so I thought I must be keeping my weight problem under control.

We were building up some money at last. We had started looking at houses and saw one we liked near the agency I first worked for, in Sutton. Easy enough to get to west London from, it was a three-bedroomed 1930s semi in a well-mannered road with respectable neighbours and fruit trees in the garden. The garden was important because we had decided to have a dog. Our closest friends Lynn and Robbie had a lovable German Shepherd and I wanted one just like it.

Shortly after we moved into the new house, we drove out to Tilbury and bought Boo from a breeder. He was a German Shepherd puppy, and he chewed our freshly laid carpets in anxiety when we first left him alone. But poor Boo; being on his own was one of those things he would have to get used to. I had not really understood. Tim probably wanted a dog as much as I did, and later events bore this out, but having a dog was for him a lot like having a child or a wife: it was a burdensome responsibility. We hardly ever saw his child. It was just as it had been from the start: I would ring up and arrange that we'd take his little boy for the weekend, and then in the week Yvonne would ring him at work and put him off. It happened so often that after three years we rarely saw Mark except when we took him birthday or Christmas presents. He was a nice, good-natured kid. And

Boo was a nice, good-natured dog, company in the evenings when Tim wasn't there.

Abysmal profits in Fields women's clothing departments were now fully explained. The culprit was a senior sales assistant, at the centre of a web of willing helpers. She was a dumpy, silent thing whose permanent air of anxiety concealed a truly criminal greed. She had shown her grown-up daughter and various friends how to go into one of the group's stores, choose some garments from the rails, and disappear into the changing rooms to stash stuff and walk out with it. This was before the days of security tags, and I was watching when I saw one of her regular customers go in with an armful of fur coats and reappear with only one.

'Not quite me . . . I'll think about it.'

The saleswoman had plenty of time to think about it in the end, because she got sent down. When I went along with the police to raid her house we found dresses worth thousands of pounds each, amazing creations in velvet and silk and exquisitely tailored suits and jackets, just rolled up and stuffed in a corner or under the bed. She had sold some, but there were scores of clothes left, and I looked at the chaos and realized that this was a metaphor for the poor cow's life. She had a problem. However, I had a job to do. When it came to court the prosecution had worked out what she had cost the store in the course of her working life there, and it was three and a half million pounds.

After that, I heard people say they always get caught in the end. They don't.

There was an old girl in kitchenware, she'd been there over twenty years and if it hadn't been for me, she'd have retired in her dotage with an unblemished reputation and a hefty nest-egg. Part of my brief was to check stock against takings, and in kitchenware the tills were always wrong. There was only one way to get to the bottom of this, so I collected all the department's till rolls for the past two months and shut myself in my office.

By the end of the first morning I realized this was going to take weeks. I came out still seeing numbers reeling past my eyes, went into the canteen and sat down to eat a sandwich. Little old Marjorie was in there, carefully carrying her tray, meat and two veg and apple pie to follow. I had my eye on her already, because I'd asked my jolly soopah friend in personnel to let me know if there was anyone in kitchenware who never took a day off. There was only Marjorie, and since she was seventy-two you'd think she'd want to put her feet up now and again and let somebody else sell kettles and cherrypitters to the good citizens of Ealing. But she never did, she came in regardless of rain or snow as if her life depended on it. Aha, I thought, hidden agenda. I was right, but it took me weeks of poring over scraps of paper to be sure.

What she was doing was taking amounts out of the till more or less equivalent to the amounts received from Barclaycard customers. She only got away with it because of the way the system worked. Credit card transactions were paper-based then, there was no automatic link to a computer centre, and you put the card into a mechanical press with two flimsy copies. Clunk. If somebody came in and paid £25 on Barclaycard, the Barclaycard bottom copy was clipped to the back of the till receipt and put in the till. When you reconciled the figures you treated Barclaycard transactions as cash. The cash total for the day would be Barclaycard transactions plus cash minus the float.

I finally sussed what was happening. Somebody, somebody whose squiggled initials on the Barclaycard bottom copy usually looked a lot like Marjorie's, was saving old low-value, uncollected till receipts and clipping them to the front of big-ticket Barclaycard receipts. So you'd get a receipt for 99p, and 99p would be in the cash to match it. But on the back of the receipt you'd find a Barclaycard docket for £25. Somebody had nicked the difference.

The records had been sloppily kept for years, in a way that skimmed over difficulties of addition, and I could not be sure that Marjorie was the only one responsible. I called in the other staff in the department. Most of them were young girls. I took them through transactions weeks old. I asked them why they had made this mistake or that. In nearly every case, the girl concerned had taken a day off when the mistake was made.

I had all the staff checked out. They were all clean but Marjorie had worked at Fields for so long that nobody could remember where she came from. An old personnel file from the 1960s, its manila cover crumbling from dry air, showed she'd worked at the Co-op for twenty-five years before turning up at Fields. I rang them up and they told me she had left under suspicion of sticking her hand in the till. At Woolworths, where she had worked as a young woman before the Second World War, mouldering records showed that she had been sacked for the same reason.

I gathered up the entire case, crumpled receipts, till rolls, the old file, the lot, took it to the CID office at Ealing and said, 'I've got this problem.'

I explained about Marjorie. How she lived on her own, had never married, was seventy-two, and how I thought she was guilty of false accounting. She had been doing this all her life and had to be stopped. I intended to go for a prosecution.

'Come on, Jacquie.' The chief inspector was shocked. 'Poor old dear won't go down for that at her age, what's the use? You don't want to nick her. Get them to heave her out with loss of pension rights.'

I shook my head. 'That'd be letting her get away with it. She's been at it too long. Look – I worked out at the rate she's been going, in the last couple of years alone she's had fifty grand out of there.'

He looked without enthusiasm at the bulging case notes I had brought with me.

'She's an old woman. Have a heart.'

'No. I came up here to tell you I'm going to arrest her. Just so's you know. False accounting over half a century is serious. She's going to court.'

The chief inspector looked grim. 'You're a hard cow, Jacquie.'

I returned to the store and had a brief meeting with the managing director. He told me he would back me in whatever I decided to do. I went back to my office. I sorted the case notes into neat piles on my desk. And I called Marjorie in.

'How long have you been working here, Marjorie?'
She told me.
'Can you tell me how the tills are reconciled at the end of the day?'
She told me.

'Do you know what this is?' I thrust a list of transactions across the desk.

'No.'

'You don't know what it is. And this?'

She was growing pale.

'Can you tell me why this figure here does not match this one here?'

'No.'

'Can you tell me whose signature this is?'

'No.'

'Why did you scratch this out?'

'I don't remember.' She took a small lawn handkerchief from her pocket and started polishing her reading glasses.

'Have you ever pinned till receipts to the wrong Visa copies?'

'I don't know.'

'Why did you pin this receipt to this docket?'

'I don't know.'

'You've made a lot of mistakes like that, haven't you, Marjorie?'

She was twisting the hanky and she stood up and said, 'I'm leaving. I don't like you.'

I stood up, too.

'You're going nowhere. You're under arrest.' I cautioned her and she sat down suddenly, in shock.

I rang the police station, spoke to CID and told them to come down. 'I've got a body,' I said.

She said hardly a word when the CID arrived. We walked out through the store in a small silent group. Other sales assistants looked curiously at her. She was taken in a police car to Ealing nick, charged and, a few hours later, bailed.

The next day at the magistrates' court she was bailed for another week. I knew it would take me that long to explain to the CID how the scam had worked and point out the crucial points of our case against her. Back at the store, I sensed hostility from a lot of the sales staff. Most people thought I'd gone too far. They were sorry for her. I didn't give a damn what they thought. I was proving I was tough. I was proving it to myself and especially to Tim, and what anybody else thought wasn't worth gnat's piss.

Later that day the old lady's nephew came in to see me in my office. He was a short, worried, fair man, a commercial traveller type with a bit of a beer gut. He pleaded with me.

'She'll never get another job at her age, she's no danger to anybody. She's not a criminal. She's always wanted to do the best for the family. Look, my brother and I have been talking about this. Can we just pay it back and have no more said?'

'Have you got fifty grand?'

He looked stunned.

I added, 'She won't go to prison. But she's been stealing from this store for years. People like her must not be allowed to think that we will let them get away with it.'

The next morning I was on my way to my office when the switchboard woman told me the managing director wanted to see me.

Richard was young to be the MD, only in his thirties. Standing behind his desk this morning, he looked grave.

'Marjorie took an overdose last night. She's dead.'

I didn't know what to say.

'Are you all right?'

I gathered my thoughts. 'Of course. What's it to me?'

I meant it. I went back to my office without a qualm. I

knew I had done the right thing. All the same, the Marjorie saga didn't do my relationship with the staff much good.

Half an hour later one of the store detectives caught the first shoplifter of the day. I had been fidgeting, putting papers away, and wanted to get out. I went over to the police station with them. As we walked past the desk sergeant he muttered, 'All right, this one, is it? No dicky heart?'

On the way up to the CID office I heard the chief inspector.

'How old's this one, Jacquie? Hope it's not feeling depressed.'

'Very funny.'

I got it for months. Tim never said a word, though. He was too busy being hard in pursuit of his own career.

7

Tim had joined the Special Patrol Group now. My God, they were unpopular. Even the police were wary of them and anyone who was more liberally inclined, like revolting students or militant trade unionists, put the SPG on a par with Nazi stormtroopers. They alternated eight weeks in uniform with eight weeks in plain clothes, doing surveillance work mostly. Tim was a big man, but anonymous; he was unnoticeable in a crowd, and he liked spying on people.

Members of the Special Patrol Group were discouraged from discussing work at home, and the fact that he could not talk about what he was doing didn't help our marriage. I'd often drive off to work on a Friday morning saying, 'Have a good day. See you tonight.'

'Yeah, see you,' he'd say, getting into his own car to follow me out on to the main road. When I came back in the evening I'd find a note to say he'd be away until Sunday. Called out on a special job, something's come up, anything. Other weekends he'd be away on a course. When he was home, we played badminton with Lynn and Robbie on Sunday mornings and had lunch with them after. 'You ain't half losing weight, Jacquie,' Lynn said to me once. She saw me every day, since she had left the police and become a store detective at Fields, but all the same she had noticed. I was glad I was losing weight. I tried never to eat unless I had to. I knew I was too fat because

Tim was always saying so, and it was easy enough to avoid food when I was working, but I had cut down my work on the tom squad a lot, and there were times when I got home in mid-evening to an empty house and raided the fridge. It was dead quiet after Boo had raced out into the garden and I was lonely. I would eat everything in the place and then stick my fingers down my throat and vomit into the lavatory. I always worried in case I hadn't got rid of all of it. Some of it might remain, go straight to my hips. I would look critically at myself in the mirror the following day and hate my bulging stomach and fat thighs and resolve not to eat for the next few days, to compensate.

One Thursday night Tim came in from work and flung down his jacket and said, 'That's it. They're sending us up to the miners' strike.'

'Up to Derby? You're joking.'

The coal miners of the north and north-east, represented by Arthur Scargill and his National Union of Mineworkers, were in angry confrontation with the Thatcher government over the Government's winding-down of the industry. Some of the miners had rejected Scargill's position and formed a conciliatory union. They were regarded as scabs and blacklegs to a man. The wives of the Scargill miners were loud and photogenic and said their piece in the media constantly. Scuffles at the pit-head were getting national television coverage, pickets were arriving from all over, thousands of man hours were being used to police the crowds at the mines and hordes of extra officers were being drafted into pit villages from the big English cities. But the SPG were something else again. They were armed and represented the State with its gloves off.

'It's a bit politically sensitive, sending you up there, isn't it?'

'Ours is not to reason why. I've got to pack for two weeks. We're going up on standby and keeping a low profile in case we're needed.'

He packed all his uniform and enough other clothes to keep him going for a fortnight, and in bed that night he said, 'I'll ring you every night at eight o'clock.'

'OK. If I'm not here I'll be at the shop or down the nick or somewhere.'

'You'd better be here. I don't want to be ringing and find my wife gallivanting about somewhere. I won't have time to mess about chasing you on the phone, they're gonna make us work all hours. Surveillance, if nothing else. Jesus, two weeks in Derby.'

Every night the phone rang.

'How's it going?'

'How you'd expect, for sixteen hours a day. It's end-less. There's nothing happening, dead boring. What a dump.'

The first Saturday he was away, I felt really sorry for him. I saw pictures of Scargill bellowing at the miners on TV and it was raining up there. London was cheerful and sunny and I had a day off. Boo bounded across the park in Sutton with me in the morning while a nice old man walked alongside me and told me what he remembered about the War. It was peaceful, contented, not the sort of day Tim ought to be stuck up there working. When Boo and I walked down the high street on our way home I lingered at Dixons' window looking at all the little black boxes of electronics with Special Offers and Discounts labelled in exciting colours. I thought about Tim and all this overtime and wished he was with me. On an impulse I went in, whipped out my credit card and bought him the top-of-the-range stereo system he'd always wanted.

'I've got a surprise for you,' I told him that night. I was happy, thinking what he'd say and looking forward to his return at the end of the week. Only another six days.

I had settled on the sofa to watch the Saturday movie when the phone rang again.

'Hello, Jacquie. Chief Inspector Griffiths. Sorry to call so late. Is Tim about?' It was Tim's boss.

'No, sir, why would he be?'

'I need to get a message to him. Would you tell him we're on standby for the miners' strike?'

'Er . . . Oh.'

'He needs to be ready to go up to Derby tomorrow. Can you get that message to him?'

'Oh yes.'

'Good. How's your annual leave going?'

'Well, I'm not on annual leave, sir.'

'Oh, I see. Well, anyway, let him know we're on standby, would you? Good night.'

The SPG work in twos. I rang Tim's partner, Bill.

'Where is he?'

'Sorry, what d'you say, Jacquie?'

'I've just had Chief Inspector Griffiths on the phone. I know what's going on. Where is he?'

'You didn't say anything to him, did you?'

'*Where is Tim?*'

'He's in the West Country.'

'Well, you'd better get hold of him, mate. Because you're

all on standby to go up to Derby tomorrow. Which is where he's supposed to be already.'

Bill didn't know what to say to me.

I did not sleep well. The next day, I was in the kitchen giving Boo something to eat when I heard Tim's car door slam and his key turning in the lock of the front door. He walked into the living-room, dumped his luggage on the sofa and was taking his jacket off when I came in. He looked round at me.

'Don't look so bloody tragic. I'm not going to have a go at you for phoning Bill.'

'Where have you been?'

'D'you say anything to the Guv'nor?'

'No, of course not. What is going on?'

He shrugged.

'I took Janine on holiday.'

'Oh. Really.'

'Yeah, really. And don't look at me like that. In the circum-stances, what d'you expect?'

I felt too helpless and inferior to yell or throw things. I minded a lot about Janine, so much I couldn't even bear to think about it, or about the scores of other weekends he'd been 'on a course' or when 'something's come up'. Now I knew exactly what that had been. But what I minded even more were the debts. He was spending money, my money from the Barclaycard account in my name of which he was a second cardholder, on hotel rooms and candle-lit dinners, petrol and cosy pub lunches, while I worked all hours to pay the mounting bills. I felt cheated because I had wanted a big strong man to look after me and it was me who was looking after him.

Tim walked out and stayed out for the rest of the day. After he'd gone I slammed through the house in tears, muttering resentfully under my breath about women with stubby legs and freckles. I put on a show of world-weariness though I was terribly hurt, and yet, in a way I was resigned to his infidelity. I worked with the police all the time, I told myself I should have known what to expect. I knew how long hours in the cosy front seats of a panda car usually end up with a recital of how the wife/husband doesn't understand me. I thought it was meaningless. But there was something about the way his name was avoided in my presence at Ealing nick. Something about the way he never turned up to the Christmas parties. People didn't attend those parties with their wives and half the male officers made it obvious they were having it away with somebody they worked with, so why should Tim be any different?

Besides, my work brought me into contact with betrayal and deceit all the time, with liars and con men and bullies.

One day not long after the Derby incident I was hanging about on the ground floor of Fields when I saw a man in his fifties in a smart suit who looked as if he had come in to buy something for his wife. He sauntered alongside the handbags, then his eye ranged along the waist-high display of gloves. He turned aside, but not before I had seen him slip a pair of gloves into his sleeve. There was something funny about the way he did it: delicate. He used his hand like a pincer. He walked towards the umbrellas and scarves, and as he looked at the umbrellas, with one deft movement he had ripped the sticky price label from the gloves.

I saw him return across the floor. He was urbane, assured. One long forefinger slid the gloves across the polished counter.

'I bought these here last week, but they're not suitable. I'm so sorry. I've lost the receipt for them, but they haven't been worn. Do you think you could let me have a refund? I'll go and find something else.'

As soon as the sales girl had called the supervisor to fill in the bits of paper, he was given about forty pounds in cash with Fields' compliments. He was on his way out into Ealing Broadway, light-stepping, head held high, when I stopped him.

'Excuse me, sir. You are under arrest. I am detaining you on a charge of deception.'

Expressions, rapid as clouds on a windy day, slipped across his face. It's the same every time. Shoplifters scan the alternatives: break for it, punch her in the gut, brazen it out. He made his decision fast.

'I'm afraid you've made a mistake, young lady.'

I was already on the radio to Ealing, asking for a police constable I knew to assist.

'If you'll just step this way, please. We'll be taking a statement from you.'

In the office he began to bluster.

'This is ridiculous.'

'What's your name, sir?'

'My name is Dirk Van Cleef, and I am a professional of good repute. I am a heart surgeon. And I can tell you that if this goes much further you will come to regret it. You have already caused me serious embarrassment.' He was leaning on my desk, two mutilated hands in view. He had no thumbs and some fingers missing. 'You may not be very good at your job, young lady, but that's a minor problem in view of the trouble I can cause. The way you approached me in public could be extremely damaging. This is defamation. I am sure your employers would rather avoid a lawsuit.'

'Yes, sir. You can say it all in the presence of a policeman in just a moment.'

The officer arrived in a car and took us down to the nick. In cases of deception, the CID has to be involved. I took Van Cleef into an interview room and left him with them. Then I went off to make my own statement.

Half an hour passed and one of the CID officers came up to me. He was a heavy man with a permanently troubled look, like an unhappy beagle.

'Are you sure about this one?'

'Not a shadow of a doubt. He whipped the price off those gloves and got a refund.'

'He has dozens of receipts in his pockets. One of them could easily be for the gloves.'

'I know what I saw.'

One of his colleagues came in.

I said, 'He lives in Ham, doesn't he? You want to get out there and search the house.'

'What, for forty quid? For deception?'

'There's something else going on here.'

'Yeah, well, maybe you just got it wrong for once. He is a heart surgeon, you know.'

'A heart surgeon.'

'Yeah.'

'He's lost two fingers off each hand and he's a heart surgeon?'

His big face crumpled into a frown. 'You're right.'

We piled into an unmarked car with the suspect and drove out to Ham. The address was a large detached house with a gravel drive, tidy green lawns and a protective fringe of fir trees. Van Cleef, or Mr Van Cleef as the CID deferentially persisted in calling him, stayed with two officers in the parked car while another CID man trudged up to the front door with me. A well-powdered smartly dressed woman, looking surprised, ushered us into a living-room.

'So, what does your husband do, Mrs Van Cleef?'

'He's a kidney specialist. At St Stephen's hospital.'

'I see. Mind if we have a look around?'

We could have waited and got a warrant but she had no objection. We skimmed through documents in her husband's study and finally decided to bring him in. He let us take several boxes of papers away and slunk back to the station with us.

I had seen the look on her face when he came in with the two officers. She was devastated. I think she really believed she was living with a two-fingered kidney specialist. I felt sorry for her, and irritated at the same time.

A few days later, the CID told me what they had found. The man had been stealing things every day, and taking them back for refunds – that was true, no question; there were hundreds of proofs of that. But there were other themes running through the paperwork: health insurance and South Africa. When they got the correspondence in order, they worked it out. He would insure himself for thousands, usually in London, against medical expenses incurred on vacation. A few weeks later he would make a claim, saying he had lost a finger when on holiday in South Africa. His London insurance company sent their request for confirmation to the box number of his doctor in Johannesburg, got the forms back duly attested and signed, and paid up. The box number belonged to a cousin of his. The two of them had done this over and over again.

The CID loved me. Two officers got to fly out to South Africa for ten days and when they came back, they brought a Johannesburg policeman with them and we had a party in the CID room at Ealing nick.

'All from one pair of gloves,' Lynn said.

We were having Sunday dinner in Sutton. Boo was lying under the table with his warm chin on my instep. Tim never said a word. He didn't like me getting good arrests. He knew I secretly hankered to go back on the Circuit and he knew the more spectacular crime I unearthed in my job, the more often the guys from the Circuit nagged me to quit and go undercover for them again. I couldn't win. If I had done a lousy job at Fields Tim would have sneered at me, and now that I was getting huge Christmas bonuses, congratulations and invitations to join the Chairman for breakfast, he sneered at me anyway.

Then one day I came home from work and he'd gone.

8

He had taken all the furniture except our bed and one rug. He took my dog, the stereo I had so fondly bought, and the car my dad had given to him.

I knew where Janine lived. I rang him there and told him he had twenty-four hours in which to bring it all back or I'd ring his chief superintendent.

So most of it came back, though not the things that mattered, like Boo. Nor my money; he had cleared out the bank account.

His first wife, Yvonne, rang ten minutes after I'd put the phone down on that first night. She wanted to know if we would have Mark at the weekend. I told her Tim had left me. I was huddled on the rug on the floor beside my bed and I must have sounded awful, because she said, 'Hold on. I'm coming round.'

She was very good. She made cups of tea while I sobbed into one tissue after another at the kitchen table. She looked as if she'd been through it, poor cow. Could have done with a good holiday, that type, the type who always seems to be waiting at life's bus stop lugging a couple of Tesco bags. She said he was a nasty piece of work, she'd been glad to get rid of him, and what he had done to me was worse because he knew I loved him. It was exactly what he'd done to Mark, ignored him when the kid needed a dad.

'Mind you, you're not much better.'

'What d'you mean?'

'Oh, come on, Jacquie. All those times he said you'd have Mark, and then you put him off.'

'But it was me who always wanted him! It was you that bottled out at the last moment.'

'That's not the way I heard it.'

We compared notes. Tim had been telling her I had to work and didn't want Mark to stay over, and he'd been telling me she was neurotic and wouldn't let him have the boy.

I went to work next day and didn't tell anybody Tim had left. I stopped buying food, since there was nobody to buy it for, and worked longer hours.

Outside Fields, in the shopping centre, there was a flower stall run by a known villain, somebody C11 kept an eye on. One day I glanced out at him from the ground floor window and saw a tall, dark, thick-set man who approached from our direction and slipped a leather jacket from under his coat to the man on the stall. Then he came right back towards the store, headed for the men's department, and started riffling through the racks of clothes. The buyer had kicked up a hell of a fuss when I said the expensive stuff should be chained, so it wasn't. When I saw him nick a leather jacket I thought, Right, I'm going to have you this time. I followed him out of the main doors on the ground floor.

'Excuse me. I am a store detective. You've got something you haven't paid for. I'm arresting you.'

I was halfway through the last sentence when he picked me up. I grabbed his lapels and hung on grimly. *I'm not going on my own, you bastard.* As we hurtled together through the plate glass window I crashed painfully on to my back. I was lying on shards of broken glass and as tottering plaster dummies went flying I had all his weight on me. He was scrambling to get up. I grabbed at the nearest moving thing, which was a tag on the heel of one of his boots. One finger was looped through it when he wrenched his foot so hard away from me that the finger snapped. I didn't feel a thing but it inflated instantly like an airbag. It was jammed in the tag so he was lumbered. I was like a ball and chain on his foot and he twisted round and I was trying to knee him. He slashed me with a carpet knife across the knee, into the bone, blood everywhere and Christ it hurt, and he was crouching, putting the boot in hard, aiming for the kneecap but clumsily because I was attached to his other foot.

By this time it was uproar in the shopping centre, somebody had called 999 and the call came out across the main set from Scotland Yard. Tim happened to be cruising around Acton in the SPG car. He heard that a store detective had been stabbed in Ealing and knew it would be me.

His team tore over, and when I woke up in Ealing Hospital hours later the bloke who had cut me was in the next bed with several broken ribs and a broken arm. Much later, in court, I demurely claimed that I'd done it all in self-defence.

I was in hospital for four months. The nurses were curious about me; in fact they asked if I ever ate anything. I am five feet ten, I weighed six and a half stone when I went in, and not much more when I left. Later, having gone back to work on crutches, I decided I had done all I had to do and there was nothing more to keep me in the job. In my tenure as head of security, Fields' annual losses from theft had decreased from five per cent to one per cent. Some of the people in the store hated me, but by Christ they'd stopped sticking their hands in the tills. I left feeling like the Lone Ranger. Who was that woman?

And without Tim's neuroses to restrain me, I joyfully went back on the Circuit.

It was a spring morning in Maidstone, early 1985. I had now been on the Circuit again for three months, I had never lacked for work and I was enjoying myself. Outside the town, there is an industrial estate. I swung my car into a space in the car park and set off for the front office.

'Hello again. Jacquie Moore, isn't it?'

'Yes. Hello.'

The personnel manager was friendly. She had interviewed me last week. This first day, I was to bring my P45 to her office and she would show me where to go. The P45 passed without comment. Nobody ever susses a fake. I followed her neat navy jacket as she bustled out of reception, through the warehouse with boxes piled high on pallets, to a set of offices at the back.

'You'll be working over here. The Ladies is that way, there's the water cooler, I'll just hand you over to Mrs Richards, she'll tell you what to do.'

My job was to be clerk to the manager, a colourless middle-aged man whose sole interest outside work was his garden. I mastered his filing system and bashed happily at the electric typewriter for a couple of hours until a coffee break seemed in order. There were two stained machines down the corridor, the kind that belch boiling brown liquid with lumps of powdered milk into paper cups, so I hoped I wouldn't have to hang around for too many elevenses before my target made her approach. I was in luck.

'It scalds, that one does,' she said, sharp-featured just like in the photograph, striding in from my left as I was juggling a paper cup over the drip tray. 'They should put a notice on it really.' 'Or get it fixed, even,' I agreed. 'Where do you work?'

'I'm in there.' She jerked her head at the main office where half a dozen girls sat at computers. 'I'm in marketing. You're Bill's new assistant, aren't you? You local?'

'No,' I said. 'I don't know a soul really. It's a long story, how I came here and got this job. What's your name?'

'I'm Lisa.'

Of course you are, dear. Ms Lisa Mailer, with £1,392 in a current account. Mortgage arrears looking desperate until just before Christmas when two grand arrived, and another thousand sailed safely into port last week. Credit card debt £742 on Access, £598.74 at Next. Pokey little flat in the top half of an old back-to-back, two bedrooms and access to a flat roof over the kitchen downstairs, on sale at £30,000 with three agencies for the past nine months. Mum and Dad divorced, both living in the town. Four CSEs, the same job since leaving school. No known boyfriend, although somebody's nicking stuff out of the warehouse like it's going out of style. And friendly Lisa has access to the company's customer database, which has almost certainly been provided, by a person unknown, to a rival firm.

'I'm Jacquie,' I said.

Friendly she certainly was. She was all over me. By lunchtime that day, with steak pie from the canteen inside us and only the horrible prospect of steaming brown tea from the machine at four to break the day's monotony, we were bosom buddies.

'So how did you end up in Maidstone, then?'

'I used to come down here for holidays when I was a kid,' I said. 'You know, when you've been through a divorce, you sort of go to earth to lick your wounds. My parents are dead and I've been an army wife for five years so I haven't got any ties anywhere else.'

'So where are you living?'

'I'm in a hotel. You know, a residential hotel – I'm looking for a flat to buy, so if you hear of anything –'

'What sort of place d'you want?'

'Small. There's only me. A balcony'd be nice, I like somewhere I can sit outside in the summer.'

'I only ask because mine's for sale. It might not be in your price range –'

'Oh, I haven't any money problems, the divorce'll see to that when the lawyers get it all tied up, but I do want to start looking. I can go up to about forty I think.'

Her pale eyes were fixed on me with wonder. Here I was, the answer to a maiden's prayer.

'Well, come round.'

'I'd love to.'

She explained to me in detail how to find it. I had spent part of last weekend driving around Maidstone, paying particular attention to Lisa's address and the bits of countryside I was supposed to have known so well at the age of ten. But it was touching to find that she was so anxious I shouldn't get lost on the way to her enticing flat. Clutching my forty grand.

Her social life began to include me. She asked me to join her and a couple of her friends for dinner. They were both women and one of them worked for our firm in accounts.

Nobody talked about work at all except to slag off the male managers. Lisa reckoned they were all as thick as pigshit and after demolishing two bottles of Valpolicella Lisa and the girl from accounts got the giggles working out which of the men would be the most disgusting to sleep with. I said I quite fancied one of the blokes in the warehouse but Lisa said he was a po-faced bugger, no fun at all, and did I want to go out with the girls on Thursday? There was a club. I did, of course. But if we were all planning to meet for a drink at seven, I wouldn't have time to go home and change.

'Can I bring my stuff over to your place after work?'

'Yeah, course you can. You can have a shower there if you want.'

On Thursday night I shut Lisa's bedroom door firmly behind me while she made some phone calls. There was no lock. The CD player was playing in the living-room, which was good. It covered up the low grinding sound made by her tacky furniture as I opened cupboards and drawers. In a shoebox in the wardrobe I found a roll of computer print-outs and an unlabelled floppy disk. This was a list of clients, all right. Names, addresses, contacts, order value –

A voice spoke so close I jumped.

'You ready?'

She must have had her face pressed to the thin wood of the bedroom door.

'Nearly,' I trilled. 'Won't be a minute.'

I swanned serenely out a few minutes later, done up for an evening in downtown Maidstone with the girls and looking as if I wouldn't miss it for the world. Lisa was skinning up, as usual. By now I knew she always smoked a joint before she went out. I began humming the tune the CD was playing.

'I really like that song,' I enthused. 'That's what you miss when you live in a hotel. I've got to get myself a stereo. I was looking in Dixons on Saturday.'

'You don't want to go there,' she snorted.

'What's wrong with them?'

'Well, nothing at all, except you work at our place. You don't have to pay for stuff like that, you can get anything you want out of the warehouse.'

'You're kidding.'

'Nobody looking after it on a Saturday morning, is there? And you know what's in all those brown boxes. Seen one stereo, seen 'em all. They won't miss a thing.'

The boxes, stacked high on the shelves, were generally accessible only to forklift trucks. I spent my days cataloguing and filing and storing lists of Japanese brand names and product code numbers for tape recorders and stacking systems, televisions and video recorders, all of them matt black and living on pallets in cosy moulded polystyrene shells within brown cardboard boxes.

'I wouldn't dare.'

'Give one of the lads twenty quid, they'll get you one.'

'Who?'

'Oh, any of 'em. They'll all take stuff out if you buy them a drink.'

By now I was getting my own ideas about who to buy drinks for. I rang up somebody I knew in the Regional Crime Squad and asked him to meet me in a pub. He was a nice man, Len, he'd been a sergeant in Peckham when I was there, and I knew he'd be interested.

'The clients asked the agency to suss out who was selling their client lists,' I explained. 'You know, counter-industrial espionage. I've got evidence, I've seen lists in her flat. But that's not all. We can get her and a whole ring of other people for nicking electronics out of their warehouse. And there's drugs involved as well.'

'What drugs?'

'She's always got hash, and she's started asking if I want to score a gram of coke before this party she's having. Look, are you interested?'

Len sipped his beer thoughtfully.

'Not in doing drugs, personally. When's the party?'

It was to be on a Saturday night. I stayed out of Lisa's way the week before. She kept ringing up the hotel and I kept having to go and see my solicitors after work, or whatever other excuse sprang to mind. I didn't want to give her a definite no on the cocaine, because I wanted to see if she would offer it to me on the night, and in any case I did have a bit of co-ordination to do. The RCS told me they'd be raiding her flat at 10.30 exactly on the Saturday night. I promised them I would get there at 9.50.

When I drove into the street where Lisa lived I passed Len and a woman sitting in a parked car. As I opened the front gate a faint thump of rock music could be heard and it got louder as I climbed the stairs. I don't know who heard the bell when I rang it. They all seemed a tad preoccupied. The door was opened by a small fat girl who seemed to have just got up. She was wearing leather jeans and matching bra that exposed a roll of midriff as white and firm as a lifebelt. Behind her stood a Myra Hindley lookalike with a whip. It was all like that. It got worse. I looked wildly around for a man. This was a party, for God's sake. There must be one. At least. A skinny bearded vegetarian cyclist, anybody, anybody would do as long as he was male and sane. But wherever I looked there were Amazonian females in rubber fondling lady partners. One of these, wearing crimson lipstick and a PVC skirt, was the giggling man-hater from Accounts. She swayed suggestively towards me in time to the music only to be intercepted by Lisa. I did a quick double-take at Lisa and hoped that 10.30 was galloping towards us. Maidstone, by Christ. I backed towards the kitchen. Her mousy hair newly streaked blonde, Lisa was wearing a sort of catsuit and smoking a joint in a long holder.

'Jack, sweetheart,' she murmured, hooking an arm round my neck. 'Here, I got you some punch.'

Punch! It probably had hallucinogenic drugs in it. I took the glass, batted my eyelashes, chucked Lisa under the chin and said something to the girl from Accounts. Lisa, close up, had gaping pores on her nose. I could see the kitchen clock from here and it was only five past ten. I could also see into Lisa's spare room, where two girls were engaged in violent loveplay on a creaking put-U-up.

'Come into the bedroom a minute,' Lisa breathed close to my ear. Her mascara was caked like a tideline on a beach and she had drawn a thick brown border around her unpleasant lips. 10.20. Time doesn't half drag when you're in a state of panic. I disengaged myself from Lisa's embrace and headed for the bathroom, where I stood watching the hands on my watch creep on for five minutes before people started banging on the door.

'OK. OK.'

I opened the door and had just got out when two women squeezed past and bolted themselves in. I hoped they stayed there, preventing Lisa from chucking her stash down the lavatory when the RCS charged in. Where were they? Why did they have to be so bloody prompt? Why couldn't they come at 10.29?

'You look gorgeous, Jack.'

Lisa had just made a desperate lunge across the sofa when in the nick of time we heard uproar in the hall. The front door crashed in and the room was filled with men in uniform.

'Everybody over there. Get over there.'

There were twenty or thirty women at the party, and we were all taken kicking and screaming to the station. It was perishing cold out, if you weren't wearing wool next to the skin, and in the police van I felt suddenly cold and very tired. The things I do, I thought. Well, it's a laugh. Lisa was giving the officers a screaming earful of abuse and she never stopped once we were down in the cells. Hours later, it must have been two in the morning, most of the others had been bailed but she was still yelling. Maybe it was the cocaine.

'You there, Jack? You all right?'

I was in the next cell, huddled in a blanket, but she couldn't see me.

'Yeah, you all right, Lisa?' I wished she'd go to sleep.

Heavy footsteps descended the stairs.

'You sad bastard, you leave my friend alone!' she shrieked as Len, unblinking, passed her and made for my cell.

'Get up, you bitch. Get off the floor.'

'Fuck off,' I said.

'Right, that's it, you're comin' out of there.' He unlocked the door.

'Where you takin' her?' screeched Lisa, frustrated. Len wiggled his eyebrows.

'It's all right, Lisa! I'm all right! Gerroff, you bastard!'

He hustled me upstairs in my trailing blanket to the police canteen.

'Len, I thought you'd never turn up,' I said, gratefully sipping a mug of tea. A woman sergeant at the next table was giving me very funny looks. Prisoners don't usually get invited to the canteen.

I asked, 'What you got, Len?'

The raid had been a great success. They had everything at once: stolen electronics, client lists, cannabis in dealing quantity and some cocaine. We had a good laugh about the state of the guests and then it was time for me to be returned to the cells. On the landing we began the sound effects and by the time I passed Lisa's cell Len and I were exchanging fierce abuse.

I was out by breakfast time and so was she. Later that morning she rang me up at the hotel.

'What you being done for, Lisa?'

'Conspiracy, theft, theft employee. And supply. They're right pigs, aren't they?' It's always the same. People do greedy things, acts of betrayal, cruel things, and then they're aggrieved when they get nicked, as if the police were the ones at fault. 'I gotta come over, Jack, I gotta see you, I want to talk, you know get it together – we've got court tomorrow.'

'You don't want to come over here, it's too public. I'll come over to you. Stay where you are, I'll be right there.'

I had already packed. I picked up my things from the bathroom, stuffed them into an overnight bag and got my luggage taken to the foyer. I checked out. Within fifteen minutes I was on the motorway back to London. As I drove

I gazed coldly into Lisa's future. When she heard my witness statement read out in court, maybe she would get some sense of what a piss ant I thought her.

9

Most of my undercover counter-industrial espionage or investigation jobs lasted six or eight weeks. The agency provided an information pack on the people concerned, the location and the background, and I had to make up my own cover story. After that, all I had to do was make the target trust me enough to talk.

I was really into it, pretending to be someone I wasn't. Partly this was because it made the job easier: it was a lot less difficult to get close to contemptible people if I wasn't being me. Partly it was because it reassured me that I was superior to them: I had a secret. And partly it was because it set me free. Being in the police force restricts your behaviour in unexpected ways. You're always watching your back and if you live with a hypercritical bully like Tim, you're always trying to live up to his image of perfection.

Now a job came up that meant I had to behave as I never normally would do. I had to be vaguely leftie, malleable, and a bit of a slob. I was repelled but fascinated as well.

The Greenham Common peace camp was famous. It was set up to protest at the US Air Force keeping ground-launched Cruise missiles on the Greenham RAF base, near Newbury, about forty miles west of London. The camp had become a magnet for troubled women. Hundreds of them, announcing that they were in favour of non-violent direct action, had been living in makeshift accommodation on common land outside the base for several years. Our client's wife had taken their children there and refused to communicate with him. My job was to find the children and the mother, so that the husband's solicitor could serve an injunction to make her return them to the family home. The mother must not suspect anybody was on her trail or she would do a disappearing act again.

I watched video footage of the camp and read cuttings. It was not going to be easy to fit in. I am tidy and organized and I've got no interest in politics. The arguments bored me, but I did my best. I even tried to figure out, without much success, what the tiny new Social Democratic Party and the Liberals stood for. I had never heard of any of these people. I had seen Brenda Dean on television, because she was the first woman leader of a big print union, but nothing else had really registered.

In the end I decided I'd just have to busk it. I got up one Sunday morning, pulled on a pair of grubby jeans and unearthed the sleeping bag I last used on a camping holiday when I was fourteen, and got a friend to drop me outside Greenham village.

The air base was about a field's distance away on the other side of a spinney. It was a nice morning, cold, and a hare sat up fifty yards away and stared as I tramped through his field. I was only halfway across when I smelt the camp. It was like the worst public lavatory you've ever been in. By the time I got through the trees I was inwardly reeling with disgust.

Thousands of tents in all colours had been erected as far as the eye could see. They were mostly low, slumped shelters for two or four people, and possessions littered the ground outside: Camping Gaz stoves, old carrier bags, toys, battered radios. Trampled mud paths ran between them and women and children ambled along as if they were in no particular hurry to get anywhere. The women wore droopy clothes or dungarees, with no make-up, a lot of jewellery and dirty necks.

I picked my way aimlessly across guy ropes until two grey-haired women offered me a cup of tea. They were making it in an enamel pot singing over a wood fire, and it was the sort of tea soldiers must have drunk in the First World War, nearly black but with sweetened condensed milk added to the churning mass of leaves and water so that it poured out opaque. It was worse than the machine at Maidstone.

I was a soulful girl, in this role, who did not talk much. I stared meditatively, smoked cigarettes, and listened. I squatted on top of my rucksack on a patch of thin grass studded with cigarette butts and when they asked politely why I was here, I told them how I had been travelling since I dropped out of college, and had decided to come and lend my support for a few weeks.

They were unquestioning, in a terribly well-mannered way. They assumed that because I was a woman I was automatically part of their system of values and we all supported each other. They obviously felt it would be indelicate to ask too many questions. This was all very kind, though foolish.

They showed me where I could sleep near their dying fire. I was offered a space in the tent, but I said no thanks. Three women already slept in there. It was dim, it was clammy, and the foetid stuffiness when it was packed with people must have been overwhelming.

On the icy trodden earth of early summer I zipped my rucksack into the foot of my sleeping bag and climbed in after it, shut my eyes against the stars and tried to ignore my freezing feet.

I woke up in moonlight with a hot shower coursing around me. Steaming liquid was splashing my face. I sat up sharply in time to see a sniggering pair of MOD policemen zipping their flies as they trotted back to the perimeter road. I yelled a curse at them and got up in disgust. I had to rinse my hair and sleeping bag in icy water from a standpipe at three in the morning, and I was not well pleased.

My new friends were very sympathetic. They might have bloody warned me, I thought irritably, maintaining my vacuous smile. It seemed these MOD idiots did it all the time, smeared faeces on the tent poles and pissed outside the tents.

The two women, Beth and Linda, and their friend Dorothy, seemed to have no objection to my staying in their tiny patch of territory within the camp. Using it as my base, I spent several days wandering about trying to figure out whether there was any pattern to the place. There wasn't. There were standpipes, field latrines which stank and, apart from that, nothing but thousands of sagging tents. I saw hundreds of children, none of them identifiable as the two in the photograph I carried in a moneybelt.

The days slipped aimlessly by. People got up early, largely because sleeping was so uncomfortable, performed their ablutions in cold water, lit a fire and put the tea on. Outside most of the tents radios would be switched on for the News. Porridge or cereal were eaten and then the morning stretched ahead with no relief except dog-eared books and conversation and washing up and washing. It was amazing. These women came from houses as I did, with central heating and hot baths and lives, if they had chosen to lead them. I mentally slapped my own wrists whenever I felt irritation rising. It was all so passive and uncomfortable and dirty, like going back to the Stone Age. I felt filthy. None of my outer clothes ever got washed, I was permanently cold, and my underwear could practically stand up by itself. I tried rinsing it under the standpipe once or twice but nothing ever got properly dry so I gave up. We were all the same. We reeked. After a couple of weeks, during most of which we had had to huddle in the tent in the evenings out of the pouring rain, I realized I'd got head lice and body lice. I scraped lines of minute white eggs out of the hems of my jacket and sat shivering while it hung dolefully on a hanger on a tree and I hoped that the problem would somehow be blown away. This seemed exactly the course of action a woman like me would take.

In role, I wasn't exactly dynamic. The others urged me to claim benefits from the DSS in Newbury and I sloped off a few times announcing that I was going to sign on but when I came back, I always told them there was a long queue and I couldn't be bothered.

Having hung out and tramped around and generally made my inscrutable face familiar for weeks I discovered that there was a school in the camp. I didn't want to become suddenly conspicuous, but I found my way over there most days. I saw no sign of the two children I was looking for.

It wasn't all boring and dirty. Oh no. Quite often we would mosey on over to the perimeter road and wait for trucks entering or leaving. A folk group turned up sometimes to lead a singalong. Very earnest, they were, and if you joined in with some all-purpose lyric about flowers and the wind, you were all right. If you got bored you'd go and tie a bit of ribbon to the high wire perimeter fence, giving it the same slightly loopy, trailing look that the camp had. When the trucks growled towards us, some of the braver spirits would lie down in the road and have to be dragged out of the way by MOD police. There was a lot of exhilarating shouting to do on these occasions and sometimes I'd clamber a little way up a post of the fence, which turned in at the top and was surmounted by barbed wire, and scream foul invective at the MOD men. I meant that part of it. That wasn't acting. I thought the way they behaved to these women was totally unprofessional.

I never needed to worry about showing my political ignorance in conversation. There was no need for discussion of the issues. Since anyone who had tits and turned up must be on our side, there was nothing to say. Apart from the crew-cut girls with big ear-rings and spangly leggings who would keep bringing up the Socialist Workers' Party, everybody wanted to talk about themselves. Not themselves in relation to the cause, just themselves. It was easy to let it all wash over you, you felt like a therapist.

When this palled, some of the women told stories to while away the long crowded evenings. I would sit cross-legged while joints were passed around, watching the storyteller and out of the corner of my eye seeing one woman take a nit comb to another's hair and thinking that this was the worst place I had ever been in. Although I must say Greenham finally put paid to my residual bulimia problem. I could never find anywhere private enough, or clean enough, to be sick in. I loathed going to sleep in the camp. Nearly every night some dyke would prowl up and try to touch me up in my sleeping bag. In the end I put about a story about having a girlfriend in the Wrens, and most of the advances stopped. Odd, really, how these women were so conventional and respectful of the idea of possession. In my view the camp was one big lesbian lustfest that went on for years, full of impressionable housewives too polite to tell the more aggressive women to sod off. There was some outright exploitation of battered wives who were lonely, but scared of men in general and their husbands in particular. But a lot of the better-off women who used the camp as a refuge from suburbia had never had a good time when they were young and were just catching up with the Sixties. They were into Finding Themselves, and could not therefore reject any of life's possibilities, just in case they missed out on an inner discovery. They went round saying things very gently, like, If that's what seems right for you, that's fine. The worst words they could use about you were *confrontational* and *judgemental*. So you could pass killer judgement on the USAF, but if some smelly bitch chose to unzip your sleeping bag you were supposed to allow her to express her true feelings.

I walked past the school every day and finally I saw the kids. They looked fairly clean and happy, as a matter of fact. But you don't argue with a client, and his wife had no moral right as far as I could see to remove their children from a secure background to this dump. From a phone box in the village I told my handler the best time for the injunction to be served. The solicitor's clerk would present her with it on the Tuesday after the Bank Holiday, so I made plans to leave on the Sunday. I promised Beth and Dorothy and Linda I'd be back. I said I was going fruitpicking for the summer.

I went to the main road and began hitching. Normally, I wouldn't. This time, I could have got a lift with a man who hadn't had sex for a decade. Nobody with a working sense of smell would have gone near me. I saw the poor bloke's nose wrinkle as I climbed into the cab of his van and he drove down to Barnet sort of leaning against his door, with the window down. He dropped me at the end of my mum's road. I'd rung her the day before, to tell her to get some nit shampoo in, so whatever she thought she didn't expect me to arrive as if I'd just spent six weeks in Claridges. However, I wasn't prepared for her reaction. She opened the front door about four inches and peered at me with one eye.

'You're not coming in here in those clothes,' she said firmly. 'You go round the back and strip off before you come in here.' So I had to do just that, huddled outside the back door. While I had a bath in four changes of water, followed by a shower and several shampoos, she burned my clothes in the garden.

A few months later, I came face to face with Beth, Dorothy and Linda in different circumstances. I was at Wapping by then, supporting a picket line, and having them recognize me by name helped my cover no end.

Rupert Murdoch, the Australian owner of *The Times*, the *Sunday Times*, the *Sun* and the *News of the World*, had moved his company's operational base out of Fleet Street to Wapping, beside the Tower of London on the Thames, and announced that from now on, News International papers would be produced using state-of-the-art technology direct from the journalists' and designers' desks. The printers had had it their own way for years. You read that there were whole families, three generations of blokes who had handed jobs on from father to son, laboriously setting lines of type in ways that were redundant thanks to modern computerized production. They didn't take redundancy lying down but set up a mass protest outside the new News International headquarters.

News International was now located behind high brick walls beside the river Thames at Wapping. A cobbled street ran alongside the walls, and other streets gave off it and led back up a slope to Ratcliff Highway, which is the arterial road running east from the Tower of London parallel with the river. Between the Highway and the river are a lot of old dock buildings, and some land that was in those days waiting to be redeveloped. It was on this land, and in the streets that ran up to the Highway, that most of the action took place.

The crowds filled the side streets most nights near News International: pickets by the gate, food vendors and the union caravan further back. A team of three of us were asked to go and mingle among the pickets to try and get proof that Sogat, the main print union, was paying for support from non-members. Once Beth and the others had greeted me like a long-lost sister, I was confident I passed as a right-on supporter.

As usual, the protest took on a social angle as well as a political one. People were enjoying themselves, in their way. The dreary folk group from Greenham Common turned up, and I stood and joined in with their familiar song of woe on a patch of waste ground outside the crowd. All the same, Wapping was rough. In most respects it was nothing like

Greenham, which was one long picnic. This was a war, with real hate in it.

There were perpetual scuffles when the trucks went in and out with newsprint, and although all you had to do was yell Filth! every so often at the police, or Scab! at the truck driver, and claim as I did to be a sacked social worker with a hatred for the Tories, you felt that if anybody sussed you for a plant you wouldn't get off with a verbal reprimand. There were minders around the Sogat '82 caravan; nobody could get near Brenda Dean. And the language was violent, the language of the SWP and other militant parties: Smash Murdoch and Kill the Pigs.

A confrontation was planned for a Saturday afternoon. I got down there and heard blokes in the crowd muttering, 'It's going up tonight.' A man picked up a half-brick from the waste ground and stuffed it in his coat. A mass of protesters was milling along the Highway already. The road was closed to all traffic except the TNT trucks that News International used, and they couldn't get through the throng. I was towards the back of the whole heaving group when we started moving slowly westwards towards the Tower. We were singing, a good few thousand of us had moved out on to the Highway and we knew what the idea was. The crowd would tail off behind us, the SPG and mounted police would follow, another group that meant business would come up behind the police and then the rear of the crowd in front would turn on them. The police would be surrounded.

That plan turned into the Wapping riot. I was close enough to the rearward group to turn and find myself facing a barrier of police with linked arms. People were chucking marbles from behind, knowing the police horses would skid and go down. They threw darts at them to madden them. Horses were whinnying and rearing. Half-bricks and lumps of concrete flew overhead and buckets of piss were being hurled into the police lines. Some of the militants in the crowd were so high on adrenalin that they tore forwards and laid into police officers with the strength of four people.

I found myself staring straight into the face of my husband.

I saw the look on Tim's face, opened my mouth, and contributed more abuse to the general uproar before a raving Durham miner elbowed me out of the way in order to chuck something. I was driven back from the front line by men who, come the real rough stuff, wanted to fight without a woman getting in the way (nothing changes, whatever side you're on), but not before I'd been seen by several surprised mates from Ealing nick. None of them said a word until the following day, when they all rang up to ask if I'd changed sides. I think I reassured them.

Towards the end of 1985 I spent many dull days sitting in a series of different cars, watching a woman in the busy London suburb of Golders Green. I didn't know who she was. She had streaked blond hair, drove an XJ6, lived above an estate agents on a main road and wore the tom's uniform of miniskirt without tights (time is money), fur jacket and chain-link handbag. All I knew was, she was the target, and she stayed in all day and drove over to Belgravia or Ealing most nights. In Ealing she went once or twice into a small terraced house in a back street, where a black man answered the door. In Belgravia she always visited a house in one of the squares. I didn't see how long she stayed, but by the time I knocked off at midnight she had never come out.

I was doing the job for Tony, a bloke I had worked with, who was being paid direct by the client, an acquaintance of his. After a few weeks Tony bought me a cup of coffee and told me he was going abroad for the next three months on a job. He wanted to know if I would take over, dealing directly with the client. I had no objection; I would get the entire fee.

The client lived in a square in Belgravia. It was one of the most desirable locations in London, four storeys, all shiny cream stucco and geraniums outside, and there was a house-keeper and a manservant, acres of pale carpeting, mirror glass and gilt with a living room on the first floor. He was a short, fat, balding Scotsman in his fifties. Very charming, couldn't do enough for me, but he had an oblique way of referring to the Young Lady. The Young Lady might be getting visitors at the Golders Green apartment, Jacquie, and he would like to know. Did I understand him correctly?

'Ian,' I said, 'I can't really help you unless I know what I'm looking for. Who is she and why do you want her followed?'

'You see, Jacquie, it's like this. She is my girlfriend, but I think she might be seeing somebody else.'

'Right.' Some girlfriend. 'If you want round-the-clock surveillance I can't do it on my own. It needs a team of three or four people at least. One person sitting in a car is bound to get noticed sooner or later.'

'I don't want to spend a fortune,' he said cautiously. 'What I'd like you to do is watch her from, let's say, ten in the morning until midnight. Don't worry about cars. I've got five, you can have three of them. The Roller and the Aston are a mite conspicuous. But you can always hire more cars, it's not a problem. Just you bill me once a fortnight, Jacquie. I'm generous and I always pay on the nail. Oh, and I want you to put a bug in my bedroom telephone. Just to keep a record of what the Young Lady is up to, you understand me?'

I checked her out the following day, and as I suspected, found that she had been cautioned for prostitution. So on the phone the next day I told him.

'I know that,' he said. My God but men are full of surprises. He'd got her from an escort agency in the first place. 'There's something I'd like you to hear, Jacquie. Come over tomorrow.'

At his house I relaxed in an armchair sipping a glass of spring water while he played me an audio tape. The microphone must have been about six inches from the bed. Either he was a great lover or she was very good at faking it. He was the client, so I was not about to decide which. Instead I fixed him with a beady stare and he took the hint. He fast-forwarded the tape to the bit where he gave her £500 afterwards.

'Ian, I don't really get it. You give her money for sex, but you say she is your girlfriend.'

'She needs living expenses. I got her the flat and the car, you understand me, Jacquie. All I expect is that she will be there when I want her, but she keeps telling me she is spending more time with her mother and stepfather. You see, Jacquie, she's had a sad life. Her mother has a drink problem. They live on some terrible council estate in Willesden.'

She wasn't driving down to Willesden in the evenings, but to the house in Ealing. She saw Ian and got £500 about twice a week, and nearly every other night she was in Ealing. After a while, she stopped leaving the Golders Green flat in the evening, and headed into town direct from Ealing, where she was spending nights. I had looked at the electoral roll and there were several names down for the house there, but I didn't know for sure who she was going to see until one day she drove from Golders Green to a car repair place near the Ealing house. Out came the black man, in mechanic's overalls, spoke to her briefly through the car window, disappeared, reappeared in ordinary clothes and got into the Jaguar beside her.

I followed them to the high street, where they parked and went into the local branch of the Abbey National building society. They were in there for forty-five minutes, somewhere out of sight, seeing a manager I assumed. I was pretty sure they were making a mortgage application, and I had a contact at the Abbey National. Within a couple of days I had the information I needed and went back to Belgravia.

'She's applied for a mortgage, along with a man called Hunter,' I told him. 'They want to buy a house in Alperton. Hunter is a mechanic who lives at the house in Ealing. He's got previous for dealing drugs.'

Ian was beside himself. He called her a lot of names, most of which reflected accurately on her profession, except for the bits about being cheap. At this stage he seemed to have overlooked my own last bill, so I was anxious to tie the whole thing up and get paid. His obsession with this mercenary little tart was getting on my nerves. A rational man would have called a halt to the affair weeks ago. But not Ian. His urbanity was sliding off him like oil off a mirror. I was beginning to see the raw man underneath.

'I'll settle the little bitch,' he fumed. 'She's not going to get away with this. Give me the Alperton address. I'm going to buy that house.'

'You what?'

'She's going to find herself well and truly shafted if she thinks she can buy that house with my money. I'll buy it over her head.'

'Ian, there are a lot of houses,' I said. 'If you do that she'll just get another one.'

He muttered something but I could see he had taken my point. 'She's a fucking tart.'

'Are you going to stop seeing her, then?'

'No, I'm going to get her into serious trouble. It's only a matter of time.'

So she went on sleeping with him for money, and I went on watching the Ealing house. I was beginning to see why Tony had made a diplomatic exit. Getting Ian to pay me for those hours of boredom was like getting blood out of a stone, only more embarrassing. Whenever he finally shut his eyes, gritted his teeth and signed a cheque, he wanted me over to his house to receive it in person and listen to another tape. They were all the same, sounds of ecstasy as performed nightly by pros everywhere. In the end I said, 'You're really not impressing me, Ian.'

'Just you listen to this.' He spun the tape forward.

She told him she wanted a thousand pounds to buy a mink coat. He asked her why it was so cheap and she said it was knocked off. She knew the bloke who'd done it. She was keeping a load of them at her mum's flat in Willesden.

The following day she rang Ian to tell him she had crashed the XJ6 on the way back from his apartment. I checked that up and found that she had actually had the accident near

Ealing, at 6 a.m. Hunter had been a passenger in her car.

Ian spat vitriol as before, but he still refused to stop seeing her. It was as if she provided the drama he needed. She gave him an emotional fix. He now insisted that I should get her prosecuted for receiving stolen goods. He was a hypocrite. I knew he had made a fraudulent insurance claim the year before. I'd once admired a watch of his, and he boasted that he had claimed he had been tied up and robbed in his own house and the insurance company had paid compensation for lots of stuff he still owned.

I was in no doubt that I had to do something, if the flat in Willesden was a stash for the proceeds of burglaries, but the way Ian kept on at me to get the girl arrested made me sick. Behind all his front, he had the mind-set of a petty crook. He rang me every day. She had said this, she had said that, when were the police going to raid the house? By Christmas all I cared about was getting paid and getting shot of the job.

I went out to Willesden on the raid with the police. She was taken down the nick and bailed for further investigations. On Christmas Day, Ian rang me from the QE2, where he was on a cruise, to ask whether she had been arrested yet. She had not yet been charged, because she had told the police that Ian had given her the fur coat, but he was going to have to make his own decision about whether or not to back up that story.

'Leave that with me. I've got another little favour I'd like to ask of you, Jacquie. You know I told you I was once married. Well, my ex-wife has got a boyfriend. I don't like the man. He is not good for her, you understand me, don't you? I want you to have him arrested for drinking and driving.'

His spite was unbelievable. I felt tainted. He was making me feel like an accomplice, not an employee. I didn't mind having somebody arrested for dishonesty, but I wasn't in the business of wrecking people's lives.

After endless nagging, I got his final cheque, paid it in and avoided taking his calls until it had cleared. When he got hold of me, at my mum's, with some new plan for making the Young Lady suffer, I said I was busy on another job.

'I'll make it worth your while.'

'Sorry, Ian. No.'

'You're making a big mistake, Jacquie. I could see you all right.'

I lost my patience.

'For Christ's sake, give it a rest, Ian. She's a cheap hooker living with a drug dealer, you pay her for sex, what do you expect?'

I was away working when he started leaving messages. My mum was always calm, she never asked me what I did or showed any sign of worrying about it, and I found that very supportive. But I was outraged when she got a call from Ian.

'Tell Jacquie not to back me into a corner. She won't like what I'll do.'

Mum said, 'Are you threatening my daughter?'

'Just tell her,' he said, and rang off.

Ambulances started arriving. They had been ordered by a caller in the West End. I finished the job I was doing and rang my mum to tell her I was on my way home.

'I've just had another ambulance here,' she said. 'They were looking for somebody at this address who's had a heart attack.'

She'd been through the real thing four times with Dad. I

was furious. I rang Ian and left a message on his machine.

'If I hear that one more pizza delivery, one more minicab, or one more ambulance has arrived at my mum's, somebody'll get a phone call. And they'll be told exactly what allegedly stolen goods were still in your house last time I looked. Do not threaten my mum.'

He was a nasty, vindictive little man. You can choose your clients, but most of the time, you don't know if you are working for the wrong side until it's too late.

10

I didn't have a weekend off the Circuit for over eighteen months. It was nearly all undercover work in lowly jobs, counter-industrial espionage or working out who'd got their hands in the till.

People who do menial jobs are often in the best position to see fiddles going on. Managers generally credit you with all the powers of observation of a pot plant. They treat you as a commodity, 'the girl' who'll post the mail or wash the glasses. They assume you're thick. The workers assume you'd go on the fiddle given half a chance. After all you're in the same badly paid boat as them, and they would. So one way or another, everybody reveals their secrets.

Through 1985 and 1986, I was living under different names, with different back stories, without a break. Most people who go undercover take time off between jobs. I didn't. There was so much work for a woman. Anyway, I had nothing else, no husband, not even my dog any more. My sisters had never shown the slightest interest in what I did and were housewives. We didn't have a lot in common. Mum was busy with the WI, the Spiritualist church and her own circle of friends. I liked seeing my own friends, but I was never quite ready to, at the end of a job. I felt I should wind down first, and get back inside my own personality, but there was no time because I always had to write up the report and open the folder on the next case.

'That's Beryl. You don't want to get on the wrong side of her.'

A thin girl of my own age was pointing out the other members of staff. We all wore blue serge overalls and sat at island tills in a big airy shop beside racks of paint and wallpaper. It was the autumn of 1986, house purchase was reaching a frenzy and all the home decorating chains were coining money. Even so, one of them, a family-owned operation with a hundred shed outlets in the south-east, was seeing a loss every month at its Lewisham store. I went on a crash course in operating their cash machines and appeared there one Monday morning as Jacquie, the new cashier.

'Is Beryl the fat one with grey hair?'

'Shurrup, she'll hear you.'

Beryl was a hefty-looking matron who was just about able to squeeze behind her till. I had seen her staring at me when I arrived. She had been buttoning her overall in the staff room and I knew her chest was looped across with gold chains under the blue serge.

There were about twenty of us: check-out girls, storemen to log in the deliveries, and half a dozen assistants who were glorified shelf-fillers. The shop was open seven days a week from eight to six with a late night on Thursday and a complicated system of days and half-days off. We ran the place. There was a manager, but the two assistant managers were the only ones who came out on to the floor. The manager cowered in his room drinking mugs of sweet tea and filling in the timesheets.

Beryl was married to a policeman. You'd hear, 'See *Crimewatch* last night? Seen your old man was on it –'

She made it clear with heavy hints that he was bent as a nine bob note. Nobody dared cross her. I was informed, after I'd been there about a day, that she was a friend of the Krays. She loved letting you know it. The Twins were inside for good, in fact the mad one had by that time been committed to Broadmoor, but you'd never know, there was a whole industry devoted to their exploits and somebody was making a film about them. She'd talk with grisly relish about Ron and Reg cutting people up. She basked in the notoriety. You'd think she was a face that made the whole saloon bar of the Blind Beggar reel back in horror, the way she carried herself. The rest of the staff lived by what Beryl did and said.

So it wasn't more than a week before they showed me how to fiddle the tills whenever Beryl's mates came in. They'd take a thousand pounds' worth of stuff and I'd have to ring up a hundred quid. Then I got offered meat from the butcher's next door. A bunch of them had a neat barter arrangement: slabs of topside for cans of paint. I reported that one to the clients as well, but avoided getting involved because although I told the other staff I was living in a room in Peckham, I was actually staying at the Clarendon hotel on Blackheath, and I didn't fancy traipsing through the foyer with bloody parcels of beef.

We had a surveillance team following the key staff to their homes and snooping round. Their houses were little palaces. They'd got half the stock of the store, from unopened boxes of vinyl tiles in the potting shed to planks of hardwood flooring stacked, ready to lay, in the garage.

None of what I saw in the first few weeks explained losses

on the scale they were running at. I had been told that takings for paint were particularly low. There was a stock check every Saturday and stuff was more or less where it should have been, so staff theft was not the biggest problem, yet the figures were down. There was some scam here that I didn't quite understand, and the clients were still mystified.

I was cautious, kept very quiet, and played a waiting game. Beryl was a bully, but conceited, and I was sure that her big mouth would catch her out in the end. I made sure I reacted with the same awe and wonder as the rest of them when she said her old man would see the manager sorted if he ever grassed her up. I could see she was busting to let me know how clever she was, it was only a matter of time.

I had been punching out the barcodes of wallpaper, putty and paintbrushes throughout most of October and November 1986 before Beryl graciously permitted one of the others to drop a word in my ear. It was a scam that eight of them were running: a couple of the warehousemen and some of the shelf-fillers and till girls. Every Tuesday, a lorryload of white and magnolia emulsion paint turned up. I used to see loads of it pass my till; it was cheap. It always sold out by Saturday. On Wednesday, the Dulux consignment arrived. This being Lewisham, where people will not pay top dollar for anything if they can help it, the Dulux never sold at all until the cheap stuff had gone. When the stock was checked on Saturday hardly any of the Dulux had been sold. On Sundays it began to go. However, the directors of the firm didn't even know they were flogging cheap paint, because it was all off the books – coming from a friend of Beryl's.

That explained a lot. The surveillance team got photographs of the paint delivery and, what with the loot in the houses, my own statements about fiddles on the till and bartered steaks, and the evidence of the paint scam, the clients were keen to prosecute. I had a meeting with the local crime squad and we discussed exactly when they would carry out simultaneous raids on the homes of the eight staff. I also explained, poker-faced, that they would find themselves face to face with Beryl's husband, a sergeant in the Force. That was their problem. The date was fixed for the following Thursday.

I had been staying in the hotel in Blackheath for about six weeks and knew now that I would be leaving for home on the night of the raid, so I rang my mum from a callbox. It was a Thursday night; exactly seven days to go. I got a number unobtainable tone, so I called my sister, who lived in Barnet as well. My sister said Mum got fed up with the phone ringing when she was trying to watch TV so she unplugged it.

'Could you pop down?' I said.

'What for? She's OK, don't worry.'

'You only live five minutes down the road –'

'Jacquie, there is nothing wrong with Mum. She is fine.'

So I rang again on the Friday and it was still unobtainable. I called my sister.

'Look, for God's sake, there is nothing wrong with Mum. I'm going up there tomorrow, all right?'

On the Saturday morning the shop was just starting to get busy and most of the others were still having the first cup of coffee of the day out the back. I was on my till, but an assistant manager came out and took over, telling me to go to the phone in the staff room.

'Your brother-in-law's on the phone.'

I went in and they were all staring at me. Nobody had got a call in the staff room in my time there. They were all standing puffing a final fag and ready to go out on the floor of the shop, but hanging about to see what was wrong. Nobody said a word. I picked up the receiver.

'Hello, Jacquie, it's me.'

It was my handler from the agency.

'Hi, everything OK?'

'No. You probably can't talk right now. I've got bad news.'

'Yeah?'

'Yes, I'm sorry to have to break this to you, love. Your mum's died.'

'Oh,' I said. I caught somebody's eye, fixed my gaze on the telephone, absently took a cigarette one of them offered me. 'Right. Right. Well, I can't do anything about that now.'

'No, it's difficult. You know what to do, then.'

'Yeah. Fine. Thanks for telling me. Bye.'

I put the receiver down. Got the cigarette lit. Kept my hand steady.

'What is it, Jack?'

'My sister's been taken to hospital. He wants me to go and see her on the way home.'

One of the assistant managers said I had better go home early. I muttered agreement.

I drove up to Barnet. The milkman had found her. Everybody was crying. The sister who had ignored me when I asked her to go round couldn't look me in the eye.

It was not a great weekend and I had to go back undercover on the Monday. There was a coroner's hearing, at which it was said that Mum had been dead since the Thursday.

The next Thursday I left the hotel knowing that the raids

were already in progress. Mum's cremation was the following day. Then I went back to work on another job.

A few weeks later, it was Christmas. I was fighting with my sisters all the time. I was even lying to them. It was as if nothing mattered. Everybody was up to something. Mum had been the one person still alive that I could trust; in the last year I'd only seen her between jobs, and there had been too many jobs.

If you asked me then what my name was, or where I lived, I hardly knew. I had spent so much time being different people, in different parts of the country, that I was a wreck. At the time I blamed the agency I was working for, because they continually sent me off on new assignments. I see now that I could have refused, taken time off whether they liked it or not, but it was years before I understood that, and understood why in those days I compulsively took everything that was thrown at me.

All I knew, by the New Year, was that I was no longer able to weep even in private. I was a zombie; emotionally dead. My family were the only ones who saw even a part of the real me, and the part they saw was not very nice. I snapped at anyone who crossed me. I was desperate, and I knew I was cracking up.

I went to see my doctor. She told me to take a few weeks off and think about what I really wanted to do. It was the sort of advice I could have given myself, but I was so weakened by this time that I needed an authority figure to tell me. So I took a few weeks off. I turned down all requests from the Circuit.

And I applied for a job.

11

Sheerness is dead flat, a low town huddled on a vast mudbank at the mouth of the Thames, so even before I drove into it I could see the Olau Line *Britannia* in dock. It was 500 feet long and eight storeys high, a cruise ship and car ferry that travelled every other day from Sheerness to Vlissingen with up to 2,000 passengers on board.

White paint sparkled, decks gleamed dull green, and port-holes glinted in smart maritime style as I dashed up the gangplank through driving sleet. Six of us had been called back, after preliminary interviews, for the ship's police force, to make a cross-Channel trip on which we would find out more about the job. When we disembarked we would hand in our own written reports about how we thought security on board could be tightened up.

Olau ferries sailed under a German flag, and under German law any ship above a certain size had to carry police officers who were also trained paramedics. The successful candidates would sign a contract in Hamburg and become members of the Olau*Schiffpolizei*, the ship's police. The posts had been advertised to English speakers, through the *Police Review*, because forty-five per cent of the passengers, and some of the crew, were English.

So we rolled off across the roaring January Channel to Vlissingen and back. A few days later, I heard that I was one of the three applicants to be accepted. They liked the references supplied by all the Circuit agencies, but even more, they liked the fact that I had gone for a walk round the ship at two in the morning and had noticed, as I pointed out acidly in my report, that the engine room was wide open to terrorist attack.

I didn't tell them I had been violently seasick.

This was just what I wanted, travel and meeting the public and, above all, being myself again, a police officer. There was nothing to keep me in England any more but I could not be happy without the adrenalin my work provided. I was good at law-keeping and at this point I lived for it. It was a dangerous state of mind. If Olau had known how dangerous, they should probably have given the job to somebody else.

By now I knew that, for me, the pinnacle of achievement was never going to be reached by becoming commissioner or the longest-serving agent on the Circuit. I was a lot more desperate than that. The pinnacle, for me, was to risk my own life in the course of protecting somebody else's. I was not exactly looking for trouble, but very deep down I wanted something to happen. When I heard that blowsy Beryl, having seen the prosecution statements, had been shooting her mouth off about what the Twins were going to do to my face, I thought, Oh yeah? Come and get me. Subconsciously I wanted to be a hero, or be in a shoot-out, or engage in some death-defying act of bravery. I had never been physically afraid. I am a believer in Spiritualism, a faith that makes worries about the temporal body pretty irrelevant. But now I was almost reckless.

If I survived with all limbs intact it was largely because

from now on I was armed to the teeth. Aboard and on duty, German ship's police carry revolvers, stun guns and PR24 side arm batons which are truncheons nearly two feet long. A gun would be of precious little use in any situation where a bullet might ricochet, but the stun guns, which put a 60,000 volt charge through an offender and knock him on to the floor, were used all the time.

Before I went on board as an officer I was required to learn international maritime law so that I would know piracy and mutiny when I saw them. I also learned some German law. My German was slight. It was mostly phrases remembered from family camping holidays. I got by somehow, and the law seemed fair enough. I was particularly keen on the rule that said I could collect on the spot fines. 'The more you argue, the bigger your fine will be.' I could hear myself saying it already.

At twenty-eight, and with more police experience than my colleague, I was quickly made up to sergeant. I was answerable only to the captain, a nice middle-aged German man who worked alternate fortnights with other captains. The officers were also German. The crew were mostly German and English and the receptionists, pursers, bar staff and so on who dealt with the public were Dutch, German or English. There were 120 of us working on board. I found myself looking after a small multinational town. It was a small town in which, every weekend, many of the English visitors acted out the *Oktoberfest* crossed with some kind of squaddie initiation rite.

The crew greeted the arrival of a woman officer with derision. On my first day I heard one of them sneer, 'She'll last till Friday night when she gets her first smack in the gob.'

He was dead wrong. Physical fear was not one of my failings. I got plenty of smacks in the gob. I got black eyes almost every weekend, my nose was broken five or six times in two years, I got broken fingers and was kicked black and blue. At first I got bouts of seasickness, but I got in there and made arrests.

There were several bars and restaurants, a sauna, solarium and pool, a duty free store, a playroom and crèche, a disco, a boutique and a casino. It was a nicely decorated ship – a lot of money had been spent on the interior finish – it was efficiently and politely run and the food was excellent. You'd think all these facilities would be enough to keep most young English working-class males occupied for the nine hours it took to cross the Channel. Not a bit of it. All they ever wanted to do was get a skinful and cause a ruck.

I had been on board about a month and was scribbling notes in the police office when, at two o'clock on a Saturday morning, a couple of skinheads came in. They were slightly slurred. (As opposed to vicious drunk, staggering drunk, puking drunk or dead drunk. I could already assess all these half a deck's length away.)

''Ere, darling,' said the bigger of the two. His forehead was wrinkled like a bulldog's and c.u.t. h.e.r.e. was tattooed across his throat. 'This bloke's just come in our cabin.'

'He tried to touch Darren up,' said his mate indignantly. 'And he had a uniform on, didn't he?'

'Yeah, the cunt'd got a uniform on,' confirmed Darren.

'Where did he go?' I asked.

'Dunno, do we, fucking pansy, he was feeling me up under me blankets, said they were looking for summat, didn't he? Fucking cunt. He just gone off.'

115

'Well,' I said carefully. 'Looking at you two, I'm surprised he's still walking.'

They were able to identify the man, who was a German purser. I had had a complaint about him before, so I got statements from them and the Watch Officer woke the Captain. The Captain agreed that I should arrest the purser for indecent assault. The skinheads strutted about all puffed up with righteous indignation, the purser was quickly booted off the ship, and I found myself suddenly popular with the crew, who had disliked him. It didn't last.

During the week, two of us were enough to police the ship. At weekends during the football season, there were always four and sometimes up to twenty police. Olau did their best to prevent football hooligans from coming on board by the coachload but they were regularly outmanoeuvred. Hundreds of pigfaced drunken louts created mayhem most weekends from October to May. As police we were always outnumbered and abused, but we dealt with them. If necessary we drafted in a support team of officers who were lowered to the deck from a helicopter off the Belgian coast.

Besides the usual run of Friday night fights, I had to deal with hookers, paedophiles, illegal immigrant rackets, porn smugglers, suicides, attempted rapes and at least one stabbing. But what the hell, I had wanted to meet the public. I had just begun to suspect that there was a drug smuggling racket going on among the crew, and was thinking about how to tackle it, when a car ferry like our own, the *Herald of Free Enterprise*, keeled right over on its way out of Zeebrugge and hundreds of people died. The skies were full of news crews taking aerial shots, and for the first few weeks the *Britannia* played host to ghouls making day trips to see the flooded boat lying in the Channel. An eerie shell, within a month the *Herald* was towed into Vlissingen.

The public were appalled by the way the accident had happened: the ferry flooded and capsized because the bow doors on the car deck were open. This was against maritime regulations but had become unremarkable. Turnaround times for a ship in dock are extremely tight. In a few hours they have to offload 2,000 people and cars and get another couple of thousand aboard. Every member of the crew has to work flat out to make this happen. Unsurprisingly, it had become normal for some cross-Channel ferries to shave minutes off the schedule by sailing out of port before the bow doors were fully shut. The *Herald*, like the others, was a tall ship and unstable if a big wave crashed in and started heaving from side to side. In March 1987, a heavy sea slumped so far over on its car deck that the whole tower, the cars, the container lorries, the many decks and bars and restaurants, mums and dads and children and crew keeled into the icy Channel.

The crew of the *Britannia* were gutted. Nearly all the English members were from Sheerness or Dover or one of the coastal ports, and had lost a relative travelling as passenger or crew. They came from a close community of small towns, full of people who were only a generation or two away from the East End of London, and if you didn't have a dead brother-in-law or wife's cousin on the *Herald*, you were a rarity. The accident cast a pall of gloom over everybody.

The maritime authorities saw with hindsight that what had happened on the *Herald* could have happened on many cross-Channel car ferries, so safety procedures were suddenly enforced with zeal. Ships no longer pulled out of harbour with bow doors open, diamond-tipped hammers became standard equipment so that glass could be broken in an emergency, and crews rehearsed lifeboat drills until they could get boatloads of people into the water within minutes.

We had all drawn together, over the week or two during which the disaster was headline news. Maybe that was why a seaman stopped me one afternoon as I was leaving my cabin and asked for a word ashore.

We met one afternoon in a pub in Sheerness. I had seen him about the ship. He was a fat little middle-aged cook with a ready smile under normal circumstances, but there was something on his mind.

'Tell you what it is,' he said awkwardly. 'I don't want to grass nobody up, but if you see something you don't agree with you've got to speak out.'

Large quantities of cannabis and cocaine were being brought on board at Vlissingen and sold in England. He named two of the bar staff he knew were involved.

'I've got nothing against them two,' he said. 'I've got nothing against 'em at all. I don't like drugs, that's all, and I can tell you there's more involved than just those lads.'

'How many?'

'Maybe eight or nine. I couldn't tell you who. I'm telling you nothing, right? We never had this conversation. I just don't want my kids to get offered no gear, I don't agree with it at all.'

I didn't agree with it either but I would have to have proof, and if at some stage I intended to arrest a large contingent of the catering staff on board I thought it might be a good idea to let the Captain know. I resolved to tell him as soon as I could. As tomorrow night was Friday night, there would be plenty to report.

Early next morning at Vlissingen I was watching the foot passengers trudge up the gangplank. I spotted a few I had seen before, but when a tall, good-looking fair man in a well-cut suit came up to me and said in a soft German accent, 'You must be the new police officer?' I was so surprised that I just nodded and muttered yes, I was. I was surprised because I caught myself thinking, *Whooah*, he's nice. It had been a long time since I thought that about anybody and I was overwhelmed.

But I quickly relegated lustful thoughts. It was Friday and I had to try and get some kip before tonight. I had only been on board for a month or two, but I knew what to expect. We turned the ship around in Sheerness late on a Friday afternoon. Coachloads of football shits would roll on to the car deck, already tanked up and thundering for the bars to open as soon as we put to sea.

It was the same most Friday nights. The fights began at about midnight. I would start arresting people for assault and criminal damage and if they declined to come quietly, I would grimly knock them out with a stun gun. A typical hooligan would slide to the floor with his eyes open, I would turn him over, cuff him, drag him down to a cell and let him lie in his own mess. The 60,000 volt charge relaxes all the muscles, including the bowels. We would keep ten people in each of the two cells, and sometimes up to a hundred cuffed to the rails outside. The ones in the cells were hosed down with icy water at intervals through the night. I often suspected that the crew enjoyed that part of it the most.

When the drunks woke up I fined them all their money. It is not possible to land on Dutch soil without a nominal sum for accommodation for every night of your stay, so, having confiscated their passports, and knowing they were potless, it was a simple matter to visit the Dutch Maritime Police on landing and have their passports stamped 'Deported'. The hooligans, still in the cells, would travel straight back to England. Back in Sheerness, after the nice family passengers had disembarked, police vans would be backed up to the ship waiting to take the damp and shivering scum to the magistrates' court.

This particular Friday night, somebody blacked both my eyes and my nose swelled up and bled. I had not been in the job long, but long enough to recognize that I would have black eyes more often than not. It's odd, the effect of a uniform on a drunken English yob. After a certain number of pints you're the sexiest thing they've ever seen in a skirt. You approach them complete with badge and guns and severe suit, and they're all glee and hands and, 'Wahay! I could give you one, darlin'.'

'If you've got one like this, come and see me,' I used to say sweetly, whipping out my two-foot rubber truncheon. 'Otherwise, go away.'

This approach worked only during drinking hours. As soon as the bars were shut they became less predictable. I once hauled a roaring blood-covered sot out of a bar, cuffed him to the bed in the sickroom, and stitched up his face, which had the nose hanging off sideways. I had just shut the door on him and turned into the narrow corridor outside when I came face to face with the four blokes who had done him over. They indicated, in the nicest possible way, their intention to get past me into the hospital room and finish what they had started.

'Uh-huh. We can talk about this,' I began, one hand on my radio and the other on my nightstick. I could see the uniform was going to have its other effect, which is: If she's in uniform she's a cow. The four of them decided as one man to give me a good kicking. On the floor, curled up, you jam your finger on the radio button that transmits everything that's happening to fellow officers so that they will come down and get the bastards off you. I survived. But uniforms don't reassure everybody, least of all the person who's got to wear one.

So, early this Saturday morning, with my suspicions about the crew newly confirmed, when I climbed all the way up to the bridge to hand in my arms at the end of my twelve-hour shift I was not feeling full of gentle benevolent thoughts about humanity in general. Surly, would have been the word. First there had been vicious Tim, then the professional thieves at Fields, then the greedy little toerags with their miserable scams in industry, and now these oafs who broke my nose and vomited down my skirt. It was a normal weekend and I had made over eighty arrests since midnight. Did I like people? Hardly.

The bridge was a wide low room with inward-slanting windows revealing the black morning outside. The captain and senior officers sat on swivel chairs at a console that winked with electronics. Conversation was intermittent, in German, in low tones. I had to call the captain 'master'; it was the German custom. I was getting used to it; and this week the senior captain of the line was to be on duty. He turned when I came in.

'Good morning, sergeant.'

'Good morning, master.'

He was tall, he was fair, he was very good-looking and he was the dish who had approached me on the gangway. I almost felt a smile breaking out.

12

'But your eyes! You must get treatment.'

'Oh, don't worry. It'll go down.'

'But –'

'It's fine, really.'

He stared at me for a minute.

'I've never had a woman before.'

'You poor devil,' I said.

'No. I mean – I mean, I have never had a woman police officer. You know what I mean,' he said, grinning. Lovely smile. Oh, crinkly eyes when he did that. I controlled my urge to beam back at him and handed him the arrest reports. As he locked away my .38 Smith & Wesson and ammunition I murmured, 'There's something I need to talk to you about in private.'

Early next morning, in brilliant sunlight under a huge blue sky, he drove me from the car park at Vlissingen dockyard to a fishing village ten minutes further north. Veere was a lovely place, cobbled, quaint and, at eight o'clock on a breezy Sunday, deserted. There was a coffee shop on the quay, one of those dark brown Dutch places that give you cheese and ham and toast for breakfast, but it didn't open for another twenty minutes, so we sat on the pebbled beach and I told him what the cook had told me.

'I thought it might be so,' he said. 'I didn't know it was so big, though.'

'It is on quite a scale. You think it's been going on for a while?'

'Maybe.'

'But there has been a police officer on board before me.'

'Ah, but a man.'

'So?'

'I have known the two sergeants on this ship before you and both of them were making love to women from the crew. Both of them were married. That sort of thing makes a policeman vulnerable.'

'Yes, I suppose it does.'

'Are you married?'

'No.'

'Good.'

As it happened, I was lying. I was, technically, still married, though separated. This may have been a factor when Olau Line gave me the job. As Thomas said, police officers on board a ferry are even more vulnerable if they are married. They are working in an exciting atmosphere, with most people off the leash and looking for a good time. Affairs are not expected to last because circumstances will drag people apart. The ship's police live cheek by jowl with the crew, but the crew are suspicious as hell because ultimately the police officer is on the side of authority. He shares experiences with them, but will never be one of them. It is small wonder that, quite often, police on board ship can't stand the social isolation, and go native.

If you're a girl working on the ferries, any male officer

with limbs and features in the conventional alignment is the most practical catch. A man with authority can protect you. All the women on board get propositioned all the time. They want to be known as the girlfriend of some-body high up in the hierarchy because then they will be left alone.

And having a lover on board changes the police officer's attitude to the job. Policemen are of course more inclined to turn a blind eye to smuggling if it's tacitly understood that the crew won't tell the wife about the girlfriend. But there is also the dependence on social contact. Very often the lover is the one person the officer can talk to in a hostile community. People get possessive in those circumstances. They will compromise themselves rather than lose the lover.

Watching and listening to Thomas, as we talked in the coffee shop and walked around the village, I was attracted by him, and I knew he felt the same way about me, two black eyes notwithstanding; after all, men want to protect a girl. But I was under no illusions. Thomas had good looks, status and oodles of charm. If I fell in love with him he could very easily break my heart. I was not going to let that happen a third time. Under the spell of a man like this, I could screw up my job. That wasn't going to happen either.

'So, about these clowns and the illicit substances. I'm going to have to keep Special Branch informed.'

'Jacquie, I am the captain of a ship, and I know how to do that; and you are a police person, you know how to do that. You come and see me when you have got all your evidence and I will back you up.'

'OK.'

'I mean that for everything. You police the ship, I won't interfere; I drive, you don't interfere. And we'll be fine. Tell me about yourself, how is it you are here?'

I told him about working under cover and how I had felt burnt out, how I had almost forgotten who I really was and wanted to go back to meeting the public. He looked wryly at my bruised face.

'But not meeting like last night.'

He was forty-one and lived in Düsseldorf. He had entered into a marriage of convenience to an Indian woman who wanted her parents to believe she was the devoted wife of a German sea captain. (She actually lived with an Indian businessman her parents knew and disliked, in Dortmund.) Her father was a senior civil servant in New Delhi, and he and her mother came to stay for a fortnight in Düsseldorf every year. Thomas stayed with his wife for the duration and together they played Captain and Mrs Happy Couple.

Before this there had been a first wife, and a divorce. He was on good terms with her, and their two children who were now at university; they too lived in another part of Germany. As a young man Thomas had been a refugee from East Berlin. His mother still lived there and there had been a father, whose life had been a tragedy. He had worked in the salt mines of the East right through the Second World War. On his return in 1945, Thomas was born, the only child. By now, the little family was trapped in the poverty of East Berlin, cut off from the western world by that cruel concrete wall. Thomas and his father had talked about getting out. His mother was nervous. At fourteen, Thomas had made his way to a Baltic sea port and stowed away. A tall, strong boy, he found work as a sailor and survived. Eventually his father had made a break for it. He was shot dead as he climbed the Wall that divided Berlin.

It was the spring of 1987 and I hadn't dated anybody since my marriage ended three years before. I hadn't given myself time; I was always working. Also, nobody had been anywhere near good enough. If a man appeared he would have to be riding on the bridge of a very tall cruise ship or I wouldn't notice him. Now my dreamboat had sailed into harbour, I was being wooed, and I was flirting right back. Every morning we met, either on the boat or ashore, and had coffee. Thomas showed me the countryside and the little old towns and ports around Vlissingen. People smiled at us, Holland glittered proudly with crimson tulips and aquamarine and white paint in the spring sunshine, and we were absorbed in each other.

'Only another four days. I have to go off duty on Friday,' he said sadly. We were sitting on the beach in deckchairs; we were never far from the sea he loved so much. The sun warmed my face. We gazed at the long white yachts moored in the harbour.

'Maybe I should stow away on a yacht,' I said dreamily. 'Sail somewhere warm and exotic.'

'The Caribbean. Have you been there?'

'No. Have you?'

'Many times. In a few years I shall work there.'

'Tell me.'

'Tell me first how you will stow away.'

'I'm talking to an expert. You tell me.'

'I don't think it's right for you. I don't think you are a stowaway. A hijack would be better. Piracy. With drama and gunfire. You could leap on to the yacht with a black scarf over your face and frighten the captain. He would put his hands up at once.'

'But you've got to come on board, too.'

'Of course. Smoking my pipe. I am the calm one. I shall take the controls after you have stolen the boat.'

'And where shall we go?'

'I think a little detour to the Mediterranean first.'

'Cannes, maybe. Or Monte Carlo. We'll break the bank.'

We planned our escape. We went around the world together, sitting on that beach in Vlissingen, and when it was time to leave and go back to work we both felt utterly happy in one another's company. We always left the ship and returned to it separately. This time I headed for the *Britannia* before him. He grabbed my hand as I stood on the beach dusting sand off my skirt.

'I forgot, it wouldn't work, Jacquie,' he said, smiling up at me from his deckchair. 'You would be seasick.'

That night I bought a card at the ship's shop and slipped it under his cabin door. Thank you, I wrote. I have had two wonderful weeks and you have been so kind. Do you know a cure for seasickness?

The next day, a little note invited me to come to lunch in Thomas's cabin. It seemed he knew just the cure I needed.

Our affair was a secret. The crew would have made all sorts of capital out of it, had they known, and with a very few necessary exceptions they never did. I didn't socialize with them; I talked to the girls in duty free and the beauticians and hairdressers, but for the most part I ate in the officers' mess rather than the crew mess. I don't know how the English sailors thought I spent my spare time. If they discussed it at all they probably told each other that any woman who was willing to risk getting her teeth knocked out twice a week regularly was probably a dyke or a masochist or both. The truth was, before I met Thomas I was aggressive outside and almost suicidally depressed inside. And without the elation of those first months of the affair with him, I would have found the rest of 1987 very difficult. Because suddenly, things began to go wrong.

The cook, my informant, met me again at Sheerness. He now knew to within a week when a large consignment of *cannabis sativa* was due to come on board. He knew who was picking it up, where it was going to be stashed and who would take it off the ship at Sheerness. What he could not say was exactly when it would come aboard. He would know very shortly, but I wouldn't be around for him to tell me. I had to appear as a witness at Maidstone Crown Court and would be on shore for five days. I told him that Craig, a colleague who had been appointed shortly after me, would be told what was going on. As soon as the cook had reliable information he should speak to Craig.

I put Craig in the picture. I hadn't told him anything before because until action had to be taken, there was no point. He was a colourless character, but efficient enough. Then I left the ship.

Five days later, when I walked up the gangplank at Sheerness, I knew something was wrong. I stopped a man I knew on his way to the car deck.

'Where's Craig?'

He shrugged and hurried on without meeting my eye. The chief purser, a Dutchman, saw me before I got to my cabin.

'Jacquie, I think we may have a problem.'

He guided me into a corner. Trippers were pouring up the stairs between decks and the noise was considerable.

'Craig is not with us any more. Captain Harman has sacked him.'

'He what?'

'For his own protection. On Tuesday night Craig started drinking.'

'He doesn't drink.'

'Oh, doesn't he? Believe me, once he starts he does not stop. He got blind drunk. Rat-arsed,' he added firmly, in case I had missed the point.

'And?'

'And he told Derek the English barman that you told him Derek was smuggling drugs. Captain Harman has also got rid of one of the cooks. The English are talking about nothing else. Derek is still here but . . . I don't think you are very popular.'

Oh. Right. I got to my cabin at last, opened the door of my wardrobe and found all my uniforms dripping with engine oil. My bed was full of cut grass. Odd to think somebody had gone ashore, mown his lawn and returned with a bag full of clippings. Bet his wife thought it was Christmas, having her old man come home and mow the grass.

There had been eight conspirators in the pathetic little plot to smuggle hashish, and there were at least seventy English crew, but they were all on the same side when it came to treating me like shit. For the next three months, nobody except the Dutch receptionists and the German officers would speak to me. If I went into the crew mess to pick up a meal to eat in my cabin and put down my orange juice, later I would find salt in it; other times I would turn just in time to catch somebody spitting on my food. At first I found the perpetual silence unnerving, but I didn't resent it. I thought they were a sad bunch, imagining themselves loyal to a stupid code and scared to step out of line.

Maybe I was indifferent partly because Thomas and I were in love; we had our own life, which mattered a lot more to me than the crew's attitude. The only effect their vendetta had on me was that I got hardly any shore leave. I was on duty more or less single-handed for about five months. Replacements for Craig quickly found that when fights broke out in the bar, when thieves tried to rob cabins or drunks fell through doors at three in the morning and attempted to rape women passengers, nobody, not the cabin staff nor the cleaners, the barmen nor the lowliest of the sailors, would help. I would be trying to handcuff a man while another one took a swing at my nose and as I peered through the blood already coursing down my forehead the crew would all turn away. Police colleagues did not stay long.

13

If I was paranoid, it was hardly surprising, but only somebody with Thomas's maturity could have put up with me in those months. I was in love with him, but I was determined to trust nobody, not even him. He said he loved me, so I had his background checked out: career history, bank details, credit reference, everything. He seemed respectable enough, but I was convinced he must have a hidden agenda. After all, he was a man, and I knew what happened with men. Sooner or later they turned and attacked you. I was damn sure I wasn't going to let myself be trampled on again. And he worked on the ferries. I knew what temptations ferry crew were prone to – he could have been smuggling porn on a large scale, or drugs, or turning a blind eye to any of a hundred rackets that would make dating the ship's police officer a great idea.

It wasn't that anything in his behaviour made me suspicious. Exactly the opposite. He was unfailingly kind. Too kind. My problem was, his affection made no sense. I couldn't quite believe it was real. When your lover sees you with a black eye nearly every week, your arms and legs covered in bruises, and you wear a plaster on your nose the way other women wear sunglasses, it's easy to feel outclassed by the competition. As the captain of the ship, he could have made love to any one of the glamorous women aboard. The croupiers were always dressed to the nines, for a start. Or any rich cultivated beautiful creature he met on shore who might find herself attracted to a sea captain who had sailed the world. He met interesting women all the time. Why me?

You could say my self-esteem was shaky. I was certainly confused. Our passion for each other was growing. I had taken a house in Vlissingen, a sweet little town in those days with a windmill, cobbled streets and a boardwalk, and we spent as much time as we could on shore as well as at sea. But there were still whole months during which we could not be together and I missed him. At such times, in self-defence, I deliberately made myself assume Thomas was insincere. If he could stand being away from me for a month, then I could stand life without him.

I could even clear up outstanding business. When I was back in London for a weekend, Tim rang me. He wanted to discuss divorce, he said. I told him I'd think about it.

'Janine's gone to Spain for a week. I'm at a loose end, can I buy you dinner?'

It was a nice dinner.

'D'you want to see where we live?'

'Sure,' I said. 'I'd like to see what I paid for.'

It was a nice house. Boo was fine. The bedroom was OK. The bed was not, but worth it to have a good look round.

A week later, when Janine was due to return from Spain, I dropped her a line. I thought it was time I said my piece to the woman who had slept in my bed while I was in hospital having a hysterectomy. *You've got a cream carpet in your bedroom*, I wrote, *and you keep your knickers in the top drawer by the window. Have a look behind the wardrobe. You'll find*

my name and address. I left it there last Saturday night when
my husband was in your shower and I was putting my clothes
on again. Funny, he's had so many women in that bed and
he's still not much, is he?

I didn't hear from Tim for a long time.

As the months passed, and Thomas and I stayed together as
often as we could, he showed me it was possible to be gentle
and tolerant without giving up your principles. I thought
lawbreakers were contemptible, and I said so. I was unforgiv-
ing and censorious. He wasn't. He disliked anti-social
behaviour, in fact he hated cruelty, but he taught me that
not everyone operates according to my own standards and
values.

'You shouldn't see everything in black and white,' he said.
'There are shades of grey.'

He said sometimes people have to dump their ideals in
order to survive. Knowing what his life must have been like
when he was a boy sailor, I thought he must know what he
was talking about and I listened to him. Also, I was impressed
by the way he treated the crew. As a boy he had been victimized
by a string of sadistic captains, and he was determined never
to be unfair. Apart from anything else, he said, you don't
often change people by unkindness, but you can sometimes
make a difference if you show you trust them.

'And you should trust me,' he said one night, as we lay in
each other's arms in his cabin.

'You think I don't?'

'No, you don't. I've got a song I want you to listen to.'

He rolled over and pushed into the player a CD with Billy
Joel singing 'An Innocent Man'. I listened to it, sleepily. All

about a man whose girlfriend is angry at him for something he hasn't done.

'Well?' he said when the music stopped.

'Well what?'

'Don't you see? You've got to stop blaming me for what somebody else did to you.'

I wanted to, I really did. I wanted to trust him. But I had been trapped before.

After the storm over Derek the barman, the crew knew they couldn't turn me, but that didn't change a thing about their attitude to the law. There was a hard core of lads from in and around the Isle of Sheppey, the vast mudbank Sheerness stands on, and as far as most of them were concerned you scraped every ounce of fat off a job on the ferries. There were so many scams going on, in and out of my line of sight, that I couldn't begin to deal with all of them. I'd walk into any pub on Sheppey and see two-litre bottles of vodka and cartons of cigarettes marked duty free, and I'd know it had all come out of crew bond, but it wasn't my problem. Unless they started to take the piss by walking off the ship with stuff under my nose, I didn't bother talking to Customs about it. I just kept on doing my job on board and let the excisemen worry about the rest.

In the end, people started talking to me again. I sat with a girl crew member for twenty-four hours feeding her fluids while she had a bad attack of gastroenteritis, and people came round a bit. Then a barman got a twisted gut and had to be taken off the ship to Holland by air ambulance, and I gave his wife and kids the keys to my house in Vlissingen. After that we were more or less back to normal. In fact, within a year of my starting the job, I was getting messages from local villains via the crew, which was progress of a kind.

'Jim drinks wiv me bruvver an' 'e says to tell you if he ever sees you again, you're dead.'

'You don't say. And would you credit it, I'm still here. Is it that hard to come and find me?'

If I got the chance I would go up to these idiots in the courthouse when they were shuffling, booted and suited, clean collars biting into their thick necks, in a huddle with their solicitors waiting for the magistrates to call them.

'I believe you've made a threat against my life. Is that correct?'

A fleeting look of panic shot across from the solicitor, every time. Their clients could get done for threatening witnesses if they rose to the bait. They never did. They were all mouth with a rabble around them, but scared little boys on their own.

Olau Line went to a lot of trouble to distract the British on holiday from beating the living shit out of each other. As soon as passengers came on board, they were plied with invitations to dance in the disco or recline in the jacuzzi or lose their money playing blackjack. Most weeks in high season there were live bands. The trip from Sheerness to Vlissingen wasn't long, but it was more than just an interlude on a journey; it was an outing.

And even the staff at Buck House get outings. One day I was watching passengers come up the gangplank when a man broke away from a party of visitors and introduced himself as an officer of the Royalty Protection Group. He was here with some maids and footmen of the Royal House-

136

hold, off to the Continent on a jolly, and said if I needed any help I must call him. I thought that was nice of him, especially since it promised to be a fairly rough Friday.

We had a live band playing in one of the bars that night and I saw one of the royal maids, a pretty blonde of about twenty, hanging around the drummer all night. She must definitely have a thing about older men. They were just the right sort of group to have playing on a family outing, but they weren't exactly babe magnets – they had been famous for about three weeks in the mid-Sixties and the singer was going bald. What remained of his hair was scraped into a scruffy ponytail. I scrutinized him carefully because he too had a girl at his feet, and she was even younger than the royal maid. I asked her how old she was because I didn't think she should be drinking alcohol, and she muttered that she was sixteen and it was only orange juice. Grandfather complex, I supposed, but that was her lookout. He was lapping up the attention and leering down her blouse. Maybe, I thought, she was a hooker. If so there was not a lot I could do about it. Under German law I should let hookers go about their business. They had to carry evidence of a recent medical check-up, and I could have a look at it, but that was all.

When the bar shut I dealt with the usual run of fights and rowdyism through the small hours. By about four in the morning all the passengers were safely tucked up in a cabin, or in a cell sleeping it off. It was a warm night and I went outside, scanning the rail out of the corner of my eye. I hated seeing lone figures near the rail in the middle of the night. Plenty of people came on board intending to plunge into the seething black water and a lot succeeded. Only a few weeks before, I had spent four hours dissuading a bloke from

Newcastle from making the final leap. He wanted to do it because of his credit card bills, he said. They were about half what Tim's had been, but then Tim was unburdened by a conscience.

We tore through a calm summer sea, the engine's low thrumming constantly audible, other ships' lights glimmering in the distance across the Channel. I was patrolling C deck, under the lifeboats, when a pale figure moved in the shadows and made a small moaning noise. I approached cautiously. C deck is far above the sea, but sheltered, with high metal walls that conceal dark corners popular with snogging couples.

The blonde maid from the royal party was shivering, weeping and cowering alone in a corner with not a stitch on. At once I took off my jacket, put it round her and led her inside. She was staggering and reeked of sick and booze.

'Wuz raped,' she gasped.

Here was my nightmare. A member of the Queen's Household raped on board the *Britannia*. And she was so very, very drunk.

'Who? Where?'

'Dunno.' She was lurching on her feet, slumping sideways and rolling into the sides of the corridor.

'OK,' I said slowly, thinking, Oh Christ, newspapers, official enquiries ... 'First I'm going to take you to the hospital cabin.'

In the sick bay I gave her a white sleeping gown and she fell into the bunk dead asleep. That was the best thing she could have done. I wanted her to sleep it off before I could get a statement out of her and the ship would have to dock before I could get a doctor on board to take swabs.

It was now a quarter to five. This was going to be a very long day. I had to marshal my thoughts. I had to eat, because I wouldn't get another chance. I could smell bacon and coffee wafting from the cafeteria. That would be a good start. One of the waiters stopped me on the stairs.

'Jacquie. Can I have a word, dear?'

'Sure.'

'I think I'd better tell you this. There's a girl's clothes in my cabin.'

'There are?'

'You may well wonder – I went out on deck for a ciggie at about three this morning and there was this girl, crying drunk, wandering about. She kept pawing my arm and saying she was lost, she didn't know where she was, so to cut a long story short I couldn't leave her on her own, I thought to be on the safe side, I'd put her in my cabin to sleep it off. So she comes in and we take her dress off and she flops into the bottom bunk. I'm in the top one, and as far as I know she's asleep. And I wake up with the lark this morning, and she's gone! But the dress is still in a heap on my floor and so's her bra, handbag, everything. So where is she? The vanishing lady.'

'What did she look like?'

'Very pretty blonde.'

'Short, tall, long hair or short?'

'Average height, about twenty, you know, bobbed hair. And all I can say is if I was a girl I'd be jealous of that figure.'

This waiter would be appalled by the idea of sex with a woman. He was no rapist. A horrible progression of events was taking place in my mind.

'Is there any ID in the bag?'

'Nothing, only a purse with about three quid in it and a lipstick. But James thinks he saw this girl last night after the bars shut. Just a minute, you really should talk to him.'

James, looking half asleep, fried bacon and talked.

'There was a blonde in the corridor necking with that drummer from the band. Then she went in his cabin with him. They sort of fell in there when I came past and then they shut the door, they was both giggling.'

In two minutes, swallowing the last of my bacon roll, I was banging on the drummer's cabin door. He opened it, bleary-eyed, and I told him to get dressed. I arrested him and escorted him in handcuffs down to the cell. He looked stunned.

'I never touched her,' he kept saying.

It was five-thirty now and, with Julia the maid in the hospital and Ron the drummer in the cell, time to inform the RPG officer. I ran up to the bridge to let Thomas know what was going on and then, my heart sinking, went to waken Alasdair from the RPG.

An hour later, with Vlissingen and its neat houses twinkling half a mile away, Alasdair and I took Julia some coffee. By a quarter to seven the ship was making those slow shifting movements that tell you it's nosing into dock. We were still getting no sense out of her. She was completely incoherent. I left Alasdair in the hospital cabin and was first off the ship. I ran across the dockyard to the office of the Dutch maritime police.

'Gotta make a phone call.'

I told Special Branch at Sheerness what had happened.

'I'm getting a doctor to take swabs from her.'

SB back in England sounded as if the sky had fallen in.

'Don't envy you this one, Jacquie.'

As I went back on board the first passengers were disembarking. I got more coffee and took it down to Alasdair. Julia was sitting up now, crouched on the hospital bunk hugging her knees in the white smock. She was slurred but comprehensible.

'Can you talk?'

'Sorry. So sorry. I'm really sorry. I went to Ron's cabin with him. I jus' need my clothes. That's all.'

'Did he rape you?'

'No. Nobody raped me. He never raped me.'

'So what happened?'

'Only remember bits. I remember going to his cabin and lying down. I wanted to go to the toilet. So I went in there. Then I was on the deck.'

'Did you have sexual intercourse?'

'No. I'd got my dress on.'

'Were you fully clothed?'

'Yes, yes, got my dress on. Then I went to the loo.'

The door from a cabin's bathroom opens out of it in such a way that a disoriented person could easily find themselves in the corridor. Drunks were always doing it. This was probably what had happened, twice, to Julia.

'And?'

'I was on the deck . . . Then somebody helped me get my dress off, then I was on the deck with no clothes on, where are my clothes? I don't know what happened – and you put me in here. You gave me this to wear. That's all I know.'

I gave her a piece of my mind. 'Do you have any idea how much trouble you've caused with your drinking?'

I phoned SB again: panic over. I got the drummer out of

the cell, which he had shared for two horrible hours with a farting snoring drunk, and apologized to him. He was quite reasonable about it, seemed to understand my predicament perfectly and was more relieved than anything else. I felt much the same. I left Alasdair to worry over Julia, who was by now snivelling about how she didn't want to lose her job, and went to my office. I was still buzzing from all the coffee. One of the receptionists dropped by with some lost property: a pair of trousers somebody had found in a corridor. I logged them in the book along with the rest of the night's paperwork and crawled into bed at ten in the morning.

It seemed like only minutes later that somebody was banging on my door.

'Yeah?'

'There's a bloke down the police office. Says he's got to see you before we go home.'

I peered out of my porthole on B deck. Vlissingen was still down there. It was 11.15 and we were leaving at twelve. I showered, dragged a comb through my hair and went downstairs in uniform.

Mike, the balding singer from the band, was hanging about outside the police office looking agitated. I unlocked the door and let him in.

'I've had two grand in cash stolen out of my cabin,' he burst out.

'Was anybody in your cabin other than you?'

He looked shifty. 'No.'

'Where were you keeping the money?'

'It was in my trouser pocket. I can't find my trousers either.'

'Right.' I took the lost property book out.

'Grey trousers labelled Austin Reed, waist size 38.'

'Yeah. That's them. Is my wallet in there?'

'Your wallet was in a pocket. Brown leather wallet, empty.'

'Shit.'

'So what's the story?'

'Eh? Well, I want somebody nicked for this. It's a lot of money. It's two thousand pounds.'

I took his passport. He was fifty. He began to make a statement.

Then I said, 'You married?'

'Yeah.'

'You had that girl in your cabin last night, didn't you?'

'What girl?'

'Mike, I'm tired. Short dark jailbait, that girl.'

'Well. It happens.'

'And you had your trousers off.'

'So.'

'So I'd say she nicked your two grand and dumped your trousers and got off the ship this morning, wouldn't you? I don't think there's a lot I can do to get your money back.'

'You can't let her get away with that.'

'All right. Let's say I make a full investigation. Police time and money in two countries. It goes to court. Witness statements. Medical reports. Press coverage. At the very least, correspondence sent to your home address. One way or another your wife is going to find out that you had a sixteen-year-old girl in your cabin.'

He looked thoughtful. I could see he was coming round to my way of thinking.

'Give it a rest, Mike. Just call it the dearest screw you ever had.'

14

Thomas and I had to snatch time together as if we were both married to somebody else. In a sense we were; we were both married to our work. These days I didn't feel the sort of death wish that had made me undertake a violent job in the first place, but still I was getting a lot of satisfaction from policing the *Britannia*. And Thomas lived to go to sea.

When we got time ashore we always had too many things to talk about and places we wanted to go. We even took pleasure in the domestic stuff like shopping for food. So when he had to spend the annual fortnight in his apartment in Düsseldorf with the Indian wife and her parents, I knew I wouldn't want to stay on my own in Vlissingen. I drove down to Marbella to see some friends.

Two weeks later, I was on my way back. I drove the convertible I had brought from England, the weather was balmy and little towns in the north of Spain were slumbering through a late afternoon siesta in golden sunshine. As the car climbed towards the Pyrenees and I breezed along with warm herb-scented wind on my face and rock music on the radio, it occurred to me that I hadn't been so happy since Mum and Dad died. I was going back to Thomas, and wherever he was seemed like home. I hadn't felt since Mum died that I had a home anywhere; now I did. My rented house in Vlissingen was ordinary enough. It was Thomas's attitude to living in it that was a revelation to me. I took housewifery seriously. I was the sort who had to have matching side plates and no balls of dust under the washing machine. Whenever Thomas caught me wiping a work surface he grabbed me around the waist and said I should stop wasting time and come to bed.

'But these things matter,' I said one day. I was worried. I had proudly produced a mug tree after a shopping expedition and he got the giggles.

'Jacquie, you don't need all this stuff. We do not need a life full of coffee mugs. We don't need ionisers or hair dryers or any of it.' I had recently bought both these items for the house. 'If we have each other all we need is a tent on the beach.'

I was starting to see life his way. It left so much more time for making love, for a start. I had probably got a soppy smile on my face as I drove along thinking about this, or maybe it was the British number plates, but for whatever reason, when I rounded the next bend on the mountain road a policeman appeared out of nowhere and flagged me down.

There was a lay-by ahead, with a Guardia Civil van parked up in it, on the edge of a drop to a green valley below. I pulled up behind the van, quietly swearing. It was dusk already, and I wanted to get to the border before dark. I still had sixty miles to go. I'd been pulled up by these types in Spain before and held in a time-wasting bureaucratic tangle. In fact, because I spoke no Spanish, I'd once been conned into paying sixty quid for a non-existent traffic offence. (I was still bewildered when a Spanish-speaking friend later read the ticket, which said I had been going up a mountainside in second gear.) And then there were girl friends' horror stories: rape at the police station, when they had gone there to report a rape, for instance. But you never really believed it. At the end of the day, the Guardia were policemen.

This one was fortyish, clean-shaven, and he wore his black hair a bit too long. I watched in the driving mirror as he approached my car from behind. There were only a few feet of gravel between my driver's door and the drop to the valley. He stood on the edge of the precipice, under the mauve evening sky.

'Get out. Out!' he said.

He was stabbing his baton in the air. Pathetic. As I got out another policeman came round the back of the van. Hatless and gaunt, he leaned on its doors to watch.

I turned my back on him and faced the first one with professional severity. 'Is there a problem?'

'You go too fast.'

'No. I don't. I am a police officer.'

I heard the gaunt driver coming up behind me. This was all wrong. By now I should be getting asked for ID, passport, car documents.

'You. Stand here. You are bad girl.'

I felt a finger on the back of my neck. The bastard was playing with my hair. I shook my head angrily and they both laughed. The one in front said something with a snigger to the one who was toying with my hair. Footsteps crunched. I heard him get back into the van.

The man in front of me was armed. I must have decided to leave and made a tiny movement in the direction of my car, because suddenly he grabbed my arm hard. His left hand was on the holster of his gun.

'There.'

'What?'

'You go there.' Gripping my arm he pulled me a couple of feet along the edge of the precipice until I stood at the back of the car. I glanced down. There was a thirty-foot drop to scrubby trees on a slope. He was pushing me on to the ground, on my knees.

'Down.'

Oh, I got it.

'You go down.'

My goodness me, but that gun was a great persuader. I slid obediently to my knees with my hands behind my back. Except for the noise of my feet on gravel there was not a sound. Christ, but the other one could creep up with handcuffs. I was listening desperately for the approach of a car. The man's fingers were on both my shoulders. Scuffling my feet round I knelt at right angles to the precipice. A kestrel soared through the cold valley sky behind him; and then the policeman was close to me, the felted cloth of his trousers smelling like warm parsnips. He unzipped his fly and stuck his erection in my face. I looked up at him. Not circumcised, yellowish and none too clean. I took a breath, took it in my mouth. His knees were against my shoulders. His hands were around his dick. His eyes looked shut, from here.

I might go over the edge. But I had nothing to lose. They weren't going to let me drive on after this. I bared my teeth and bit hard.

It was like snapping a big carrot. A wild scream rang out. I forced his legs sharply towards me at the knee and heaved. The scream pitched as he disappeared. I saw the sole of his boot vanish. I scrambled to my feet, dashed to my car and, grabbing the heavy Krooklok, tore round the van, yanked the driver's door open and swung the thing violently at his forehead. As he lunged at me I smashed his head hard between the door and the metal side. He slumped. I stretched past him, took the van keys, and ran.

The keys hurtled over the valley, a tiny black arc in space. I drove like a maniac, the first few zig-zag mountain miles without lights in the dusk, hoping that somehow this would make it easier to hide. I was scrabbling in the back seat as I steered, trying to grab rolling cans of Coke to wash out my mouth.

The bastards. The policewoman part of me wanted to drive to the nearest nick and report them. I saw myself rushing in, distraught. 'I've just castrated one of your blokes and shoved him over a cliff!' That'd go down well.

I would have to put headlamps on soon. It was sixty miles, well over an hour on these roads, to the border, and ahead of me were several towns big enough to have a police station. The creep in the van was probably only momentarily stunned. He might make a radio call within minutes. They would send out an army of Guardia Civil. I had seen what they were like when they had no quarrel with me; I couldn't bear to think how they'd treat me if they had.

I didn't stop until I was ten miles inside France.

When I got back to Vlissingen, Thomas told me I should have shot them. I told him I would have done, if I'd had a gun. I guessed I was in trouble enough in any case. For weeks afterwards, I expected somebody to come and arrest me for murder. I would ring up English police friends in Marbella to pass the time of day and casually interpose, 'Umm . . . Nothing in the paper about Guardia Civil in the north of Spain, is there?'

'No. What sort of thing?'

'Oh, you know. Accidents. Deaths.'

'No-o. What you been up to then?'

'Nothing. Just wondered.'

I was convinced that somebody must have seen my car, with its British registration plates, and taken the number. I imagined how they'd prove it had been me and realized with horror that they'd have to do it from my teethmarks. As an ever more gruesome series of events unfolded in my imagination, the days passed, and, after a while, I dared to think that the man must have survived the fall. If so, his wounds would have healed. He would be a Whole Man again.

He must have had a few awkward moments explaining his injury to the wife, but maybe this sort of thing was a regular occurrence in police marriages in Spain. I shouldn't be at all surprised.

Tim rang me. Again he wanted to discuss a divorce. My letter to Janine had made it all the more important that he should be free to marry her, he said. I'd have thought that Janine, having got written proof that he routinely knocked off anything in a skirt crossing his field of vision, would have refused him at any price, but it seemed nothing short of matrimony would cement their love. He was welcome to a divorce. I told him I had no time to talk about the details on shore, but if he would like to bring a few mates for a free cross-Channel booze cruise we could meet for an hour. He was delighted with that idea, and so was I. I could have fun with it. The endless rivalry between police, Customs and Immigration at ports could be exploited if you knew how. The

Customs at Sheerness had recently arrested an Immigration officer returning from Amsterdam with the boot of his car stuffed with hard porn, and in their current frame of mind they would search Mother Theresa if they got a whisker of a hint about a breath of suspicion. I told them that Tim, of the Territorial Support Group, would be bringing his car. It should be searched.

'How searched?' enquired my nice friend in Customs.

'Mmm . . . searched,' I said.

I kept wandering into the Customs shed.

'But I'm a police officer,' I heard Tim protesting. He was standing helplessly by as they wrenched the passenger seat out. Later in the afternoon they had a sniffer dog nosing at the wheel arches and next time I went in they had the engine on the floor.

I couldn't bear to look after that. It was all so greasy and dirty and they were under no obligation, of course, to put any of it back.

I was always wary when somebody went out of their way to be nice to me because, as a police officer, you get used to the idea that the public don't like you much. So, when a middle-aged man with a child came up to me as I stood on the gangplank watching foot passengers embark at Sheerness, I didn't quite know what to make of him. I had certainly seen him at least once before. He was tall, fair, slightly hunched, with a London accent. He held a small boy by the hand. He was a quiet little boy.

'My nephew,' the man explained. I was almost sure he had been with a different little boy the last time I had seen him. Three weeks later I was certain. Again he greeted me, again he had a boy with him, and this time the boy was red-haired and freckled.

On the way back from Holland there was a fight in the bar. The man was on his own, though I had seen him take the child down to a cabin earlier.

'I witnessed that fight,' he said to me. I stared into his pale, eager eyes. He wanted me to like him. He wanted me to think he was a righteous citizen. He was trying too hard.

'Good, I'll take your statement,' I said. 'Come into the police office and bring your passport.'

I copied down his details. Dennis Michael Harris, aged 45. When we berthed, I had Special Branch check him out. There was nothing in Criminal Records about him. I asked around, and one of the barmen said he had sold Harris alcoholic drinks which he had taken down to the cabin. He had shared the cabin with the nephew. Whether he had given the child anything to drink, of course, I had no way of knowing.

Next month Harris was back again with another child. As the *Britannia* rode out of the Thames Estuary I spotted them in the queue for cabin bookings.

'Hello, Jacquie.' He smirked, glad to have the surrounding trippers see he was on familiar terms with the ship's police officer. I decided I needed to get the little boy alone to ask him what was going on.

'Hello,' I smiled, and squatted on my heels next to the latest little nephew. He had a sweet face, freckles again and floppy hair. Harris glared at me.

'What's your name?'

'Paul.'

'How old are you, Paul?'

'Ten.'

'Are you having a nice time?'

The boy nodded.

'D'you want to come up to the bridge and meet the captain?'

'Yes, please.' He beamed for the first time.

I took his hand and got to my feet.

'We're just going up to –'

'No, he's not going without me,' snapped Harris. Suddenly agitated, he grabbed the boy's shoulder.

'But – don't be silly, we're only going to the –'

'No. I promised his mum I wouldn't let him out of my sight. Sorry.'

'Suit yourself,' I murmured. 'I'm sorry, Paul.'

I had to do something. However, it was Friday night, the usual uproar commenced and hours slipped by. At about midnight I was hurrying along a corridor when I got a call over the radio.

'The bar's gone up again!' I could hear screaming in the background. A bar steward raced towards me.

'One of your lot's getting beaten to a pulp in there.'

I tore up a flight of stairs and was about to climb another, two at a time, when somebody seized my elbow. It was a middle-aged German woman.

'Yes?'

'There is a man in the lift with a boy –'

'And?'

She was plainly confused. She couldn't get her words out. I could imagine the policeman upstairs getting glassed while I stood here.

'The little boy. He's . . . he is –'

'I'll deal with it in a minute,' I yelled, dashing upstairs.

When I got back to the spot an hour later, the woman was nowhere to be seen. But the following morning I saw the little boy. On deck with Harris, he looked petrified. He wouldn't meet my eye when I spoke to him. They were going to disembark at Vlissingen together, however, and there was nothing I could do to stop them.

When we got back to Sheerness I went to the Special Branch office.

'I really need help with this,' I pleaded. 'I can't prove anything. I don't care if he hasn't got a record, there is something wrong. That boy was scared. He's not the first one either. He always takes them to Holland for two days and brings them back and they never have a word to say for themselves.'

'Nothing you can do about it, love. No evidence. You should know that by now.'

Well, thanks for your tireless support, guys. Flabby bunch of useless piss artists, I thought, splashing angrily across the dockyard in the driving rain. As far as I was concerned, the Sheerness office was the elephants' graveyard of Special Branch. Once I had bought myself lunch and got over my resentment I began to think constructively. I went to a public callbox and made an anonymous phone call, to the Child Support Unit of Kent police.

Next day, in dock at Sheerness, there came a knock on the door of the *Britannia*'s police office. A man and woman introduced themselves as a detective inspector and a detective sergeant from the Child Support Unit.

'And how can I help you?' I asked.

'You made the phone call,' the DI said.

'Did I?'

'What do you want to tell us?'

'If I had phoned you I couldn't admit to it,' I said. 'I would have had to go over the heads of Special Branch to do that. You know I could be in deep trouble.'

I told them what I had seen. I had the child's name and address, from his own passport, and they interviewed him and his parents at home in Chatham.

Harris had met the boy's father in a pub about six weeks before. He was looking for lodgings and was offered the living-room sofa till he found some. And then – and it happened this way every time, it had happened with all the boys – the bloke and his wife were having words and Harris said, Look, mate, you need some time on your own. I've got contacts on the ferries, I can get free tickets [he couldn't, he paid]. Why don't I take the kid away for a weekend?

The CPU interviewed the little boy. At first he said Harris had tickled his tummy; and then he told the truth, which was that he had been sexually assaulted, in the cabin. Harris was a known paedophile. The records had somehow been mislaid. He had also been interviewed about the murder of a homosexual twenty-five years before.

I had to go to court to give the main evidence. The jury looked at me with utter contempt. I felt like a worm. I had made a split-second decision to sort out a fight instead of going to defend a child, and it had been the wrong decision. The defence lawyer tore me apart; he was right.

I have to live with my mistake. Harris got two years.

15

The bar had just shut, and there was a full moon. Six of them stood in a noisy group on D deck, all about twenty years old, all male, with a good few pints inside them. The seventh man was strung spreadeagled between them, slumped like a sagging wineskin and yelling his head off. They were clutching his ankles and wrists and swaying back and forth with the rocking of the boat, roaring,

'We are sailing

We are SAILING . . .'

The seventh man twisted around, his teeshirt riding up over his paunch, and they were hoisting him higher and higher towards the rail against the windy night. The Channel churned past fifty, sixty feet below.

I had dived off that deck twice. It was part of my training as a police officer and paramedic. I had dived into a calm harbour from a stationary vessel and was perfectly fine. Once out to sea, if you went over the *Britannia*'s side, night or day, you were fish food. If you survived the fall, the water temperature even in summer was so cold that you'd be dead in eight minutes. The ship would have travelled about three miles before it was going slowly enough to turn back for you. Not that it would turn back. Nobody was ever seen going over – that was half the problem; we lost people over the side, but the first I'd know about it would be three or four hungover white faces when we docked and 'Our mate's missing.'

We lost a boy scout that way once. He was only eleven and disappeared around the time of the paedophile case. I was very upset. Dennis Michael Harris had made me depressed. Or maybe it was the fact that I had failed to help. Whatever the reason, it was the last straw. I was no longer happy in my work.

Of course it could have been something to do with being beaten up every weekend. I was getting sick and tired of having the same drunken yobs vomit all over my uniform, doing things they thought were funny. Like grabbing a mate and threatening to chuck him overboard. And now here I was again, Friday night, grasping my radio, ordering the six of them to stop arsing about. I was near the stern of the ship, it was blowy and cold and it had just gone midnight. There were other people on deck, twos and threes hovering in little knots of anxiety.

'I'm a police officer. Put him down.'

'Oh!'

They were giggling, they continued to lift him but when I shoved into the middle of the group with a baton they dropped him sharply on to the ground. I was close by them now, close by the rail, handcuffs at the ready. I said a few choice and vehement words to the two ringleaders.

'We wouldn'a done nuffink.'

One of them caught somebody's eye over my shoulder and sniggered. The other four were behind me now, crowding me. A sixth sense told me what to expect. With a surge of anger I snapped the cuffs on to my wrist and the rail and turned to them with my thumb on the radio button, but I was too late. They'd got me by the knees.

'Wo-aaAH!'

I was over. One hand grabbing the rail. Christ but I wanted to let go that radio. But I resisted. I screamed into the transmitter. The cuff was holding but my hand was sliding on the rail and my wrist felt as if it was being cut. My legs were dangling into space. Christ let the cuff hold. Somebody from the crew grabbed my arms. I was pulled back on board. Oh and didn't those bastards get a few choice off-the-cuff remarks.

Not long afterwards, Thomas took me out to dinner. He knew I was getting increasingly fed up with the violence on board. Thomas himself now had the chance of the career move he had wanted for a long time. He could spend winters as the captain of a cruise liner in the Caribbean, and summers sailing from Hamburg around the Baltic and Norway.

'I think it's time I left the ferries,' he told me.

'I won't stay when you go,' I said. 'I think I've paid my dues on the *Britannia*.'

'Come with me, Jacquie. We can do what we always said we would. We'll sail around the Caribbean together.'

'You know I can't. What would I do?'

'Be a *hausfrau* for a change.'

We smiled at each other. It was impossible and we both knew it.

'I'm thirty-one. I'm too young to spend the rest of my life baking apple pie.'

'What do you want to do?'

'I want to go back on the Circuit.'

'I will never know where you are. They could send you anywhere.'

'I don't want another job like this one, Thomas.'

'I don't want you to have another job like this one. I hate to see it when you are hurt. I want you to be with me, where you are safe. The Circuit isn't safe, you get menaced by nasty people. Look at those criminals the Krays. You had threats.'

'Most of the time I shall be sitting in a car following some boring businessman. It's a lot safer than the *Britannia*.'

He sighed. Neither of us had any appetite and our glasses of wine stood untouched.

'When will we see each other?'

'We can meet six or seven times a year. We can call each other, you know we can. I can come to you in the Caribbean. I've got to do this, Thomas. I can't stop working at thirty-one.'

'But when will you stop? I want you to promise me. You must stop one day, we must be together all the time.'

'Yes, I want to be with you all the time. But not until I'm ready. I'm not ready yet. I've thought about it. I'll do five years. I'll stay on the Circuit until 1994 and then I will come to you for good.'

'You promise me?'

'I promise.'

A few months later I left, and so did he. When we gave up the house in Vlissingen I very nearly cried.

All the same, something in me returned to the Circuit with guilty delight, like a woman returning to a secret lover.

I had been only too right about sitting in cars. The first jobs I did were mostly surveillance. I like surveillance because, however well trained you are, there is usually something to learn. People's behaviour is unpredictable, technology changes. And you're working with a team. Eight of us on to one target, more if there is a group to be watched. Everybody can do everybody else's job. Some are better at undercover work, some at desk-based investigation, some at bugging phones. All of us can do any of these things if required. We are used to taking orders as well as giving them, and can judge when to take the initiative.

It costs a lot. A team following a target in London is generally two or three cars, a cab, an observation vehicle (the 'obbo van') and a motorbike. I watched Roger Levitt, for example, a businessman who was on bail for allegedly defrauding individuals of millions of pounds, though he was later acquitted. Boring life he had too, stuck in his flat in Maida Vale with nothing to do but pop out for a pint of milk and sign on at the police station once a day. But we had a typical team: a couple of guys in a scruffy builder's van parked up near his apartment, myself and a few other cars round about, and a cab that would conveniently appear if he wanted one. My job was to wait for a radio message that he'd driven away in my direction. Then I'd pick him up, stay a couple of cars behind, see where he went.

A target might go to the airport. In the boot I'd have a bag packed. I'd have my passport on me. Other cars would follow in formation, taking over from each other at intervals. When you first do surveillance, the least hint of a dodge and you think the target's on to you. They never are. Partly, that's because they're intent on what they're doing. Mostly, it's because surveillance techniques have been honed over the years so they're pretty well foolproof.

You start from a point where you want to see and (often) hear everything that the target is doing. Let's say you're putting the hearing part in place. A phone can be bugged in various ways. You might have a hard-wire tap from the junction box in the street; there are people on the Circuit, as well as moonlighting telephone engineers, who do this. Or you have a scanner in your parked car or a room nearby, and a pair of headphones, and you listen in to calls to and from the target's mobile. Maybe the phone in the house or the hotel room has been bugged. Inserting the tiny bug is a purely mechanical job, it's just a question of gaining access in advance. You can listen in to that up to half a mile away. Then again you can leave a bug in almost any office without anybody noticing. One three-way adaptor looks much the same as another. Or you can replace a wall socket, leaving a bug behind it. Let's say the target goes out of his office and takes a cab. If you know – because you've been listening – that that's what he's going to do, then your own cab turns up. It's got a microphone in the back seat, so he won't be well advised to entrust his confidences to a companion there.

If you spend enough time and money you can overhear just about anything, unless the target whispers into a confidant's ear in the middle of Dartmoor or a lead-lined room. The more money you spend, and the more advance warning you have of where people will be, the less likely it is that you will be flying blind in an investigation.

By 'flying blind', I mean getting surprises. You don't always know by bugging or other means what a target is up to. You might be following somebody along a dual carriageway and they suddenly do a U-turn. You can't know whether they've left the central heating switched on, or whether they're surveillance conscious. Suspected drug dealers are usually surveillance aware. Sudden unexpected moves are a dead giveaway that they've got something to hide. You find out on the first day. If it happens, surveillance might be abandoned for the day, while a bigger team is brought in: more frequent changes of car, another cab, another bike. People tend not to suspect bikes. They always think they're couriers.

If you're following a car, you don't want to be right up his chuff, but in London, with traffic lights and lane changes and zebra crossings it's almost inevitable that you will be, some of the time. In the countryside, following a car presents a different set of challenges. You're a bit conspicuous if you want to pull out behind the one guy who leaves a sleeping village at exactly 6.40 every morning. You just plot up and make plans for it. There'll be team members on all the roads out, probably lying in a ditch while their cars are hidden behind a hedge. Everybody's in radio contact. Before the team's in place, in fact before they're hired in most cases, the desk research has been done. Where the target works, who his wife is having an affair with, the number of his offshore bank account – it's all known. So when your colleague hidden in the woods tells you over your radio that the target's northbound on the M2, you probably know where he is going and who he is going to see.

Roger Levitt had months to wait for his trial and led a blameless life, outwardly at any rate. As one of his watchers I was well paid for sitting in a car in a street in Maida Vale. That was it. If Levitt didn't go anywhere, I didn't budge. Maida Vale is a smart residential area just north of central London, with wide tree-lined boulevards of tall mansion blocks and massive Victorian terraced houses. The street I was in had parking down the middle as well as both sides. Day after day, I admired the architecture, ate my regular breakfast of four Mars bars and a chocolate milk shake – a girl, even a thin one, needs go – and scanned the paper. I was in radio contact with the obbo van. I learnt the dog-walking habits of various old ladies and Filipina maids. I listened to the racket coming out of the house across the road – the thump of bass guitar, and there was a singer in there somewhere. It began about eleven in the morning and was still banging on when I quit in the evening. I watched a parade of frazzled blokes in jeans and shades trailing up to the front door. Well, it takes all sorts. I was beginning to worry about whether the council dustcart was late this week, it was that interesting.

A man with designer stubble and dark glasses tapped on the window. I slid it down.

'D'you mind telling me why you're here?' He had an Irish accent and a pleasant enough manner.

'If you've any worries, just call the police station. They'll set your mind at rest.'

'Oh. Fine.' Looking taken aback, he returned to the house. I thought he probably would ring the police station. The local nick is always forewarned by surveillance teams – you'll explain which streets you're plotted up in so if Neighbourhood Watch do any curtain-twitching they don't get too bothered – but you can't do much about traffic police. They're inclined to ask you out to dinner in return for going away. Always accept, is my motto. You can cancel later.

Next day the designer stubble came out in a woolly hat with a cup of tea and some muffins. I declined the muffins but the tea was very welcome.

'I made the cake meself,' he said. I hoped I hadn't offended him. I gulped my tea. The din from inside had stopped, briefly.

'What are you doing in there anyway?'

'Practising.'

'That what you call it? Ever thought of getting a proper job?'

He grinned. I wish somebody had told me that he was Bono from U2, but I didn't find out for days. It keeps on happening to me, that sort of thing. When you're working, you absorb everything around you without being consciously aware; you're entirely focused on the job in hand.

The secrets of good surveillance are in the detail. For instance, learning to dip headlights, then put them on half beam, or full, and back again, when you're following a vehicle at night; that way they think it's a different car all the time. Keeping a bike or a cab closest to a speeding car in town so that it can run a red if it has to – couriers and taxis do that all the time anyway, so the driver of the car in front won't be suspicious. On a motorway, a target who isn't surveillance aware can be followed in any lane, you don't have to be behind him. If he pulls into a service station some of the team can keep on along the motorway, get ahead and be ready to pick him up when the team in the car park say he's leaving. Radio and telephone contact is constant.

In cities especially, most of the team may be on foot. There are signals you give to each other, to tell each other to move up, take over, get back in formation; you can form a triangle behind the target, or a box shape, or any one of a dozen others. You'll take a hat off or scratch your ear or make a sign behind your back to indicate where you're going or tell one of the team to take over from you. Often you're after somebody who runs down to the Underground. In a crowded ticket hall you can get right behind the target in a queue, find out where he's going and tell the rest of the team by phone while you're following him down to the platform. You won't be seen as long as you stay close.

Also, personally, I find it easy to disguise myself. I am tall, thin and dark. Like most women, I can make myself unnoticeable or draw attention to myself by the clothes I wear and the way I do my hair. With make-up on, I've suddenly got a face; without it, you could pass me by. And stance and deportment are everything. In my time I've worn a wig and aged up to sixty. The boot of whatever car I have contains day clothes, night clothes, evening dresses – you have to be able to run into a loo or a bush and change. Once I was pulling on my tights on the floor of a surveillance taxi in Park Lane when a punter in a hurry yanked the door open yelling 'South Ken!' at the driver. We stared at each other in mutual amazement. Another time, I was plotted up in a parked car waiting to serve an injunction on a notorious gambler when I got a radio message that he had taken a room at the Ritz and had ordered a call girl. I was into my party frock and eyeliner like lightning, and up to his door. A couple of guys were positioned either side, out of sight. I knocked.

'Hello?' came a cautious voice from inside.

'Good evening. You sent for me.'

The door opened and he stood there smirking and scratching his chest. I smirked right back and thrust the documents into his hand.

'You're served.'

Thomas and I met, whenever we could, all over Europe in the first few months. I set the rules of engagement early on:

I didn't talk about work. I learned very quickly that it would only make him uneasy. He had no basis for sexual jealousy, and I don't think that it ever bothered him. He knew me well enough to realize that as far as rivals on the Circuit were concerned, I'd already tried the insecure aggressive type, and wouldn't do so again. I valued Thomas because he was kind and wise. The longer I worked on the Circuit, the more I appreciated how rare these qualities are. However, if I talked about work Thomas started to think I might get hurt. So I never mentioned it, except for once when I needed his help.

I had been asked to fly to Nice, where I would stay in a little town on the Côte d'Azur and be part of a large surveillance team subcontracted to one of the international security companies. On jobs like that you don't get the whole picture. I vaguely understood that a credit card company was suing our target for millions and he was pleading bankruptcy. The investigation we were part of was supposed to lead to the seizure of his fraudulently obtained assets. Assets that included a yacht, cars, houses and works of art. The sort of trinkets we all overlook in moments of crisis.

I envied him, living here; sun sparkling on deep blue water, bougainvillea in the garden and platefuls of *fruits de mer* on snowy tablecloths in dockside restaurants every night. What a life. His wife was an art dealer, and it seemed that he had obtained valuable sculptures which were now held in her name. When the bailiffs turned up the sculptures were not in their villa; they were on permanent loan to the Principality of Monaco. I was told to retrieve them. Three brass sculptures, said the brief, and at least one of them was easy to get at as it was on public view in the open air, at a roundabout near the casino. Ever obedient, I cleared the boot of my trusty hired car, nipped along the Corniche and whirled around the roundabout a couple of times. And home again. The sculpture was there all right: a solid brass abstract, probably of deep artistic significance, but it would have to stay right where it was. It was about eight feet high and twenty feet long. I rang my handler and told him he would have to conceive Plan B.

'One more damn thing,' he said gloomily. He was having a hard day. He had just heard that goods were being loaded on board the yacht in the marina as if it was about to leave. It looked as if the swindler had decided to shift his possessions somewhere we couldn't find them.

'They might sail away tonight. It's a lot of bloody sea to lose them in.'

'You want the yacht followed?'

'We want the yacht kept there. Don't suppose you know how to disable it, do you?'

'No, but I know a man who does.'

I rang Thomas and explained the problem. He was in Southampton, berthed for a couple of nights, and he sounded lonely. I wished he was here. But we talked business, just this once.

'To make it stay? A chain around the propeller shaft. With a heavy chain, it will go nowhere.'

I got one of the guys on the team to buy about four metres of chain from a ship's chandler's. After dark, with scores of wealthy yachtsmen and their consorts carousing on shore, the water in the marina was as quiet as it got. Portholes bounced long glimmers of light on to the inky Mediterranean. There was nobody to see me slip into the water. The target's yacht was about 150 yards out. I had slung the chain over my shoulder. It wasn't so heavy in the salt sea and I crawled out to the yacht sideways, as if I was life-saving. I felt safe once I was in the shadow of its sides. I took a huge breath and dived down, following the line of the hull with my fingers until I found the propeller shaft. I quickly slung it round as well and tightly as I could. Which wasn't very tightly, as once I had put half of it on, I got my arm stuck. Refusing to imagine what would happen if they started the propeller while I was floundering about, I tugged, wrenched and tore my bruised arm out from under, broke free and burst up to the surface for air. That was a bad move. There was turbulence near the surface and as soon as I broke cover I saw that a much more impressive yacht was almost on top of me. I squinted through salt water long enough to read *Trump Princess* written on the side before I had to dive again. When I got back to the beach I was not in the best of tempers.

16

For at least a year, just by coincidence, I kept getting sent on surveillance jobs around Maida Vale and Little Venice. They are pretty much the same place, Little Venice being the swanky part of Maida Vale, with canals, cherry blossom, lots of cream stucco and even higher property prices. I was staked out there to watch a divorced woman whose ex-husband suspected that she was getting entangled with a bizarre religious cult. No doubt he wouldn't have minded, only they shared custody of their ten-year-old son and the cult members were supposed to go in for paedophilia.

She certainly didn't look like a Moonie. No headbands, thonged sandals or floating silk frocks here. Towards lunch-time most mornings she would swan down the elegant steps of the Victorian villa I was watching, a vision in Chanel and Gucci, and step daintily into a BMW. From then on it was one long exhausting round of getting one's highlights done and one's nails painted, massage therapy and light lunches with friends. Often there would be a hard afternoon's shopping at Harvey Nick's or an evening supper at San Lorenzo. Oh, the endless search for a parking meter. Such a strain.

Occasionally, on the alternate Friday nights when her son was spending the weekend with his father, she'd have a bit of a bop at Annabel's in Berkeley Square. The rest of the time she didn't socialize a lot. The little boy boarded at a prep school from Monday to Friday. She had male company, however, in the person of a society masseur called Jonathan Clark. A royal princess was among his clients, so he must have been checked out by the security services. He didn't fit the usual profile of a pederast.

Clark never stayed the night. He lived not far away in Hampstead, and the two of them spent many an afternoon trekking up and down the high street nipping into bookshops. They were in each other's company most evenings, and at weekends they took the boy out walking on the Heath, or to the zoo in Regent's Park. I watched them. The child was cheerful. They looked like a happy family group.

For the first couple of weeks, watching this woman was very dull. Parking was difficult and we had to be plotted up by six in the morning or we'd never find room for the obbo van. The back of that airless, windowless metal box was usually occupied for eighteen hours a day by Dave, an old mate I'd worked with on dozens of jobs, and the listening equipment and cameras and an ice-cream bucket (to piss in). It got hot in the van. You could see out, though nobody could see in, but there was not a lot to look at since our girl rarely left the house till midday. However, one Wednesday evening there came the breakthrough that would later make it all worth while. (For me, at any rate. I like a good laugh.) About ten people, including Clark, turned up at this woman's house in ones and twos and stayed until eleven o'clock.

They came every Wednesday night after that. We got photographs of them, and their car numbers were checked out. All of these individuals had at some time had links to minority religious sects. They looked as conventional and well-heeled as the target did. But we had established that at least part of the rumour seemed to be true, so the client decided to proceed. We had to get closer.

There were two reasons why everyone concerned turned to me at this point. One, I was a woman. I could get my back professionally rubbed by Mr Clark and try to define exactly what his charms were. Two, I was a Spiritualist. I have always been a Spiritualist. My mum and dad were, and so was at least one of my grandparents. I am also psychic. Everybody on the Circuit who knows me knows this about me. And as far as they're concerned, most of these religious freaks are vaguely heading in the same direction and it takes one to know one. I was going to have to play a major part in the infiltration of this cult.

I made an appointment to see Jonathan Clark. Frozen shoulder, I explained on the phone to his receptionist – which was true enough. He had a nice house, with a consulting room upstairs, and he seemed pleasant. He was a holistic masseur, he said. His long fingers pushed and palpated my shoulders while his voice, soothing as he hovered above the nape of my neck, instructed me to cleanse my system from the inside out. He was a skinny, tall, ethereal sort of man in his late thirties, with curly brown hair; not my type, but you could see what some women saw in him, because he was unctuous. He flattered. He was so slick, you could have slid off him. He came a cropper with me, though. He spent twenty minutes telling me to rid my body of coffee and cigarettes because it would clear my cellulite, he said. My tranquillity hit the floor like a rock. If there's one thing I don't have, it's cellulite; never have had. After that I didn't volunteer to buy any of the balms and aromatic oils ranged on the shelves in the consulting room. I could see how, after a session with him, a woman with regular alimony and nothing better to do would find herself parting with good money for whole racks of potions.

The religious group hadn't come up in our conversation, but one of the other watchers had had a brainwave. He had been muttering since the first Wednesday that he knew one of the women visitors from somewhere, and now he remembered where. He had briefly worked on an investigation in the States that indirectly involved a cult, and he had seen her then. She was a Chinese American who gave talks and conducted seminars on inner spiritual health and mind over matter. She was a professional spiritual leader and, like any other salesperson, she did exhibitions. There was one coming up very soon: a psychic fair at a West End hotel. I bought a heap of magazines in the field and found a ticket offer. We were in.

Two of us went, me and Mike, the guy who had recognized the woman in the first place (though he looked a bit bemused by the experience). We wandered about between stalls that were genteelly promoting everything from incense, ouija boards and crystals to six-month courses and weekend retreats in Northumberland. It was all a bit rarefied. I went into a side room and listened to the Chinese American woman whose name was Louise Tan, giving a seminar. She used the usual brain-washing techniques of repetition, but there was no sinister reference to small children. My only concern was to find out whether children were concerned in the group. So far, I had seen no hint of malpractice. After the seminar I told her how interested I was, how inspiring she had been, and she invited me to the group's meeting in Maida Vale.

The following Wednesday I turned up at the house. The lads stayed outside in the van and a couple of cars. Inside, the wide marble-floored entrance hall gave an elegant impression, with tall mirrors and a huddle of potted palms. The target occupied the first floor. I was ushered into the living-room, all vermilion paint and soft furnishings in flickering candlelight with a drift of incense. There I was introduced to the other guests by their first names. Most of them were women in their early forties. Everyone was conventionally smart. It could have been a rather repressed dinner party anywhere in north London, except that there was no food or alcohol. Jonathan Clark recognized me and said he was glad I could come. He must have thought he had invited me himself.

We perched on chairs, sipped mineral water and listened with rapt delight as Mrs Tan held forth for a while. Then we began to chant with our eyes shut. I sneaked a look at the radio mike taped to my chest; still firmly in place. The guys wouldn't have got a lot out of what they had heard tonight. I had to get more. After the chanting there were prayers, and then mingling. I mingled hopefully.

'Will you come again?' an earnest woman asked me. 'Will you become Integrated?'

'Tell me what's involved.'

They couldn't wait to explain. I would be born again. I would be returned to the nakedness in which I was born, boomed one of the men, and released into the world as a baby. A joyous rebirthing, he called it. There was enough of a hint of some connection with children to make me wonder. I said I'd think about it.

*

'Well, will you do it?' asked my handler on the phone. 'I think you should.'

'If you want,' I said cautiously. 'But you know what I said about returning to nakedness and all.'

'Yeah?'

'Where shall I put the mike?'

There was a thoughtful silence. Finally we decided that my handbag was the best place for a microphone and transmitter.

Next Wednesday I turned up again. It was a hot night and, as I drove past the obbo van in the street I knew that at least four of the team were huddled in the back, probably stripped to their Y-fronts. As I ran up the front steps I averted my mind.

My Integration was to be the highlight of the evening. There was no sign of any children and everybody greeted me warmly. The more I saw of these people the more I thought they were perfectly decent. Sad and daft, maybe, but not child molesters. Tonight, like last time, there were three or four men and the rest were women. We began the evening cross-legged on the floor, with silence, relaxation and a few choice mantras being chanted around a Persian rug. Joss sticks wafted pungent smoke from the hearth. After half an hour of this I was timidly invited to go to the bathroom and remove all my clothes, jewellery and make-up so that I would be in my original, unpolluted, childlike state. I reappeared, a modest neophyte ready for Integration, wearing a kimono and clutching my handbag.

'Take off your robe and lie on the carpet,' commanded Mr Clark. I put my handbag on the sideboard. The others had already started chanting soulfully. I hoped the lads in the van were enjoying this. Everyone stood up around me.

Two of the men rolled me into the carpet with only my head sticking out. Twelve pairs of eyes gazed down on my startled face.

'Allelujah.'

'Allelujah.'

My Inner Being was then commended to a Higher Power. Everyone said Ommm and lit candles and swayed about a bit. The carpet was horribly scratchy and chanting doesn't half get tedious. Just when I was daring a wistful hope that they would suddenly break into a conga, I got signs that the process might be coming to an end. The two men stepped forward smiling beatifically. I was now Integrated. With a flourish they unrolled me. I rotated one more time to make sure I was face down on the carpet. My eyes were watering, I could feel my neck going crimson, and I was getting a pain between the shoulder blades from the effort of stifling hysteria. Hefty male feet in sandals were tramping around me in a sort of dance. I could tell who was who by their toenails. The women kept on chanting and the men pulled me to my feet. I rolled my eyes to the heavens, sucked in my cheeks, waved my arms sinuously and swayed to and fro. Good thing I'd shaved my armpits. There was a good few minutes of this and, squinting through half-closed eyes, I could see that the others seemed to be attaining a trance-like state. I loped gracefully along the wall towards the door, swiped the handbag and kimono from the sideboard and headed for the bathroom.

'I'm getting dressed,' I hissed into my handbag. 'See you in the pub in half an hour.'

I was offered a reviving mineral water in the kitchen and shown back into the living-room, where I lay down with the others, who were now all prone, staring at the ceiling. Jonathan Clark sat cross-legged contemplating his hairy toes. I remained motionless for five minutes. At last Clark trod softly to my side of the room and knelt beside me.

'How do you feel, Jacquieline?'

'I feel so cleansed. So pure, it's amazing.'

The others were starting to sit up.

'That's exactly how I was. It's really weird, how you get rid of all the baggage.'

'You're reborn.'

'Gosh, yes,' I agreed. 'It's so wearying, though. You feel you've sort of plumbed hidden depths.'

'It's like soaring up from the bottom of the ocean.'

'Yes.' I yawned.

'Is it too much for you?' Clark asked sympathetically.

'Well, it is rather a lot to take in in one evening. It's an amazing experience. I'm going to sneak away. I need to be alone to take it in properly.'

'That's so true.'

'It's all about growth, isn't it? You need to rest. It's kind of strenuous.'

With their well-meaning cries of encouragement ringing in my ears, I went off to deepen my spirituality down the pub. The lads appeared, sniggering, ten minutes later. What an insensitive lot they were.

I was glad when a job ended without the client's suspicions being proved right. It didn't often happen. Usually things were worse than you'd been told to expect.

The team I was on had been following a company employee around London for about a week, listening to his calls and having a good snoop around whoever he met. He was definitely dodgy. A little fat bloke with greedy eyes, always dapper, surreptitiously meeting people from rival companies and talking on the phone about 'packages'. It was just coming up to lunchtime, and he'd gone from a meeting at his corporate HQ back to his house. He stayed inside in intriguingly total silence for an hour before he reappeared with two suitcases and hailed a cab. I drove behind it, and soon we were swooping over the Hammersmith flyover. He was definitely on his way to Heathrow. The two guys in a car behind me agreed.

'Client want me to stick with him?' I asked.

My handler confirmed. Outside their own countries, men of any nationality are easily picked up by a compatriot; behind the bluster they're lonely and nervous, and you have the language in common. I was supposed to get close and scan as many documents as I could. The radio went quiet as we drove on. I kept up an annoyed monologue inside my head. This would happen, always did when I hadn't had time to collect my dry cleaning or grab a camera, and in the boot my case was half empty. Nothing except summer frocks, and he would probably turn out to be heading for the Arctic Circle. In the past week he had met Danes, Finns and Norwegians. The cab dropped him at Terminal 2 Departures. I jumped out, leaving the keys in the ignition, and grabbed my bag from the boot. As I followed the target into the booking hall I saw Richard running across the forecourt ready to park my car for me. Dave was already heading for Long Term Parking. I hoped he could get on the same flight. I tapped his code into my mobile.

'He's heading for the BA check-in at C. That's a Copenhagen flight. Can you get somebody to book a rental car at the other end?'

I queued behind the little man at the Priority, Gold Knobs On, Gee You're Important Mr Murgatroyd desk. He was going to Copenhagen all right; I was behind him, looking confused, when he picked up his first-class ticket. I wittered. The girl looked at me pityingly.

'Over there for ticket collection, madam. Boarding starts in half an hour.'

I crossed the booking hall to buy a very expensive ticket and Dave, behind me in the queue, muttered something.

'Check this in for me, Jacquie.' He put his suitcase on the ground. 'I'll pick up the car at the other end.'

I smiled at the target in the departure lounge, stood a little too close behind him as we boarded and stretched myself languidly over two seats in Business Class. I turned, caught his eye and slowly crossed one leg over the other. He sent champagne across. (And they said I'd lost my touch.) I sat next to him all the way, sweetly gushing. Was he going to Copenhagen on business? Where would he stay? He had some very dull meetings to go to, and was staying at the Tivoli. And me? Oh, as for me, this was a spur of the moment decision. I only decided to come a few hours ago.

'You see, I think what most people have lost is spontaneity. I like to do what feels right for me. I'm writing a romantic novel with a scene set in Denmark, and I've never even been there. So I got in my car and came to the airport.'

'You're obviously a woman who's in tune with her impulses.'

'Never nurse an unsatisfied desire,' I agreed, glancing at him Princess Di style from beneath my eyelashes and sipping my champagne. He was gulping eagerly at his. I counted three glasses in the first forty minutes. I would have to have a word with Dave soon, before we landed.

The man said, 'Where are you staying?'

'Oh, well, you can imagine, it's typical isn't it, of course I haven't bothered to book. I expect I'll find some little place that'll put me up.'

'I've got a suite. Two bedrooms.'

'How nice.'

'I'm sure you'll be comfortable at the Tivoli. Why don't we see how you like it when we get there? I'm being met. You can come in my car.'

I waited for the toilets in Business Class to be occupied and then made my excuses, squeezed out and queued between Business and Economy. Dave slipped out of an aisle seat in Economy and came to stand behind me.

'He's giving me a lift to the Tivoli. That's where he's staying.'

'Keep him in the baggage hall as long as you can, I'll get a car and follow.'

'Where're you gonna stay?'

'There must be a Hilton.'

'If there's a Hilton I'll try that first. If not I'll ring the other chains so make sure you get a room in a Sheraton or something.'

The occupant was emerging from the toilet cabin. I hissed, 'If all else fails, leave a note for me at the conciergerie.'

I let Dave's suitcase swing past on the carousel twice before I noticed it. The man was very patient. His meeting wasn't until four, he said. A limo met us. We swept off to the Tivoli and I was installed in the suite while he departed for his meeting.

Dave and I met at a coffee shop.

'You got them in there?'

'Yup.'

Dave opened the case and produced a small plastic bottle from the First Aid box. A scruffy folded photocopy was wrapped around it and secured by a rubber band. We unfolded this and stared at it.

'What's fourteen stone in kilos?'

'I wouldn't think he weighs that much.'

'You're kidding. More like sixteen.'

'It says 500mg per 50 kilos body weight. Where d'you get these?'

'Pakistan. Giz a pencil, I've got to work this out.'

I selected three gelatin capsules and one for luck and wrapped them in a napkin from the café. Then I went shopping for clothes. This was to be my big night.

We went out to dinner in a little restaurant with the sort of shaded pink lamps and long white tablecloths that let you rub a man's leg in complete concealment. Two bottles of wine were emptied, mostly into him. Back in his suite at the hotel, he drank another couple of glasses of champagne before disappearing into the shower. I broke three of the gelatin capsules into another glass of champagne, swizzled them urgently until they dissolved, and took the drink to him in the bathroom. I drank Perrier between gropes, and wouldn't leave until I had seen him swallow his champagne to the last drop. I returned to the drawing-room.

Female Operative Jacquie now had to keep the target occupied for twenty minutes before he passed out. Smoochy music was playing. He emerged clad in a thick white towelling robe and we began to waltz around the room. His stomach sat solidly against my new black cocktail frock. I shouldn't think he'd seen his dick for years. For twelve minutes exactly, we shuffled back and forth with my lipstick reflecting like a peony in the shine off his bald patch. I murmured sweet nothings, bent and nibbled his ear. *Right*, you fat bastard, that's your lot. I began to steer him tenderly towards the bedroom. At seventeen minutes we were in a clinch on the bed. Hands everywhere until at last, thank God, the enthusiasm waned. He's going, going . . . Thank you, God.

With a gargantuan heave I rolled him over, pulled the covers back, and rolled him between them. Then I dropped the rest of my clothes on the floor. He was deeply unconscious. I put the lights out and tiptoed from the room with his briefcase.

Dave was somewhere in Copenhagen doing his bit for England. His job was to gain sight of all the faxes reception took in for the target. The easiest way to a woman's fax machine being through her libido, he had invited the hotel receptionist to spend the evening in his company. As I quietly slipped the catch on the briefcase I hoped he would get more joy than I did. The material inside was mostly bank statements and, without a camera or copier I couldn't do a lot with those. I memorized what I could, took a few notes and put it all back. Then I replaced the briefcase and went into my own room for a few hours' sleep.

At five, I got up and returned to his muggy bedroom. There he lay, snoring and farting as I climbed between the warm sheets. If Thomas could see me now . . . It was disgusting. After a while I quietly rang room service, asked them to deliver breakfast at seven, and got up. I was in the shower when the tray arrived and by the time I came out, dressed and perky for the day, he was sitting up drinking his coffee and asking how good it had been. Oh! I breathed, it was wonderful.

In the course of the morning, Dave checked with the man's employers. They were extremely interested to see the faxes Dave's efforts had obtained and confirmed that they needed copies of the bank statements. Dave arranged with the receptionist that he could use the hotel's photocopier in the middle of the night. Again I had dinner with the target, slipped him the knockout drops and took his briefcase. This time I waited until exactly two in the morning and handed it out of the door to Dave. At two-thirty he was waiting in the corridor to give it back, having photocopied the lot.

I woke up late on the second morning in the target's bed.

'Morning! Rise and shine.' The curtains were flung back; it was Dave. A pot of fresh coffee was steaming on the breakfast tray.

'What are you doing here?' The bed beside me was empty. 'Where is he?'

'Checked out at a quarter to six. Flew to Zurich, I followed him out to the airport. No worries, we've got what we need.'

'Oh.'

Would you believe it, walking out on a girl like that.

17

Using a fly to catch a spider is a very old idea. I can't say I was crazy about being the fly. People wanted to use me like that too often. Once, in Hamburg, a man stayed wide-eyed and fumbling long after I'd given him enough powders to put a horse to sleep. I kept smiling through gritted teeth and expecting him to wilt, and the more I smiled the harder things got. I ended up banging about downstairs at two in the morning pretending to make coffee. As the machine roared and gurgled I slipped into his study and stole proof that he was buying pharmaceuticals under six company names from his home office. He was certainly taking an antidote to whatever it was I gave him. I kept imagining I heard his tread on the stairs. And then there were Arabs, people like the Kuwaiti suspected of passing information to Iraqis during the Gulf War. I was getting quite expert at dosing lamb kebabs with knockout drops. I told myself it would all look good on my CV. But if I was going to spend time in bed with a man, I wanted it to be Thomas.

He and I met in Miami for a week, and talked. I hadn't gone on the Circuit to become Mata Hari. I wanted to move on, pick and choose work, and the Circuit needed more women. Back in London, I began to train a few, mostly ex-policewomen or girls who'd been in the Army. I set up by myself and started taking specialist work for female bodyguards. My company joined ASIS, which is the American Society for Industrial Security. There are members all over the world. The idea is that if a member is in trouble in an unfamiliar country, he can look in the ASIS directory and find a fellow member who will help. It works brilliantly.

It wasn't long before journalists got to hear about my all-women agency. I was interviewed and articles appeared. One day I heard a familiar voice when I picked up the phone.

'Hi, Jacquie.'

I felt my face freeze.

'Hello, Tim.'

'Been reading about you.'

'That's nice. How are you getting on?'

'Very well. I'm in the DPG now.'

I knew this perfectly well, as I had seen his picture in the paper, guarding the Prime Minister. It was good to know that the future of civilization was under Tim's protection.

'And Janine's just had a baby girl.'

'Congratulations. I'm pleased for you.'

'So there's still something she's got that you can never have, isn't there?'

I put the phone down. What a sense of fun the man had.

Some of the articles about me were syndicated abroad. This led to my being approached by an ex-Circuit man who knew that I knew journalists. At this time a large civil engineering project was being undertaken in Britain. It was overburdened with debt and constantly having to run to the banks for re-financing. This man's friend, he told me, had been official photographer to the construction consortium responsible for the project. He had been sacked for whistleblowing. The photographer wanted to go to the press with his story. Did I know anybody who could get it in the papers?

I met the photographer, a jumpy young man with bad skin and long hair. He talked incoherently about scandal and corruption and bad safety standards but I thought he was a man with a lot of problems. He was too volatile to trust.

And I had a friend, too. The head of security for the consortium was an ex-Metropolitan Police chief superintendent whom I knew slightly. His department was also a member of ASIS. Given a choice, my loyalty had to go to him.

I went to security at the construction company and laid my cards on the table. I had this photographer, he could do some damage: he was mouthing off about how the chairman squandered company funds and how health and safety regulations were routinely overlooked at the site. According to his allegations, men were being injured on the construction site because short cuts were being taken to get the job finished on time.

The head of security went into a huddle with some big cheese at the consortium and came to a rapid decision. There was an AGM in a few weeks' time and if these stories got out, there would be an uproar at the meeting that the big institutional investors and banks wouldn't be able to ignore. The firm would pay whatever it cost to keep the photographer's mouth shut.

I devised a plan. I told the photographer to hang on while I organized an appointment with a key journalist. As it happened, I knew an investigator from the Circuit who had once worked with the *Daily Mail* and the *News of the World*. He regularly sold stories even now. I contacted him, and said the photographer must be interviewed but the story must never be used. We agreed his price.

We hired a conference room in a hotel outside London. I picked up the photographer and drove him there. The person we were going to meet, I told him, was a *Sun* reporter. He happened to be having a big meeting at the hotel today about a story, and he had agreed to give us ten minutes at the end.

When we were shown into the conference room I realized I'd hired a true pro. The long table was a mess of empty coffee cups, used water glasses, ripped memo pads and filled ashtrays. The Man from the *Sun*, tie awry, greeted us in an atmosphere as fuggy as if ten argumentative smokers had been closeted in with him all day.

He arranged to do a series of interviews with the photographer. He took him out to dinner to encourage him to talk, not that the photographer needed much prompting: it all tumbled out. Board members with paintings in their homes that had quietly disappeared off the office walls, non-executive directors whose wives were somehow able to earn a fortune in consultancy fees, parties with hookers and cocaine at the chairman's home. He had finally been goaded to speak out, he said furiously, when one day he had been at the chairman's London house and some birdseed for the parrot had arrived by special delivery in a Harrods van. He was determined to disrupt the AGM brandishing some of his incriminating photographs.

My 'reporter' shook his head regretfully. The story wouldn't be an exclusive then, would it? The photographer saw the point. When the interviews were complete, the reporter had promised that he'd approach the *Sun*'s editor.

There would be big money in an exclusive on a story like this.

That was probably true only, unfortunately for the photographer, every word he said was being transcribed and biked directly to the head of security at the consortium. On the day of the AGM the shareholders were as quiet as mice and the directors had a very nice lunch, while the photographer talked long and hard at one final, all-day meeting with the reporter who was to make his fortune.

A week later, the photographer rang up. Sorry, the reporter told him, the editor didn't think it was a story they could run. The public wouldn't be all that interested. The photographer accepted this; he gave up. The consortium continued unscathed and I got paid. I dare say the chairman and the board were more security-conscious after they'd read the transcripts. Personally, I felt it had been a question of loyalty. Mine had been to a fellow member of ASIS.

I had up to five trained women bodyguards working for me at any one time. Not a lot with about 2,000 men available on the Circuit, but it was a 500 per cent increase on just little old me. I was pretty happy. Though, often when I thought the ice underfoot was solid it had a nasty habit of turning out to be very thin indeed.

An Italian rang my office one morning from Rome. He needed security for his visit to London the following week. I faxed him a routine enquiry form, which he filled in and returned. It gave details of his blood group, the name of his doctor, his height and weight. Was he on a known hit list? Did he have any aliases? Please fax a copy of your passport. All this came back at once. Nothing to declare. I rang an

FBI friend at Quantico and asked whether this man was known or affiliated with any political group. He wasn't.

There are three categories of client: High, Medium and Low Risk. High would be somebody against whom, for instance, a *fatwah* had been issued, or who represented a country at war. Medium could be a celebrity who had attracted a stalker in the past. Low Risk was somebody like this Italian, who could get by with a single bodyguard and driver. I didn't ask why he wanted protection. As long as he wasn't on a hit list, and was far from home, we could assess the risk of some nutter or rejected mistress taking a pot shot as pretty slender.

The form also told me his itinerary and personal details. This was to be largely a business trip, although he had a few errands to run. He wanted to buy a particular breed of dog and export it to Italy, so we had to find out where to get one and how he could take it out of the country. He wanted to go to a restaurant in Notting Hill with paintings on the walls and a piano; he had been there before but could not remember the name. This was the normal sort of research we had to do and I thought no more about it.

A bodyguard met him off the plane; he was a well-dressed dark middle-aged man about five feet nine with a pleasant manner who spoke good English. He immediately asked if he could come to the office to use the photocopier and fax. That was fine. He produced our fee for the three days in cash and drove away in the back of a limo, with a male chauffeur and a female bodyguard in front, to Buckinghamshire to buy the dog, a bewildered, expensive puppy which would one day grow into a bewildered, expensive bull mastiff. We took him to his hotel. He had not asked for overnight security, which would cost more as it would mean taking other rooms for the driver and bodyguard; instead, our people were to pick him up every morning at eight. On the second day we took him shopping. Our girl escorted him the length of Jermyn Street and accompanied him to buy clothes. At night he dined in the restaurant in Notting Hill. The chauffeur stayed outside with the car, to make sure nobody planted a bomb under it, and the bodyguard followed the client into the restaurant and dined at a separate table – omitting a first course, as is usual, as she would have to stay one course ahead.

On the way back to the airport, the Italian stopped off at my office to tell me how pleased he was and how safe he had felt. Everything had gone according to plan. We took him to the airport. We said goodbye. That was that. Until the next day, when he sent me a fax.

He hoped I wouldn't mind if he wrote an article about my agency. Under his real name – he had been travelling on a false passport – he was quite a well-known journalist in Italy and, as it happened, was also a Member of Parliament and on a Mob hit list. He had round-the-clock protection in Italy. He had simply wanted to know whether a woman could offer effective protection, he said. He had been impressed.

I wasn't. I wasn't impressed at all. I picked up the phone, dialled his number and screamed at him. I was livid. If he had given us his real name we would have given him a full bodyguard team; he was obviously in a High Risk category. Sounding surprised, he said that he would have no hesitation in recommending my agency or using us again. I told him if he went down on bended knee, we would never be available to look after him. I couldn't understand how he could be so dim.

I specialized in close protection work for celebrities, and got a long-term contract for the *Challenge Anneka* television series. One Friday afternoon, at the end of a shoot in the West Country, just when we were all winding down and looking forward to the BBC version of a wrap party (a pint in the local), my mobile rang. A good friend, an ex-policeman with his own security firm in London, had been asked to investigate what a certain woman was up to in the South of France. Her husband suspected that she was spending time with another man. It didn't seem necessary to deploy an entire team. Could I fly to Nice tomorrow morning at nine?

I drove back to London. My office was in Grosvenor Place overlooking the gardens of Buckingham Palace. There I found that the case file, complete with blurry photographs, had been faxed through. The woman was a bridge player, there was a tournament at Juan-les-Pins and she had told her husband she was going to participate in it. The Cannes Film Festival was on at the time and she had said it might be difficult to find accommodation. My ex-police friend Eddie had booked me, with difficulty, into the Belle Rive at Juan-les-Pins in the expectation that the errant wife, who knew the hotel, was already there.

I arrived at Nice airport at about midday, hired a car and drove happily along the Corniche. The sun sparkled on the Mediterranean, wind-surfers showed off in the little bays and expensive motor cars crawled past seafront hotels that gave on to private beaches. The air was a heady mix of thyme and mimosa, petrol fumes and Ambre Solaire. The roads were invaded by a flotsam of roller-bladers, cyclists and tanned posers of both sexes. If my target didn't fetch up at the Belle Rive or participate in the tournament, looking for her was going to be a challenge worthy of Anneka.

When I arrived at the hotel, I couldn't believe my luck. I recognized her at once from the faxed picture: a glossy brunette in her thirties wearing a floppy white hat, standing beside me at the reservations desk. There was a man with her – not bad looking, I thought – and they called each other darling. I took a long time filling in forms and messing about losing things in my handbag, and heard them give a room number. She was tired, she said as she took the key, and needed to rest.

I was escorted upstairs. Because there was a shortage of rooms Eddie had had to reserve me a suite. I wasn't complaining. The bellboy stopped the lift at the top floor and picked up my bags. I stepped out and saw at least two bodyguard teams guarding different doors.

'Yes?' said one of the men, looming over me. 'Do you have any business on this floor, madam?'

'I have a suite,' I snarled. 'So fuck awf.'

I decided that the target couple would probably have a hectic afternoon ahead in the bedroom, so I could afford to potter about a bit. I found the hall where the bridge tournament was to take place and photographed the list of participants on a notice outside. Her correct name was on it. By this time it was late afternoon, so I showered and settled in the lobby to wait for them to emerge from their room.

They ate together in the hotel and I rang London to say I had found them. Next morning, I got up at six to sit on the terrace, which they would have to cross to get to the sea. The hotel overlooked a glorious little bay with rocks on the sand and a jetty. It all looked perfect, like a stage set. A scruffy bearded man emerged from the lobby a few minutes later and sat a few tables away from me looking at the menu. He asked the waiter for toast. The waiter was clearly confused by this American who didn't have a word of French and I offered to help. The man invited me to share his table. He was very friendly, wanted to know why I was here and was interested when I told him I was researching a book. I steered him off the subject. We talked a bit about movies. He seemed very knowledgeable.

'Are you here for the film festival, then?' I asked.

'Well, yes. You don't know who I am, do you?'

I peered at him, quickly reviewing all the American films I had seen in the last six months. Not a clue.

'Sorry, no. What's your name?'

'Steven Spielberg. What's yours?'

Friendly as he was, he must have thought I was suspiciously anxious to loaf about on that terrace, because when he finished his coffee and left for his first meeting of the day I was still there. I had been at my table for nearly three hours before the target couple drifted out at nine o'clock to munch croissants. The trouble with being the sole investigator is that you do such a lot of hanging about.

When the man and woman headed for the beach at last I got out my camera and began to take pictures of them with a zoom lens. There was quite a sprinkling of hotel guests on the sands already. The man and woman found a secluded spot under an umbrella near the jetty.

But not for long. Half an hour later, I was lying ten yards away from them, sunbathing topless like most of the other women on the beach. My eyes half shut, I watched the woman's boyfriend dive into the polluted Mediterranean. You wouldn't believe how tough it is, working in the South of France. You smell the ozone and listen to shrieks borne across the water while the sun soaks right through to your bones and if you're not careful, the worst happens, and you're asleep on the job.

I leant up on my elbows and looked out to sea. An American couple scrambled to their feet nearby.

'You mind looking after this stuff for us?'

They left their Nikon and Raybans on their beach towels and headed for the water. When they came back I had just finished taking a few casual shots of the target couple embracing. Now she was heading for the sea. The Americans, returning dripping wet, got talking to me and within ten minutes the boyfriend had somehow fallen into conversation with the three of us as well.

'So what are you doing here?' he asked. He had been watching me curiously.

'I'm doing the research for a romantic novel,' I said. I had an inkling that he wasn't entirely convinced, in fact that he might have noticed me loitering on the terrace, dining across the room the night before, taking his picture or listening as he gave his room number. You need a team for these jobs.

'Who's your publisher?'

'Penguin,' I said glibly. The woman came up the beach just then and was introduced. The boyfriend and the Americans did most of the talking after that. The American woman asked him to take our pictures. I handed my own camera to her.

'Will you take a picture of us?'

She took a shot of all of us together; me, the grinning targets, and the American. They asked me a few more questions about my job. Did publishers generally pay so well that I could run off and bask in the sun at Juan-les-Pins whenever I felt like it? The boyfriend thought he must be in the wrong business. I fudged some sort of reply and thought I was getting a searching look.

'My wife didn't send you, did she?' he said suddenly.

'I beg your pardon?'

'Oh, sorry.' He smiled. 'Didn't mean it.' He put his arm around the woman. 'It's just that we're not married.'

'Oh I *see*,' I said, eyes widening. Gosh. What some people get up to.

I got the pictures developed that afternoon. They were perfect. On the Sunday and Monday, before returning to London, I had breakfast with Spielberg again. By Monday he too had started to ask questions.

'I give up,' I said, in the end. 'I can tell you. I'm not really researching a novel at all. I'm an investigator.' He seemed fascinated. I didn't mind telling him the truth; I would probably never meet him again, and he was such a nice man it seemed petty to deceive him. Besides, he had a close protection team and I didn't want to make anyone suspicious.

Back in London Eddie asked me to go with him to see the client. We arrived at a huge house in St John's Wood where we were let in by a butler. A manservant brought tea. The client was a dapper, effeminate, jumpy, fussy little man of at least sixty-five. He wore rings on perfectly manicured fingers. The room was high-ceilinged, with pale carpets and slippery, formal Regency sofas. I sat down.

'Oh!' he cried.

I leapt up again. Had I sat on the cat?

He rushed to apologize.

'That's where my wife sits, you see. No, no, sit there by all means. Do. Please sit down. Tell me.'

I told him. He perched on the edge of a chair opposite twisting his wedding ring. It was cruel. I had to tell him how they had arrived together, taken a room together, kissed on the beach. I was hating this. I showed him the photographs. He looked very pale and sad.

'What should I do?'

'I can't tell you that. It's up to you. My job was to find out whether or not your wife is having an affair, and I've done that.'

'Yes but – as a woman. What do you think I should do?'

He was surprisingly feeble. I suppose I had felt just as vulnerable when Tim hurt me. I had wanted somebody to confide in. I looked around the room. It was full of antique furniture and its high windows overlooked greenery. He had enormous wealth, yet he was utterly miserable. My job hadn't given me the skills of a marriage guidance counsellor but at least I had learned to move on. Feeling deep sympathy for the poor man, I said at last, 'Decide whether you want to stay married. And if you don't, find a good lawyer.'

I never knew if he took my advice. You don't. You go on to the next thing.

18

Rich men also check up on their mistresses. He was in a clinic in Switzerland, she was going on holiday to Dublin, and he was about to leave his wife for the newer model but wouldn't commit himself entirely until he'd had her spied on for a few days. If I concerned myself with his moral position in these circumstances, I got dizzy. So I didn't. I hired five men and got on with it.

The client seemed happy to spend any amount of money on this investigation, so I assumed he must have grounds to feel tortured by suspicion. I half expected her to land in Dublin and immediately head off to some distant bog for a passionate affair. We would probably have to hire cars and follow her to the furthest reaches of Galway. The reality was rather tame. We flew to Dublin and checked in, as she did, to the Westbury.

The good thing about working in hotels is that somebody on the team usually knows the head of security. You can get a room on the same floor as your target. Or if you need to dope food, one of you can borrow a uniform and wheel the trolley in pretending to be the room service waiter. Even if they don't know you, hotel staff are usually amenable to inducements of one kind or another; it's part of their job to expect them.

I sometimes thought I must have worked or stayed in

most of the hotels in Britain by now. Lonrho, the company that owned the Metropole Group, had commissioned me to spend regular weekends at Metropole hotels and write reports on the service. I also had to test purchase drinks in the bar to see who was fiddling. Just about everybody on the staff from Hendon to Harlech seemed to be at it. I would order half a dozen items, sneak off to the loo to scribble a note of what I'd had, and submit the note to be checked against the till roll. Thanks to me, thieves were getting sacked up and down the country. In fact once, undercover as a participant, I had to attend a function in a Metropole banqueting hall that turned out to be a knees-up for the mayor of Barnet and the local Conservative Association. I found myself sitting next to the man I had been engaged to when I was seventeen. He was very nice about it, told everybody I was a school-teacher.

One of the Metropole managers had left under a cloud, but quickly found a job nobody else wanted. He took over the notoriously bomb-damaged Europa in Belfast. One of the first things he did was ask me to go in and report on the place. I spent an uproarious weekend there with a party of drunken Russian hockey players and an IRA man I picked up in the disco by pretending to be a French tourist. Great crack, as they say, but the hotel was filthy, with torn carpets and, to my horror, no blast protection behind the plate glass windows in the lobby.

Security work doesn't make you universally popular, and I was quietly told that the IRA knew who I was and would not give me a warm welcome if I ever returned to the North. North, south, it made little difference to me. Ireland, to my mind, meant trouble.

In the Dublin hotel, we had been asked to record all the mistress's phone calls. The guys bugged her phone, took the room next door and listened on headphones.

She behaved like a model city tourist. On the first day she shopped. Six of us traipsed after her up and down Grafton Street until she took her packages back to the hotel. At teatime I sat in the lobby waiting for her to reappear for afternoon tea. The Westbury is a superb hotel, which manages to make its guests feel cosseted and at peace. Sunk in a deep sofa, awaiting a pot of Earl Grey and an arrowroot biscuit, I was enjoying myself. The mistress didn't turn up but the pianist was good, I thought. He was playing 'Happy Birthday'. I went over to him and asked him to play 'La Mer', one of my favourites. He was a pleasant young man and obliged with a smile. The other guests taking tea seemed mildly amused by my request. I had no idea why. The young man disappeared after that, and it wasn't even five o'clock yet, so when the waiter brought my tea I asked him why the pianist had left.

'That wasn't the hotel's pianist, madam,' he said, deadpan. 'That was Johnny Logan. Your man's won the Eurovision Song Contest three times for Ireland. He's here with friends for a birthday party.'

I blushed, but worse was to follow. On the second morning the woman we were following took herself off to Trinity College library to look at the mediaeval illuminated *Book of Kells*. We shuffled after her into the grounds of Trinity College, up a zig-zag path frequented by members of the public. I have forgotten exactly why all six of us had antiquated radios on this job, but we did. We had the kind that need a stubby plastic receiver in your ear, connected by cable to the main box at your waist. We were in a conventional pursuit pattern, Dave and Robert ahead, Mike and Ian behind and me in the middle, when my receiver came loose and Robert's voice boomed out at the idling passers-by. My mind flashed in neon: IRELAND! Acting instinctively, I hurled myself over a low wall and down a slope, rolling to rest against a thorn bush. Breathless, I opened my eyes. A couple of red faces in woolly hats were peering over the wall at me. I wasn't rational. I must have looked like a rabbit caught in headlights.

'Are you all right, miss?'

I didn't answer. I was too busy trying to stuff the receiver back in my ear.

'Ah, God love 'er, can ye not see the poor girl's deaf. Are ye roight?'

I nodded and gulped.

'Lovely,' I shouted. 'Looks like rain later.'

I scrambled back on to the path with a hand from Mike.

'Felt like some physical jerks, did you?' he muttered. 'You want to get into that library. Plenty of jerks. Robert's in there, I don't think he's going to fit in. He'll be looking for the Noddy section.'

At about seven that night I joined the rest of the team in the room with the phone transmitter. They seemed to be taking turns to put on the headphones and listen in to a call the woman was making. I intercepted meaningful looks passing between them. It slowly dawned on me that I was being excluded from some joke.

'What's going on?'

'You don't want to know.'

Mike, who was wearing the cans, made a sudden explosive noise, took the headphones off and dashed to the bathroom.

He met Robert on his way out. They were muttering something to each other. The door slammed behind Mike. Robert looked dazed.

'What is it?' I insisted.

Dave was a sensible man. He was the lean, clean-living, vegetarian, non-smoking master of the ironic comment that I usually ended up working with. I knew and liked his wife. She was one of the few wives of men on the Circuit who felt secure enough not to worry about me working with her husband. But now even Dave was pink and spluttering.

'Think you'd better take over.'

He flung down the headphones. I listened.

'I'm wearing the black silk. I'm moving my finger just there, and –'

This was an erotic phone call. She was talking to the client. And he'd asked for the tapes. The cunning bastard knew all this was being recorded. My team needed buckets of cold water thrown over them.

On the third day she arranged by telephone to meet a man that evening. At half-past seven she walked the hundred yards from the hotel to the restaurant. We hung about outside. In the centre of Dublin, a reasonably security-conscious city, this is not as easy as it might sound. A thunderstorm began. Darkness fell. Rain teemed down. Hours passed. We moved, singly and occasionally together, from one shop window to another, keeping the restaurant in sight. Behind its long net curtains we could vaguely discern steaks flambéing in butter and bottles of vintage wine being uncorked. We were cold and wet. She didn't come out. We were starving. Ten o'clock passed. People began to leave the pubs. There was a lot of getting into taxis and driving away of cars. Still the rain splashed on the pavements and the rich man's mistress stayed cosy, dry and well-fed in the restaurant. At last, at midnight, she and her friend walked back to the Westbury. He left her at the entrance. The rest of us, damp cloth flapping around our legs and dirty rainwater dripping on to the exquisite carpet hand-woven by leprechauns, tramped into the hotel and foregathered in my room. There was still work to do: we had to go over the final report together. We were all flying back to London the next day.

We were dying for something to eat and I rang room service. There was no reply. I tried again ten minutes later. Still no reply. I stomped off to the lift and down to the lobby, where a fat man was leaning on the counter talking to the man in a dinner suit behind it. I barged up to the desk and let fly with a few choice words.

'I do think that at £180 a night it's not too much to expect 24-hour room service. There are five cold, tired, hungry men in my room –'

'Eeza private party? Or can I come-a too?' interjected the fat man.

I was not in the best of tempers. 'It is entirely private.'

'I can seeng-a for my supper.'

'Well, is that a fact. You can sing. Really.'

I gave him an icy look and turned back to the man behind the counter with my sneer still in place. He seemed suddenly uneasy.

'Madam, may I introduce Mr Luciano Pavarotti.'

I could have sunk through the floor. The trouble is, I was so focused when I was working that I didn't notice anything in the world that didn't immediately concern me. Thank goodness, I thought, that Thomas was nowhere near when

I was on these jobs. I was completely absorbed to the exclusion of all else.

Next day, I found that Mr Pavarotti had left two tickets for me to the concert he was giving that night. It was extremely generous of him, and I would have loved to go, but I had to fly back to London to do another job.

The Victoria and Albert Museum is a vast edifice not far west of Harrods which contains literally millions of artefacts from all corners of the globe. Prince Albert, the husband of Queen Victoria, made sure it got built with funds from the Great Exhibition of 1851. The V&A is a national treasure house. In the early 1990s, visitors could still get in free, as Albert had intended. However, its miles of corridors and cathedral-like rooms, stuffed with displays of everything from priceless statuary and chunks of whole churches to fabrics and jewellery, cost a fortune to maintain. By now, government money and donations barely covered new purchases, never mind repairing the roof. So, amid great controversy, the new woman director of the museum had dared to instigate a voluntary entrance fee. This was rung up on tills as visitors went in. All went well until the management noticed that, although most people paid, the tills never returned a lot of money.

I got test purchases made by some of the women I had trained. Even at the august V&A, people are not above being on the fiddle. One man alone was pocketing about £120 a day in cash.

Maybe this made the administrative staff wake up, I don't know, but shortly afterwards something even more suspicious was reported. A woman in the public relations department got a phone call from a photographer concerning Ham House, an historic building about twelve miles out of London which is run by the V&A. He wanted to hire the place for a location shoot but hadn't been able to get through to the curator there. He'd spoken to her last time.

'So you've been to Ham House before?'

'Yes.'

'Could you give me the date?'

He gave it readily. She checked the records, to make sure no damage had been done and no fees were outstanding, but there was no entry. He was adamant that he'd got the date right.

'It was the curator I spoke to last time. I paid cash.'

The correct fee was more than he had been asked for, as the PR woman knew. The director smelled a rat and called us in.

Next week I rang the curator saying I was PA to a photographer who would like to use Ham House's grounds for a fashion shoot for a day. I spoke to her personally and we fixed a date.

'It'll be twelve hundred pounds.'

'Ah. In that case I'd better consult him and get back to you.'

'Eight hundred for cash.'

'That'll be fine.'

I turned up on the day with a guy from the Circuit, strung about with cameras, and two of my blonde, six feet tall nieces. They strutted on steps, glared moodily at urns, and clutched trees.

'Give me vital!' yelled the photographer. 'Give me wind!'

I was Hair and Make-up. The curator, a tiny woman and

ever so refained, hobbled out to greet us on four-inch heels. As soon as the bit o'wedge was placed in her hot little palm she motored gaily into Kingston to deposit it in her Halifax account. I knew this because I had someone waiting outside to follow her there.

I put the information in front of the V&A and they asked me to build the case further. Everything fell into place. Although she lived rent free in an apartment in Ham House and earned only about twenty grand a year, she had a half share in a property in Dorset which was worth a quarter of a million. I call that living beyond your means. And she agreed to another photoshoot.

'When you come this time,' she instructed me, 'Ai won't be available. Ai've got meetings all day. So please give the money to the security man you'll meet near the entrance.'

The security man approached us in a spirit of co-operation, took his eight hundred and nipped off to deposit it in his own account. I was surprised, but then at that stage I didn't know that he was her father-in-law.

The local CID were ready to move. We agreed that we would turn up at Ham House to make the arrest at eight-thirty on Friday morning.

I rapped the knocker on the imposing front door. With me were a DS and a uniformed constable.

'She's gone to a meeting up town,' said the cleaner who answered it.

'We are police officers,' said the CID sergeant.

'Well, I can't help you, love. She went out to the museum first thing.'

I rang the director and asked her to carry on with the scheduled meetings, but to keep the woman in the building on some excuse. We slugged our way back to London through rush-hour traffic. At the V&A, the curator was in an upstairs office on her own. We knocked and entered. She was on the phone.

'What do you mean by barging in here?'

'We are police officers.' The sergeant asked her to confirm her identity. She put the phone down and stood up. We all towered over her. She was told she was under arrest. She sat down, white as a sheet. Then she stood up again and came round the desk.

'Get out of here. You can't come in. You haven't got an appointment.'

She stood there squeaking at us on her high heels, then she glared, puffed herself up, lowered her head, stamped her tiny foot and made a run for the door. We were all ten inches taller and in the way. Amazing what fools people make of themselves. The detective bundled her flailing form away by one elbow as if she were some weak wild animal.

I was very happy. Christie's had asked me to do a job for them; thanks to me snooping around the stallholders in Camden Lock, they had caught a bent van driver who was flogging their valuable auction catalogues before they went on sale to the general public. And then there was another job for the V&A and I was asked to run instructional courses on security for the ladies of Christie's auction rooms. Work was coming in all the time; I could pick and choose. I met Thomas for a few days in the Caribbean.

'It's nearly 1992,' he said. 'You've only got two more years on the Circuit. If it keeps going like this you'll be rich when you retire.'

'It's downright sinful,' I agreed. We were sunbathing. There was plenty of that; we met in all the best places. 'Think of it. Retiring at thirty-six with enough money to keep both of us.'

'Seriously, I worry about you.'

'What, making all this dosh?'

'No. I never know what you're doing. It could be dangerous.'

'Not really. I know what I'm doing. Besides, I like it. Stop worrying and start planning where we'll sail on our yacht.'

My life as a company director was not entirely trouble-free. I had to deal with some pretty odd people, and not just neurotic clients. Most of the guys on the Circuit had all the resourcefulness and phlegmatic competence you'd expect from people who had been in the Regiment or the Paras or the Secret Service, but there were others, and this type would have you believe they played frisbee with landmines for fun. You had to be wary. I was always looking for promising contacts and after years on the Circuit, if I needed an expert in most fields associated with surveillance, protection or investigation, I generally knew where to look.

Although I was running my own agency, I was still doing jobs for other people. Paul, whose job it was, knew I spoke some German and asked me to take part in a surveillance operation near Hamburg. On the plane out of Heathrow at five a.m. my companion and I got talking. I'd never met him before. His name was Rob, he was forty-five, balding and stocky. He had been a major in the army and then in MI6. We made friends over the next few days, in the classic way you do on a surveillance job – sitting for long hours together in the front of a car. He was an open type, straight, and I liked him. He told me he had been married, two kids and a big house in the country, wrought iron gates and a long drive up to the front door, all that – but that he was now divorced. He had left his wife for a travel agent called Ruby, and they had a new apartment in Docklands. He didn't talk much about the army or MI6, but I didn't expect him to. He thought discretion was important and also honesty; he said he would never look at another woman, now he had found Ruby. I thought that was nice. As to expertise, he spoke passable French and could go into houses as a telephone engineer and plant bugs, so I expected to use him in future.

Hanging about in a Hamburg suburb, our conversation ranged over all sorts of things, so I was pleasantly surprised when he rang me up at home before Christmas. He remembered that we'd talked about Strauss and the New Year's Eve gala concert in Vienna that Thomas had told me about. Well, there was Strauss at the Albert Hall on New Year's Eve and he could get a box, so did I want to come and bring a few friends? I was delighted. Five of us went. Ruby wasn't quite what I had expected. She was very nice, though. From Clapham, and worked in a travel agent's. She told me she'd met Rob through the Meeting Point column in the *Evening Standard*. He hadn't told me that part, but still, it was none of my business and we had a great evening. Waved Rob and Ruby off into the New Year in their XJ6.

Rob didn't see much of his own children, since they were in the big house in the country and he was in London, but he had started a judo club in Streatham for underprivileged kids and he asked for support from some of us on the Circuit. I was only too glad to help and went along one night. I was surprised when I saw him. For a sixth dan he seemed entirely lacking in skill, speed or grace. He had a class of ten-year-olds and if he hadn't been a major and a crack spy and all the rest of it, I would have thought he hadn't a clue what he was doing.

However, I needed somebody to bug phones and he seemed pretty good at that. Another V&A job came up – they suspected a couple of employees were taking backhanders from construction companies. It would be necessary to investigate and track both the employees and their contacts at home and at work, so I would need several vehicles and a lot of people. Rob would be one of them. One of the V&A managers was pulling thirty grand a year and yet managed to occupy a £2 million property out in Kent, so I wasn't surprised they'd put the finger on him. I started by checking the electoral roll, the Land Registry and so on just to see if he or his wife could have come by such a house by inheritance or some such. That drew a blank. Then I got a couple of guys to sift through the dustbins at his home for old bank statements and credit card transaction slips.

We had a surveillance team outside the staff entrance on the east side of the museum in South Kensington. We started by following people home. There was a cab rank opposite, so I put a couple of taxis there, and the rest of the team plotted up round about. I was co-ordinating the whole thing from my office a mile away in Grosvenor Place. At the end of the first day they were all going to report back to me for a debriefing: two ex-MI5 guys, a couple of ex-army men one of whom was Rob, a woman who had been an army sergeant, and a former policeman in the Met. All professionals I had worked with before.

It was getting on for eight o'clock, everybody had turned up at Grosvenor Place but I thought there was an odd atmosphere. Rob said he had got to go, couldn't stay – something was on at home. The minute he was out of the door, Charlie, who had been in MI5, said, 'Where d'you get that wanker from?'

'Why?'

Dick had been in MI5 as well. He was disgusted.

'Jacquie, he hasn't got a fucking clue what he's doing.'

It seemed Rob had decided to go and sit in a café on the far side of the road opposite the staff entrance to the museum. He stayed there much too long and the others could see him, gawping out of the window with his camera equipment out on the table.

I thought it probably wasn't as bad as they said. After all they were ex-5, he was ex-6, and the rivalry between MI5 and MI6 was notorious. I told them I'd have a word with him, give him a few more days.

The next day, the police rang me and invited themselves round. A couple of plain clothes men came in suspiciously.

'What's going on?'

'I've got a surveillance team out there. It's fine, I've informed Special Branch.' Princess Margaret is a patron of the museum and you can't be too careful.

'Yeah. Well, we've had a call from this beefeater.'

The man who owned the café had once been a beefeater, a yeoman warder at the Tower of London, and he had rung the police because some nutter (stocky, balding, 45) had sat in his café for two afternoons running and when he asked him what he was up to, he had got the old finger-to-the-lips, hush-hush, nudge-nudge, I'm Carruthers from MI6 treatment.

I nipped down to the café myself. The beefeater was gentle but concerned.

'He said he was from MI6. He had this radio crackling on the table, it felt like a minicab office in here. Well, you've got to watch it, haven't you, there's all sorts about –'

I pulled Rob off the job straight away. As it happened, I could do that without a confrontation because somebody had come into the office and asked us to bug his home phones, which is perfectly legal, so I sent Rob off on this new mission. The others made a great job of the investigation once he'd stopped embarrassing them. I had a couple of them dug into one of the suspects' back gardens, and they taped conversations taking place within the house and photographed other goings-on.

When it was all over and I'd handed in the report and the evidence, I turned my attention to the conundrum of Rob. By this time he had disappeared – and for the second time he hadn't done the work that I'd asked him to, and paid him for. I asked Paul about him. I should have asked sooner; but then, that's typical of people in this business, everybody else gets pulled apart but once we've decided on the strength of an introduction that we're 'one of us' we trust each other. It seemed that since I had first worked with him, Rob had turned over a few other people in the industry, taking money to set up work and then not doing it. That was not all. One of the guys on the V&A team now told me that Rob had boasted he could get stun guns and other illegal weapons. He was bringing them in from abroad. This is highly illegal and I don't like it.

I wanted something done but I didn't necessarily want him to know it was me who'd instigated action against him.

Karen, who had also worked for me on the V&A job, knew a woman crime reporter on the *Sunday Express*. She told the reporter what I knew and left her to follow it up. She snooped around, traced his family, and came up with a few surprises. The first wife lived in a council house on income support. She wasn't at all surprised to hear she was supposed to be living in a mansion. Rob had Walter Mitty syndrome, she said; he'd always been the same, ask his relations, they'd given up listening long ago. She'd had the bailiffs round already about payments on the XJ6. As for his glowing army record, it consisted of six weeks in Purbright camp.

It's not unknown for Walter Mitty syndrome to afflict people on the Circuit. It's an extreme form of the mind-set I noticed starting in myself when I first did close protection work in the Intercontinental. You live the high life, you start thinking you are really part of that world. Only in Rob's case he believed he was James Bond.

19

Rob's nasty little attempt at arms dealing was somebody else's problem now, and I hoped he got what was coming to him. I turned my mind to other things.

A world-famous Danish optical instrument manufacturer had been investigating one of its executives. He was involved in a conspiracy to counterfeit their products. To cover all the angles in court they needed proof that he had spent time in New York within the last few weeks. I was asked to gain access to his home and rootle through his personal effects for any kind of paper trail that would show he had been there.

I flew to Copenhagen with Karen, we hired a car and checked in at a monumentally snooty hotel which fifty years before, somebody told us, had been the Nazi HQ in Denmark. For two days we watched the suspect's house. It was a pretty, detached double-fronted place with steep eaves and a long back garden. The house stood close to the road but its porch and front windows were shaded by tall fir trees. In the evenings, police drove along the street at regular but very infrequent intervals. There was no visible alarm system.

After dark on the third day we left the hotel, sashaying across the marble entrance hall in cocktail frocks as if we were going out to dinner. Karen drove to a quiet, hidden car park. We changed into work gear – black tracksuits and trainers – and drove past the suspect's house. Tonight was Friday. We had been told there would be nobody there tonight or tomorrow and there was no light in the house, just a faint bulb in the porch. The street was quiet: a few parked cars, other secluded houses with curtains drawn, people presumably indoors having dinner. It was about ten o'clock.

Karen parked away from street lamps in the next side street. I put on gloves and took some binliners with me. I crept silently up to the house wall, a dim circle of shaded torchlight bobbing on the path ahead, and followed it to the back garden. Three black polypropylene dustbins stood beside the garage. I switched off the torch and listened. Nobody was about. Gingerly I lifted the lid of a bin and stuck my hand inside. Something unpleasantly squidgy was in there, and it stank. Hastily I withdrew my hand, realizing that I had uncovered a used nappy. These people didn't bother to wrap their rubbish. I quietly tipped the bins on their side and filled the black bags. Listening all the time, I hauled the bags back through the front garden and left them behind the hedge. This took about ten minutes, during which time there wasn't a sound, except for a faraway lovesick cat and the low grind of traffic on the main road.

We loaded the bags into the boot and Karen set off back to the car park, complaining bitterly about the smell.

We parked in the darkest corner of the car park and began changing back into our finery. I had just got my trousers off when a police car glided in and circled around. Then it made a second little tour, and stopped and focused headlights on us. We were two women, one dark, one blonde, blinking guiltily and struggling with our zippers in the front seats of a parked car. Having seen all they wanted, the police drove off.

'Greetings from Denmark,' Karen murmured.

Back at the hotel she rolled polythene sheeting over the carpet while I sneaked up the fire stairs with the rubbish. We put on rubber gloves and set to work. After all my effort, there was nothing. Not so much as a Macy's carrier bag. So I took it all back downstairs, drove the rubbish away and dumped it, and decided to do something I never liked: breaking and entering.

The next night, Karen drove me back to the house and parked up again. I sneaked over the fence. In the darkness all the windows and doors were firmly shut but I had provided myself with a set of lock picks. I felt thoroughly annoyed at having to do this. Well, I would. In my time I have arrested people for less.

No one could see the dimly lit porch from the road unless they were standing right at the gate, but there was always the chance that I might be spotted and I was glad when the pick worked quickly and I slipped inside. I shone the Mag-lite down the corridor; it was long, wide, dark, and there were several doors off it, some of them open. Stairs led to an upper floor.

I had been told his study was the first room on the right. I crept in and shut the door behind me. I knew there was nobody else in the house or garden but there is something unnerving about being where you shouldn't. You are half-listening for somebody else's breathing in the room. A computer stood on a huge old-fashioned desk. Also a telephone, a Copenhagen phone book, a notepad with doodles, something scrawled on it in Danish. I pulled at the drawers one by one;

they were not locked. There was no sign of any recent visit to New York. On the shelves, only books. I fumbled about for over ten minutes, and I still had nothing.

As I was about to open an old plan chest in a corner I took a last look at the very top drawer of the desk. Above it was a slide-out tray for paper clips and business cards. It was locked, but I tried a tiny key I found lying in the drawer underneath. *Gotcha*. In one of the compartments, he had stashed the cards from three or four massage parlours in New York and a two-week-old credit card voucher for ear-rings bought at a Manhattan jewellery store. I held the Mag-lite on to the front of my spy camera and photographed all the cards on the slide-out tray. I could now, thank God, get out of here.

A peal of laughter rang out. I froze, switched off the torch and stood motionless. If I strained very hard I could just hear conversation. Where the hell was it? Outside or inside? I left the room as I had found it and sneaked into the corridor, barely daring to breathe behind the balaclava. The laughter must have come from deep inside the house. I tiptoed along close to the wall. The kitchen door was open, with the faintest possible light inside. I got closer; I could smell cooking and hear a murmur of voices. I got nearer still, and peered through the crack between the hinges. Ten feet away, a young man was talking to a girl whose face I couldn't see. They must have been having a candlelit supper.

I crept back down the hall and held my breath as I got out of the house.

'Go go go!' I said as I leapt into the seat beside Karen. My heart was pounding. I found out later that the suspect's stepson and his girlfriend had taken the house for the weekend. Somebody might have told us.

Back in London the following day, I found an odd call on my answering machine. At 01.07 that night, 'Amazing Grace' had been played through a distant telephone on to the tape. Very weird.

Two days later, somebody told me what had happened to Rob. At some time shortly after 1 a.m., according to a pathologist's report later presented at the coroner's court, he had shot himself.

Earlier that evening he had checked into a hotel near Heathrow airport. Two women, one blonde and one dark, had arrived from an escort agency. He had ordered dinner for all three of them in his room; the waiter remembered the little party quite well, as Rob must have known he would. The next morning a chambermaid came in to clean the room. She left again, having seen Rob apparently asleep on the bed in an odd position, crouched with his forehead on the bolster. Five hours later she came in and saw that he hadn't moved. That was when staff at the hotel realized he was dead.

He had placed a pillow underneath his body and shot himself through the heart. The pillow soaked up all the blood.

The more you thought about it, the odder it seemed. Nobody had ever heard of a suicide quite like it. But he died as he had wanted to live, the man of mystery.

I began to run courses. I conducted a seminar for accountants about fraud, and then there were the ladies of Christie's who learned from me how to spot rogues, my deah. Thomas was relieved that I had set off in this new direction. We spent a week near the northern coast of France, looking for a house to buy, and I told him about it. He looked terrific these days, with a permanent tan from the months in the Caribbean, and I said, only half joking, that it was getting harder to stay at work for two more years and not retire now and stay in bed. He said, at least while I was teaching people about security, nobody was going to attack me. And I agreed with him. At the time.

I was part of a team that was invited to instruct the Sri Lankan government's bodyguard squad. I thought I could look forward to r&r on a beach under some coconut palms, but in the end we didn't go to Colombo; the squad arrived for a residential course at the Hereford training centre for eight days.

Eight thin brown policemen in civvies, all of them with pretty good English, turned up on Monday morning. We four instructors were introduced. Unfortunately, the party had been led through the green lanes of Herefordshire by a sulky individual from their embassy. There was nothing politically correct about this guy. He took one look at me and curled his lip in disgust. He muttered to my colleague.

'This is a woman. She cannot teach our security team.'

'Yes I can,' I said pleasantly. 'I'm fully qualified.'

He gave a derisive snort. The policemen sniggered.

'No,' he announced, still addressing my colleague, who looked highly uncomfortable. 'This is completely unsatisfactory. These men cannot be taught by a woman.'

'I can teach them,' I repeated. The man turned to me angrily.

'You think so? Sergeant Samaranayeke –' One of the smaller policemen stepped forward.

'Attack this woman.'

I knocked Sergeant Samaranayeke on his arse and stood

216

on his windpipe. The man from the embassy looked sick. My foot remained firmly on the guy's throat.

'All right,' said the embassy man through gritted teeth, lifting his hands in submission.

'Please go away and let us start the course,' I said. He took a few paces towards the prone policeman under my boot and backed off, furious.

'Enough!' he barked at me. Sergeant Samaranayeke was now blueish. I folded my arms, kept my boot where it was and stared into space.

The embassy man had to storm off in his car before I would release the sergeant. He recovered pretty quickly and, although most of the others were equable enough in my company, for the rest of the week I detected strong animosity from him. He did what I told him with a suffering air. He thought I had humiliated him. Stupid, really; it was nothing personal. I had only been making a point. As the week went by I kept telling the whole lot of them not to get into fights with women. Men always hold back out of chivalry, and we fight dirty, I pointed out. Samaranayeke glared.

They were a smart bunch, fit and quick on the uptake. In fact, by Saturday night we were all delighted that the course had been such a success. We took them down to the pub for a drink and joined in with the locals singing karaoke. One of the Sri Lankans was on stage bawling,

'I'm leaving
'On a jet plane –'

when I nipped out to the Ladies. When I came back two of them shyly stopped me in the bar. They had bought me a wooden cross covered in shells. I was really touched. I thought that was sweet of them and was just saying so when Samaranayeke came over, fortified by a couple of pints of bitter.

'Well done,' he said scornfully. 'You have turned two men into women.'

There's no pleasing some people. I set off on my own back to the camp. It was a fifteen-minute walk down an unlit country lane and I was very much aware that Samaranayeke was up for Round Two. However, he didn't seem to have followed me. I washed my underwear and did some packing and then had to collect something from the supply hut. I knew somebody was in there; I heard a noise as soon as I opened the door. Knowing I must be silhouetted against the light from outside I shut it behind me and stood still in the dark.

'You are a woman and you think you can cause me problems?' said Samaranayeke, up close. He sprayed my face with pepper dust and punched me in the stomach. My face wrinkled like a prune and my eyes flooded with salt tears. I was curled up on the floor getting a good kicking. It was just like old times on the *Britannia*. Only this time I had no radio and I couldn't bloody see. There was no alternative: I began to wail. He stopped at once, switched on a light, helped me to my feet and apologized. I was snivelling, genuinely, because of the pepper, but I was getting my eyesight back.

'I'm a woman in a man's world,' I sobbed. 'I'm sorry. I had to hit you. I have to be like this.'

'That's all right.' He looked embarrassed. I blew my nose and tucked my hanky in my pocket. Then I decked him.

'You soft bastard,' I said, and walked off. I'd told him. I'd been telling him all week. But did he listen?

*

Three of us were invited to go to Egypt, where the Ministry of the Interior wanted us to inspect and advise on anti-terrorist measures at the airports and in international hotels. I was the hotel security expert; Bob, an ex-Para who founded an agency I'd done a lot of work with, was to advise on dog handling, and Brian, a charming ex-SAS lieutenant colonel, was to lend a bit of gravitas to the proceedings and take the larger view.

We turned up at Cairo airport in baking heat to be met by a beaming under-secretary and a large official car. Flunkeys took our passports away, muttering something about the need for visa stamps. We hung about in the VIP lounge being polite for twenty minutes, and when at last our passports were returned, we were driven to the ministry. They didn't ask us in, but the boot of the official car was opened and half a dozen carrier bags clanking with Glenfiddich were swiftly transported through a side door. We continued to the hotel. I looked at my passport, which had some odd squiggles around the visa. Bob and Brian had the same hieroglyphics in theirs. Eventually it dawned on us that foreign passports had been necessary for the interior ministry civil servants to buy alcohol from the duty free shop.

The Egyptians were very hospitable and took pride in showing us round. It was rather a shame, really, that we were there to point out shortcomings in their system. There were quite a few. I started to feel downright churlish and carping. Even when we were taken to see the changing of the presidential guard we saw security problems. It was hard to miss them. Anywhere else, overhanging branches next to the perimeter wall of a secure building are cut down. But the Egyptians had a novel solution. They posted sentries in the trees. The changing of the guard meant some sentries climbed down and some other ones climbed up.

We ran a course from eight in the morning until four in the afternoon. I was treated with respect for eight hours: the deference accorded by pupil to teacher meant that all the officers we were training looked me in the eye, spoke carefully to me and tried to impress. After four, when classes ended, it was as if I'd turned into a pumpkin. There was no more eye contact and I got rudely elbowed in the corridors.

As a woman I was treated with the utmost paternalism. The three of us had asked for neighbouring rooms so that we could meet easily to discuss course work and solutions to other business-related problems, but although the rooms were close together I might as well have been on another floor. No men, including room service waiters or other staff, were allowed across the threshold of my room. A male guard observed my door day and night. If such a big strong man hadn't been there, heaven knows what I'd have done. I might have lain awake for hours, worrying and trembling. Sweet of them.

Cairo was hectic, noisy and full of curious locals. Physically, all three of us stood out as we were taller than the general population, but Bob caused a sensation wherever he went, as he was six feet six and blond. This got to be rather a nuisance, and anyway we had work to do, so we tended to spend evenings in the hotel. The Gulf War had not long ended, and one night we were taking coffee after dinner in the poolside restaurant when a party of Kuwaiti princelings sent over a bottle of Johnnie Walker Red Label. To our allies! We smiled and nodded and expressed our gratitude. One of the royal party, a skinny prince with an overbite in a white dishdash, rose with a meaningful look at me and approached the stage. He whispered something to the band, got up on the dais, the music struck up and he performed the sand dance with great passion and verve. His manservant leaned over my shoulder.

'This is for you, madam,' he whispered. 'Our prince dances for the beautiful lady.'

'Gosh,' I said. I was jolly impressed. The prince tossed back his head-wrap, flashed me a sultry look over his Bugs Bunny teeth and wiggled his hips. When it was all over he stepped down from the stage to polite applause and I slipped away. Returning five minutes later I came face to face with him.

'I danced for you.'

'It was wonderful. Thank you so much.'

'You join me now for a drink.'

'I'm afraid not. I'm working.'

'Ah, you are the secretary?'

'No. I am the anti-terrorist expert.'

A sort of flicker, like a mild electric shock, affected his mouth. He bowed.

'It has been a pleasure to meet you.'

That's got rid of you, sonny.

A few days later we flew to Luxor. The idea was to inspect airport security there, but Luxor was kind of off the scale. It didn't actually have radar yet: the army base down the road phoned the conning tower to say when a plane was about to land.

Cairo airport, of course, was different. On our arrival the men from the ministry had boasted about the millions of pounds' worth of German scanning equipment that had recently been installed. Thanks to these high-tech measures there was now no drug or terrorist problem in Egypt. Since the equipment went in there had been not a single arrest.

Impressed, we went to see the system in action. Luggage was heaved on to the rolling ramp as we watched from the other side. We were quiet for a few minutes. At last Brian cleared his throat politely and said that the alleged lack of smuggling or terrorist crime could be – and it was only a suggestion, mind – because the screens weren't switched on.

As we peered at the blank screens, passengers had been treading nervously through the metal-detector arches. They needn't have worried, as these were not plugged in either. When our hosts confirmed that nobody had been trained to use any of this stuff, we had to design additional course notes in rather a hurry.

I had discovered that there was a circuit over and above the Circuit. It consisted of the international exchange of expertise and information. None of us could do anything to combat crime unless we collaborated and learned from one another. And of course, expertise could be a valuable export. My company received a DTI enterprise grant to finance my attendance at COPEX, the Covert Operational Procurement Exhibition, in Baltimore. There I made contacts that would profoundly affect the work I undertook in the next three years.

20

Covert operations fairs take place in Miami, Baltimore and in England. Women are not well represented at any of them. At COPEX in Baltimore there seemed to be about three thousand men, and me. On the first morning I went for a walk away from my exhibition stand, down endless aisles crowded with guys whose lapel badges proclaimed their status. They were officers in the FBI or the CIA, or Vice Presidents with arms manufacturers or Japanese electronics companies. The few who wore no badges at all, out of arrogance, I supposed, turned out to be from MI5 or MI6.

Promotional videos boomed and glared unheeded in every corner. Business cards disappeared into a thousand wallets. There were displays of guns, surveillance cameras, communications systems, rigid inflatable boats, CCTV, tanks, tents, telescopes and survival equipment of all kind. Stuff I wanted, stuff I needed but couldn't afford, and stuff I couldn't have found a use for unless I had started a small-scale war. All the salesmen ignored me unless I approached them. I was the wrong sex.

After half an hour, what with all this hardware and being treated like the Invisible Woman, I was a bit dazed. But then I spotted another alien, just like myself. It was a shock, like Stanley finally meeting Dr Livingstone. I had given up any expectation of seeing another female and I think she had, too. She was a friendly, dark-haired woman from North Carolina called Ann Walker. She introduced me to her husband, Buddy. We stood talking for five minutes until she was interrupted by insistent enquiries about their firm, ISS, International Security Services.

We were all staying at the same hotel, and in the bar that night I met them again. We'd been speaking for twenty minutes when I told her I was going on to New York after this. I would be driving there. She asked where I was staying, and when I explained I'd find a room when I got there, she opened her purse and handed me a set of keys to their Fifth Avenue apartment. I couldn't get over such kindness.

They arranged for me to be shown around New York by guys from the NYPD; I put them up later in London; we got to be friends, and started helping each other professionally. Ann turned up penniless once at Heathrow with a mother and a little girl they had rescued from some horror in Bangladesh, and she stayed with me. That was typical of the sort of thing that happened with ISS. Ann and Buddy had work that kept them abroad a lot.

They had accidentally cornered a market I had barely come across until now: child rescue. When two people from different cultures marry, the children too often end up trapped where one of the parents doesn't want them to be. ISS helped mothers – it was usually mothers – get their children back. I had read about tug-of-love cases in the papers, but I didn't know there was anybody who would help a parent to snatch a child back. But after the first few successful rescues, publicity had snowballed.

'We get three hundred letters a week,' Ann said grimly.

'It's killing me. Most of these women we can't help. We can't afford to. Can you imagine what it costs us?'

'Well,' I hazarded. 'Fares, accommodation –'

'Bribes, equipment,' Buddy said. 'You start thinking about how to get kids out, you start getting into real serious stuff. You might need a chopper or a boat.' Buddy had been in the crack Delta Force, the American equivalent of the SAS. He was a heavy-set man with a nice smile who didn't talk a lot. I wondered if this wasn't a bit over the top.

'Choppers and boats? Come on.'

'No kidding. There's often no way else. When you start reading some of the info packs we get and hear the case histories, you'll see.'

From the first job I did for ISS, I began to see what he meant. It was really two jobs one on top of another, both in Saudi Arabia. The first one was typical, because there was literally no way out.

When I was staying in North Carolina, a woman rang Ann up after seeing her on television. She had recently been to Saudi and had met an American mother called Myra who was being held against her will, with her children. The two women had only managed to talk when they met at a supermarket.

Myra had met her Saudi husband at university in Washington State. He was charming, earned a good living when he graduated, and over the years they had five children: three boys and two girls. The youngest were coming up to school age and the eldest was about ten when he suggested they take the family home for a holiday. He had never taken her or the children to the Middle East, but it was part of the children's heritage, he said. They should meet their cousins and grandparents. There would be a large villa in Riyadh, servants to do all the work, a chauffeured car, and trips to the beach when they went to the family's second home in an oil town near the Gulf. It seemed a wonderful prospect.

That had been two years before. Within weeks of their arrival the husband altered. He was permanently ill-tempered and insisted that his wife remain in purdah like an Arab wife. He confiscated her passport, took a permanent job in Riyadh and announced that the children were his property and so was she; none of them were ever going back to America. He employed servants who reported everything to him. When she tried to get to the Embassy, he found out and broke her ribs. When she attempted to telephone relations in America, he broke her arm.

Ann insisted that Myra herself must ask for this rescue. With the intermediary's help, Ann managed to speak to her. The sad story was true enough. Myra was desperate to leave. There was one chance to escape. She was to take the children to the Gulf house for the summer while her husband spent six weeks in Indonesia on business.

Money was available but it was hard to see a way round the practical difficulties. Myra told Ann she was guarded by servants and armed drivers at all times. There were checkpoints on the roads. Women were not allowed to drive, and not allowed to be driven unless the man could show proof that he was a paid employee, a relative or a cab driver. She could not get to the embassy in Riyadh with her children and even if she could, the embassy staff would not be entitled to protect them there. Under Saudi law, children were their father's property from the age of seven. Even if she got to the airport she had no passport for herself and certainly no travel documents to cover five children who looked like locals. Not only that, but her husband's job kept him in close contact with airport staff who knew him and might recognize their family name.

Ann, Buddy and I discussed the possibilities. The only scheme we could come up with was to hire a boat in Djibouti, sail along the Yemeni coast and into the Gulf, and effectively snatch the mother and children off the shore. I could sail a boat and was pretty confident about the Djibouti part, so we despatched a couple of men to recce the set-up at the holiday home.

It was hopeless. They did their best to get close to the tall American robed from head to toe in black, but she was under armed guard all the time and they, as westerners, were too conspicuous to carry out any proper surveillance. They said the boys were driven back and forth to some kind of school, but in separate cars and at different times of day. Road blocks were everywhere. Women were routinely questioned. Western women in the town, wives of expatriate oil men, stuck together in their compounds so Myra hardly ever came into contact with them. She dressed like a local woman. Her sons were not allowed out with her alone; if she went out with her children, there were male servants around. Myra, on the telephone to Ann, confirmed all this. Ann explained the difficulties. She suggested that in this impossible situation, Myra should take the girls and leave the boys.

'At least you know the boys won't be ill-treated. With girls it's different.' Ann had heard that female circumcision was practised in Saudi Arabia.

'I couldn't do it. I can't leave them here.'

It was one of the first child rescue cases I had come across and one of the most harrowing. We could do nothing. The institutions in Saudi Arabia prevent women from having any power over their own lives. If this brute of a husband wanted to keep his wife prisoner, he had chosen the right place.

I had heard Saudi horror stories years ago on the tom squad. Guys on the Circuit would come back from a stint guarding the royals in the Gulf, and they'd say to each other, 'Remember Tina?' or Nicky, or Vicky, or one of the other girls who had hung around the casinos. 'Blonde girl from Cardiff, married a towel-head? Saw her in Dharhan last week.'

'How's she doing?'

'Desperate. Hanging round the hotels, face wrapped up in a yashmak, I saw her. Christ, she looked rough.'

'What happened?'

'He divorced her, she married a bloke with a Toyota dealership, then he divorced her, she's got two kids and no passport. Kids are Saudi, aren't they? Poor cow, eh?'

That sort of story made me believe the white slave trade still flourished. As far as I know, Myra and her children are still in Saudi Arabia.

While we were looking into Myra's case, a Saudi woman rang the ISS office. She was from Riyadh but had got out by marrying a man who took her to live in America. She had been desperate to marry to get away from her father, who used to beat her mother, her sister and herself. After some years the mother had gone to England for medical treatment, and had found a way to stay there. This left just the younger girl. She was now twenty-six and taking the full force of the father's bullying.

The sisters spoke often on the telephone but now Dina, the

one from California, was beside herself with anger. Something more terrible than usual had happened in Riyadh. The younger sister had accepted a lift from a neighbour and they had been stopped unexpectedly by the religious police, who enforce the laws of the mullahs. When these policemen had discovered that she was an unmarried woman travelling with a man she was not related to or married to, they had given on-the-spot notice of punishment. She would have to report to them and receive forty lashes.

The girl was distraught, and Dina had reached a decision. She said her family would spend whatever it cost to get her sister out of the country. She had the germ of an idea, which sounded as if it might work. It would cost a lot of money. We calmed her down and told her we would at least go there and recce the job, to see if we could put the plan into action.

There were times in the next couple of months when I thought we must have been mad to hope we could ever do this, but after poor Myra and her five children, anything looked easy. From North Carolina, that is.

In London, I and one of the guys I knew from the Circuit concocted a visa application, along with a friend of a friend who had contacts in Saudi. I couldn't go into Saudi alone as a woman, and if Richard went by himself and tried to speak to the sister he would probably get his vital parts cut off for attempted rape, so for the purposes of this job we were a man and woman with a mission to sell machine parts. Our contact got us an invitation as the sales reps of a firm that made parts for machinery that extruded high-density polypropylene pipes. That should be a conversation-stopper, I thought.

Our visas came through. They were for six weeks; most

of the time I was going to be in purdah. I dropped into an optician's on the Edgware Road, got my eyeballs sized up, and ordered prescription-free brown contact lenses.

There were a lot of stressful aspects to the Saudi job – the heat, the imminent danger of flogging, and so on – but the thing that set us all on edge was the race against time on several fronts at once. We had a six-week entry permit. The punishment lashings had been postponed until the following month but the date loomed.

The brutal father was in Hanover, where he usually stayed for several months in the summer. Our contacts kept him under surveillance there. He was seeing a lot of one woman, so all we could hope for was that she would retain his interest. If he took it into his head to return at any moment we would get advance warning.

At the house in Riyadh a 28-year-old brother remained as chaperon. By all accounts he was a lot like his father, though nobody knew what he did or where he went.

And in America, we had a Saudi supplied with a false passport on standby to arrive at Riyadh airport, collect his 'wife' – Amina, the younger sister – and leave. This was the major complication. Because his job and family demanded his attention, there were only three weeks in which he could come from California to do this. He was getting paid $25,000 but he was doing it reluctantly and we knew he meant what he said about the time window. He would arrive on a flight from Los Angeles, plant himself in the departure lounge until the next flight out, and leave with or without her; that was the deal. We would have to co-ordinate flight plans.

Then there was the paperwork. Without the right documents, Amina would never get out alive.

To get on to a flight, she had to have a passport as a wife. No Saudi woman could leave the country without a passport, if she was unmarried, issued with the permission of a male relative, or if she was married, with the permission of her husband. The back story we came up with was that she had left legitimately on her unmarried woman's passport, met this guy, married him in America, come home to see the folks on her new married woman passport, and here he was to take her back.

We had bought a false marriage certificate. We were waiting for a false passport to be made up in the right name at a cost of $13,000. The passport would get stamped with an exit visa when she left. All this was organized and then somebody pointed out that they'd smell a rat at the airport because as a US resident she would have had an entry visa when she first came back. That had to be put into the passport as well: a further $5,000. Everything cost.

On arrival we stayed in an international hotel and wore our usual clothes. Richard and I drove past the family house in a taxi. It was in a district where wealthy people lived, near our hotel. All we could see were high whitewashed walls around a courtyard. The street offered a surreal view of parched palms, sand gathering in runnels beneath walls, yellow sky, no noise, no windows, nothing parked, nobody about; Maida Vale, it was not. You couldn't sit around with a Mars bar and the *Sun* crossword to keep you company.

After a few days I bought a chador in a market, we changed hotels, and I stayed in my room all the time. I practised putting on the yashmak, the robe and the contact lenses. I walked up and down the room, eyes downcast, the chador swaddled around me.

I knew what Amina looked like; I knew she spoke English; I knew what she wanted to do. I was now two streets away. But I couldn't just ring up and arrange to meet. The servants reported everything she did and every call she made and received to the father and brother. I also had to assume that my calls from the hotel would be monitored by the internal security services.

I spoke to Dina in Los Angeles, and she told me that a package would be waiting for me at the post office on a certain date. So at least I knew where and when I would meet her sister. What I didn't know was what progress we were making on the passport. Ann and Buddy had to talk in oblique terms and I was never quite sure what was holding it all up.

I was powerless. I was waiting, and had to stay out of sight. I could go nowhere for two, three days on end. Meals were deposited on trays outside the hotel room. I wondered what Thomas was doing, but I had told him not to expect a call from me for a couple of months. I watched CNN. I read every magazine on the hotel's rack. I looked out of the window. From high up I could see swimming pools glinting blue in the gardens of rich people's houses. Stuck in my room, I lived from one meal to the next, one telephone call to the next. I remembered the Sheikha that I used to bodyguard years ago at the Intercontinental. If this carried on I would be scratching my name on the wallpaper.

When the time came to scuttle down the back stairs and into the street to the post office, I kept my eyes lowered. It was absolutely not permitted for a woman to look a man in the face. Outside, the traffic noise and dust came as a shock. Troops were everywhere. At busier junctions, religious police patrolled in pairs. They were squat bullies with long night-sticks, white uniforms and blue bands on their headdresses. I concentrated on my own feet, moving rapidly under yards of black cotton. I had been told that if they caught sight of your bare legs they sprayed them with yellow paint. If they nicked you masquerading as a devout Saudi woman when you didn't even speak Arabic, I guessed they might think up some even jollier wheeze.

I followed the crowds into the post office. The main room was high, cool, grubby and full of people, like a railway station and nearly as noisy. I looked for the girl. The little swathed figure was in the right place, and instantly recognizable amid the crowd of identical bundles because she was so tiny; anorexic, with little bones and big eyes like a mouse. I stood next to her and murmured through my yashmak that I was Dina's friend. She nodded. I told her I needed to know when her brother came and went from the house. She promised to write this down and pass me a note, in the same place at the same time a few days later.

That was all the excitement there was. It was enough, since we were both so threatened, but I expect an adrenalin high to build and maintain. This job meant alternating short sharp bursts of danger and concentration with long interludes of tedium. It went on like that for nearly six weeks. We got the information we needed, inch by inch. There was tension on both sides. I never walked the streets in a chador again. Richard got me a cab every time. It was safer.

The brother left the house for three hours in the morning, two hours in the afternoon and three hours late at night. We had to get Amina to the airport and out of the country before the brother realized she had left. If he alerted the airport, she was a goner. I pored over flight timetables.

At long last we received Amina's passport. It looked perfect. The Saudi 'husband' was flying in from LA on a morning plane. He was booked to leave for London, with his 'wife', that afternoon.

For several days, Richard had been keeping an eye on the brother's movements as inconspicuously as he could from a taxi. The driver had been well paid and would assist on this last day. We were both pretty sure the brother was out of the way for several hours.

When I left the post office I knew Amina was following me, clasping her two small bags. She got into the back seat of the taxi beside me. Richard was in front beside the driver. We nudged through heavy traffic, music sawing away on the car radio, strips of red and gold fringe wobbling inside the windows and a gold cardboard Hand of Fatima swinging by the driving mirror. Nobody dared say a word. In the yard behind the hotel, our luggage was loaded into the boot. I ran indoors to the powder room and changed into western clothes. We were off to the airport.

Richard had warned me that there would be three checkpoints on the way out of the city. At least the guards were not difficult to distract. They waddled self-importantly across, peered into the car as they glanced at our documents and then their eyes bulged. They were riveted. I was wearing a skirt the size of a hand-towel wrapped around my waist, and three-inch heels. I got out of the car to stretch and strut unconcernedly every time we stopped. Then I wiggled back in, flinging my legs about in case they missed anything. Whatever they were concerned about, it wasn't Amina's papers.

In the miles between road blocks we hurriedly filled her in on the details I had never managed to make clear in the post office. We were supposed to be travelling together because, as an acquaintance of her husband's, I had agreed to escort Amina as far as the airport. She would be taken into a cubicle where a woman security officer would make her take off her chador to check if she was who she said she was. I was going to distract the male guards again. But she might get questioned.

Dina had always known that suspicious officials might ask her sister about life in America, so she had spent a lot of time on the phone enthusing about Malibu, how warm and sweet-scented it was, how she would be driving this afternoon to the beach, not far from the house, along that lovely street with the palms swaying, to the wide sands and those big houses on the shoreline with decks overlooking the Pacific.

Dina knew the Saudi community in LA was not large. People sent letters home, people gossiped across continents. Any of the security people at the airport could have had relations in LA who would surely have known and spoken of this couple had they been genuine. I didn't point this out to Amina. She looked terrified enough as it was.

At the airport Richard and I checked in her small suitcase with our own. I handed my passport to an elderly official. Amina was a few feet away. The official peered at me. He flicked a fly from his nose with one end of his white headdress. He looked at the visa stamps. He asked me about the firm I had been visiting.

'You do good business with Saudi, yes.'

'Very good.'

He glanced at the tiny bundled figure.

'Why do you travel with that lady?'

'She is meeting her husband. He asked me to bring her here.'

Out of the corner of my eye I saw a woman in uniform taking Amina by the elbow. They disappeared into a cubicle with a long green curtain in front, like a changing room. A younger official peered over the old man's shoulder. He picked up my passport, looked at me. He started asking where I had stayed in Riyadh. Inwardly I let out a great sigh of relief. I could spin this along, he was just talking to me out of boredom. Another guard came. They both started flirting. One of them stamped and returned my passport. Then he smacked my bottom. They had taken not a blind bit of notice of Amina. She came back, they barely looked at her documents and waved both of us through with Richard.

In the departure lounge stood the man I had come to recognize from his photographs as the 'husband'. He was several shades paler than the man I had been expecting but I knew it was him. He was shivering convulsively. The aircon wasn't that good; he was just the most scared person I had ever seen. I didn't blame him.

He nodded to me and to his 'wife' – which if this had been a genuine Saudi marriage would have been absolutely the right thing to do – and shook Richard by the hand. We hung about for the flight to be called. When I saw that British Airways jet on the tarmac it shimmered. It wasn't just a heat haze. If a yellow brick road had suddenly appeared across the tarmac to that plane, if it had sprouted pepperpot turrets and a rainbow over the cockpit, I wouldn't have been at all surprised. We were two couples now, crossing to the aeroplane and climbing the steps. I was carrying hand luggage with the sister's jewellery in it. When we got to the top there stood a stewardess in her perky hat, looking passengers straight in the eye and smiling like a normal person.

'Good afternoon, sir. Good afternoon, sir. Good afternoon, sir. Good afternoon, madam.'

'Gimme a drink,' I said.

We had taken our seats in First Class and were taxi-ing along the runway. None of us were speaking, when the crew curtain began to riffle and move. I stared, fascinated, as a hand appeared, and passed me an uncorked bottle of wine and a glass.

21

I had two years to go before I was supposed to 'retire', and work obsessed me. When I saw Thomas after Saudi, I was euphoric. After the child snatched from the ox cart, I was on a different kind of high. The ox cart incident – looking back on it – could have gone horribly wrong.

I was working with a friend of Buddy's called Dan, who had been asked to get a child back from the Middle East. The Arab father was a violent man, divorced, who had no legal custody of his daughter but had snatched her from her school in Florida two years ago. The American mother seemed at the same time vague and single-minded. She'd spent several weeks with her husband's family in his home country when they were first married, but now she couldn't even remember the name of the village where they lived. All she could give us were photographs of some ruins taken in 1978 from the balcony of the family home. Dan sent a couple of guys to the capital on a recce, and they identified the place from those ruins: a hillside hamlet about thirty miles from the Turkish border. The house was a two-storeyed place with the usual black-clad women pottering about in the courtyard. There were several children. One of them was blonde and looked like the last picture of the daughter, taken two years ago. Some time between two and four every afternoon, the women and children left the house and were transported in the back of a bullock cart along a desert track to another village, where they helped to pack dried tobacco leaves.

We had decided to bring the child across an isolated border post and head for Adana, where there are tourist flights. Dan and I and the mother had to organize visas; she must be present when the child was rescued, or we could be accused of kidnapping. Money changed hands behind the scenes. Our documents were in order. We hired a car, and early one morning drove to the flat plain away from the coast.

Journeys are monotonous in this part of the world. We got out of Turkey without a problem, and the car grumbled over rough road for about ten miles until it met a decent metalled highway that stretched from north to south. We kept straight on, and Dan's two operatives met us at a small town on the hill road east to the capital. They drove ahead of us past the house. It was early afternoon and the flat-bedded cart stood on the track outside, with no animals between the shafts.

We all wanted to get it over with. We could not park; the way from the house led over dusty tracks, along about a mile of tarmac, and over dust again. There was no reason to stop, so if we did, any other driver would think there was something wrong. On the other hand we couldn't keep cruising up and down the single tarmacked road through the town. There were about ten cars a day in this part of the world. We were horribly conspicuous. Despite occasional ruins baking in the sun, it wasn't a tourist area and we felt that if we hung about for more than an hour or two, the police would come snooping. Dan, the American mother and I were in a car with Turkish plates, the two Americans in the hired car they had been driving for a week. We made a big circle around the district.

We were all tense and three of us were armed. There was no other way.

At last, far ahead on the empty main road we saw that the ox cart had started moving, and it was full of people. The two operatives slowly overtook it. We approached, but hung back a long way. It was an old, sandy cart creaking on iron wheels, travelling at about five miles an hour. There were probably twenty women and children on the back, and none of us could see the little girl among them. The car ahead drove carefully off the road, on the track to the tobacco village, and disappeared over a hill; the ox cart lumbered after it. We hung back and then drove after the cart. The guys in front should have pulled sharply across the road at the brow of the hill. Sure enough, the ox cart stopped when it got to the top. We tore up and braked right behind it. In a second I was out of our car and running forward with the girl's mother. Ahead of me, one of Dan's mates had already got a gun trained on the ox cart's driver.

On the cart it was pandemonium. The driver, a filthy-looking old party with one tooth and a turban, was screaming in Arabic and brandishing his fists in the air. Half a dozen huge black-gowned women wobbled to their feet on the cart, all shrieking and grabbing at me as I jumped aboard. The mother saw the little girl first, and hauled her from between the obstructive women and out of the back. I held the women off. I saw Dan running round looking for some way to disable the cart, but he gave up. It was a bit low-tech, as transport goes, and that sort of thing confuses Americans. We slammed into our car. The front car rocked round to join us. And we were off, back to the junction near the border where we swapped cars and drove in different directions.

Dan drove north. The mother and child were tearful in the back seat. He and I said nothing. We were too busy concentrating on what might happen next. Both he and I were conscious that we were carrying guns and might have to use them. We were racing.

The whole operation had taken under two hours. The American investigators had assured us they had paid for no questions to be asked at the border crossing. When we got there, a workers' bus would be waiting; we were to cross in that. We veered off up the grotty road back to Turkey.

The customs post amounted to not much more than a couple of scruffy buildings and some scratching dogs. The bus was the only one there, stationary and baking in the sun. We clambered on to it. And waited.

Dan sat on one side of the aisle, I on another. I was gazing through the muzzy fly-spattered windscreen at the barrier, fifty yards away. Behind us the mother and child whispered and murmured. The driver, it seemed, was inside the police post having his lunch.

Another bus arrived. Wizened men and women, mostly carrying what looked like their week's laundry, climbed out of it and began to heave their possessions into our bus. We had been sitting in silence for twenty minutes when a couple of armed soldiers ambled out of nowhere, chucked their cigarettes on the ground and climbed in. They stared the length of the bus. I was near the front.

'Papers.'

I handed the soldier my passport. My right hand crept

behind my back. I could feel the heavy pistol stuck in my waistband.

He looked at me, shut the passport and handed it back. The two of them moved down the bus, checking documents. The driver returned. The soldiers got off, the bus jerked forward and crawled across the bridge, and half an hour later we were in Turkey, negotiating a taxi fare to Adana.

Thomas and I ended up discussing it. I never usually talked to him about work. I had made a rule. But there was a bit of an uproar about that rescue. Dan had been informed that the State Department might have to make an apology for the behaviour of its nationals in a sensitive part of the world, and it was on my mind. Thomas and I were together in the Caribbean, I was obviously preoccupied, and in the end I sketched the event in outline. Not the details, but the fact that guns had been involved inevitably came into it. He looked grim.

'I just want you to give this up,' he said. 'I admire what you do but there is no cause worth getting shot for.'

I thought of his father, killed crossing to the West. Thomas knew what he was talking about.

'I won't get shot. It's only a couple more years, Thomas.'

'You keep saying that. You're no good to me dead.'

By the time Neil Livingstone's book recounting some of ISS's exploits had hit the shops in America, I was discovering that there is more than one way to fall flat on your face in this business. Back in London, we were approached by a woman called Jo Clark who wanted to get her sons back.

Her story had already been in the news because of an

abortive rescue attempt. Ten or twelve years ago she had married an Egyptian and had a daughter and two boys by him. Quite recently he had taken the children away to live in Egypt. She hired a bunch of thugs to retrieve them. As operations go it must have been a fiasco, because when she grabbed the little girl, the child's grandfather came roaring at her with a knife and stabbed her eighteen times. Harry Arnold, a journalist from the *Daily Mirror*, got on to the case. He may have told her about ISS; I'm not sure. By now we had had a lot of publicity. However it came about, Jo Clark contacted Buddy and he promised to go and see her, with me, when he came to London.

Jo had been in hospital in Egypt for some time after the stabbing. She must have been an embarrassment to the Foreign Office, but somehow she had got the little girl out. Now they lived in Coulsdon, Surrey, in a council house. Coulsdon is one of those dull suburbs that function like cross-hatching on the map of a city, filling in the gaps between landmarks. Jo and little Poppy had nothing; there was a fusty smell, a threadbare carpet in a bare and cheerless front room, and I felt sorry for whoever found themselves in such horrible circumstances.

She was a lot older and thinner than I had expected. I was almost sure I was looking at an alcoholic. If not now, then at some time in the past, drink must have given her that grey haggard look. But I wasn't about to pass judgement on her for that; she must have suffered terribly when her children were taken.

She told us she had been looking for a legal way to gain custody of her two sons still in Cairo, but it seemed hopeless. Buddy advised her to keep the case going through the courts.

He told her any kind of covert operation would cost a lot of money. I backed him up. We had already brought an American child out of Tunisia by boat, and although all I had done was sail the ship across the Mediterranean, I knew how much that had cost. Given how jumpy the Egyptian family must be, this was not going to be a straightforward matter of putting Jo and the boys in a cab to Cairo airport.

Jo was not going to let mere financial difficulty put her off, however. She said she was getting paid by a newspaper, but because most of that money would go on the lawsuit, she claimed she had accepted an offer of extra help. The Al Fayed brothers, owners of Harrods, who were Egyptian, had read about her case and promised to finance any rescue attempt. They didn't want to be associated with the case, for obvious reasons, but they would pick up the tab.

Buddy was still a bit doubtful. He told her that if she really wanted us to rescue the boys, she must carry on with the lawsuit otherwise suspicions would be aroused. She agreed. She was sure she could get the children from their school; all she wanted was somebody to go with her and help her work out a way to get them out of the country in due course.

We drove back into London. I decided to send Karen. I had trained her, she had been in the army and she could certainly look after this woman.

That's what I thought. The fact is, you can only protect people who aren't living out some kind of death wish; and I should have got the message about Jo a lot sooner than I did.

I should have got it when I found that she had no friends or relations who could take Poppy for a week while Karen went to Cairo with her. Poppy was eleven, a quiet girl, and one of my nieces was good with kids and would cheerfully look after her for a week. Poppy would stay up in north London with me. The school gave her four hours of work to do each day. So that was all settled.

Three days after Karen and Jo left, I came home from the office and had just said hello to Poppy when the phone rang.

'Jacquie?'

'Karen, how're you getting on?'

'It's a nightmare. She's been drunk since we got here. She's smoking cannabis. She's fucking the wine waiter –'

'Calm down. Karen, calm down.'

Poor Karen was sharing a hotel room with Jo.

'You've only got to tough it out for a week. If she hasn't got her act together by then –'

'No, it'll be next week because the boys are away.'

Every couple of days I spoke to Karen and every time she sounded more disgusted. In the end I got hold of Jo herself.

'How d'you think you're helping your case, behaving like this?'

'What do you mean?'

'Sleeping with waiters –'

'I never slept with a waiter in my life. You want to ask Karen if you think it's me that's putting it about. You should see her. She's all over them. Flashing her tits at anything in trousers.'

Since I knew that Karen was a lesbian, Jo failed to convince me. I got to the point.

'What about the boys?'

'It's really hard. I'm looking out for them and they're never there.'

'What shall I do about Poppy?'

'Don't worry. I've got an idea, I'll be back with Karen in a few days.'

Two days later Karen rang.

'This is the last straw. I get back and there's a note on my pillow. Listen to this: "Staying Nile Hilton with Achmed. Will call later."'

'Who the fuck is Achmed?'

'New waiter. She met him last night. Specializes in room service, apparently.'

'I think you'd better come back, Karen. And bring her with you, for God's sake.'

Jo Clark refused to come back. She had no money so how she kept herself for the next six weeks I have no idea. She didn't bother to ring me to say where she was or ask after her daughter. I was giving my niece £20 a day for child care, and the school was getting anxious. Poppy said her aunts, Jo's sisters, had refused to have her.

Poppy didn't cost a lot to feed, but I drew the line at buying new clothes and the child had only come with enough to wear for a week. A couple of guys from the Circuit went into the house in Coulsdon to collect some fresh stuff for her, and came back looking shocked.

'It's disgusting over there,' one of them muttered to me. 'The bedrooms are filthy. The sheets are grey, no kidding. Fancy bringing a kid home to that.'

Poppy didn't like living with her mother. She said she was fed up with having different men around the place all the time. The stories in the paper made her embarrassed and her mother was always drunk. She had been in the car once when her mother had crashed it after drinking. I began to feel a lot of sympathy for the Egyptian father. I was sickened by the whole situation: we had misjudged it, and now we were landed with the consequences. Poor Poppy. I was going away soon, and she couldn't stay here for ever. I got her aunt's telephone number from her.

'Never again,' she said. 'Sorry she's done this to you, but we've been had before. She's dumped Poppy and gone off for months on end.'

'I'd keep her here, but I can't,' I said. 'I have to go away. I won't be here at nights and she can't stay in the house on her own.'

'You'll have to sort it out for yourself. I told you, she's a nice kid and we're sorry for her but we've had it up to here with her bloody mother.'

Days were going by with no call from Jo and I had to be abroad next week. I contacted Social Services. They said if no family member could help, Poppy would be taken into care.

At the last minute one of the sisters relented and Poppy went to stay with her. I was abroad for a few weeks working, and when I got back to England I got a call from Jo. She was in Coulsdon now.

'What's your sodding game, you smart-arsed cow, getting my sister on the phone? Who asked you to call her? Leaving me out there in bloody Cairo on my own. Call yourself child rescue –'

I was almost too annoyed to speak. I simply told her I wanted nothing more to do with her and sent her a bill. Our out-of-pocket expenses alone ran into thousands. She has appeared on television since, flourishing the bill and complaining. It was never paid. The Al Fayeds made it clear that they had never made any agreement to finance Jo Clark's lawsuits, rescue attempts or anything else.

As for the boys, they now live as far as I know with Jo and Poppy. She eventually got them back in Miami, through the courts.

22

In 1992 I took 175 international flights. I worked on divorce cases, fraud investigations, surveillances, recces for child rescues and the rescues themselves. I got work from ISS, off the Circuit, and independently. Thomas and I didn't meet for months. On the telephone, he no longer asked what I was doing because he knew I would always say the same thing.

'Working, but I can't talk about it.'

'It's dangerous. I don't understand. Why do you feel you've got to do this?'

'They need somebody.'

The child rescues were hardest to justify because they were the most dangerous. At worst, I could get shot at, or arrested and charged thousands of miles from home. I knew Thomas didn't understand how desperate some of these women were. If we didn't help them, there were people out there who would offer to commit murder for much less than the cost of a genuine child rescue. And having an ex-husband bumped off was a short-cut many of these women would be prepared to take. I couldn't explain to Thomas how half-crazed and despairing they were. Thomas stopped talking to me about it. He knew that I knew his silence meant he disapproved.

I didn't care much what the State Department thought, or the Foreign Office, or the newspapers for that matter, but when the one person who really mattered to me began to have reservations, I got a bit defensive. I told myself Thomas would just have to tough it out for two more years until 1994 when I would keep my promise to retire. Right now I had other men to deal with, men with an entirely different set of problems.

I had already done a recce in Pakistan for ISS when I drove to Sheffield to meet Anne Lewis. She was a middle-aged woman, introduced to me by mutual friends. We met in the lobby of a hotel and for the next two hours she poured out her story.

'I can't believe Mahmood would do this to her,' she kept saying. 'I'd never have thought he'd be like that. He's the last person. He was always so kind.'

I stifled an impulse to ask whether Mahmood had ever thought of joining the SPG. It was another of those cases where a sweetheart turns into a beast the minute he is married. Laura, Anne's daughter, had been whisked off to Islamabad shortly after marrying him in Leeds six months ago. And then – silence. Apart from one worried call from a female relative of Mahmood's, saying that Laura was losing a lot of weight, there had been no contact at all until a letter came two days ago. Or rather, a note. Anne handed me a crumpled bit of lined paper torn from a pad.

Dear Mum, I really hope you get this. I have got to get out of here. I am locked in the house 24 hours a day. I've got no key and no money and the servants spy on me. M. says I must stop living like a western woman. He hits me every single night. I am twelve weeks pregnant. I stopped eating to get back at him but then he stopped giving me food.

I have got to get out and he has got my passport. Please come and get me. I'm going crazy. I can't have my baby here. Love Laura.

There was a row of Xs under the signature and a big blotch, as if she had wept on to the paper.

'I don't know what to do. I can't get her back on my own. I thought maybe the Consul could help or I could write to Benazir Bhutto.'

I had to tell her that in my experience, consuls don't intervene in domestic dramas like this one. They are there to promote trade, and if they start criticizing the Muslim way of life, even indirectly, by taking a wife's side against her husband, it's bad for business. So they don't take a lot of notice when English girls get locked away by local men. As for Benazir Bhutto, I had bodyguarded her in the past so her name had come up in conversation with ISS. She had often been approached to help American wives and mothers, without positive results.

'So can you get Laura back?' Anne asked.

'I can try, but it'll be expensive. It'll probably take three or four of us and we may have to hire a boat.'

When I had been in Pakistan before, it had been to recce a rescue out of Karachi by sea.

'I'll remortgage my house,' she said at once.

By cutting costs to the bone I could barely do the job for the money she could afford. I got visa application forms and started ringing around. At the low rates I was willing to pay, and with all the paperwork, it was four weeks before I had a team in place. Anne sounded more worried every time I spoke to her. Laura wasn't getting any less pregnant; time was precious. Also, she would need a passport and she couldn't hang about in Pakistan waiting for one once we got her away from her husband. I would have to get Laura into India.

There would be three men and myself. Mike and I flew out to Karachi first. As I saw it, I had only two options: either to get her to Srinagar by walking across the border through the low foothills of the Hindu Kush, or to get out by sea.

I rejected the idea of a long trek over rough terrain with an undernourished woman who was expecting a baby. My idea was to rent a Zodiac, a rigid inflatable boat of the kind used by armed forces all over the world, get Laura out of Karachi in it and land with her on the Indian coast.

Mike and I were in Karachi for three days. We tried hard and got nowhere. I hadn't exactly taken to the city on my first visit and this second one didn't alter my view. I found it dusty, noisy and the dirt and poverty appalled me. You stayed in a hotel, in proper rooms with clean sheets and running hot and cold water, but the chambermaids and the man who cleaned the pool could be living in tarpaulin-covered shacks within a hundred yards of you. We couldn't hire a car without a driver, so we gave up and took taxis everywhere, which got on my nerves but was typical of Pakistan: you were constantly having to interact with helpful people you wished you'd never met. Down at the harbour they took us out in fishing boats, they begged off us, they tried to sell us everything from camel rides to snide watches, but none of them actually showed us a way out. The harbour was partly blocked by a big concrete chicane that nobody except a local pilot or fisherman could navigate around. The beaches up and down the coast were crowded with holidaymakers whenever we took a taxi there to have a look.

And on the morning when Roger and Dave were to arrive from London, we heard gunfire in the streets. Mike said a man in the lift had told him it was an uprising. Whatever that meant.

So when Mike went to the airport to meet the others I was pondering other ways around the problem. With half a mind on what I was doing, I pushed my way down a bustling garish market street and bought *shalwàr kamiz* from a towering display in an open-fronted shop. These are the trousers and knee-length tunics that the local women wear, usually in vivid colours with embroidery, with wide shawls looped gracefully around the face. I chose brown, black and navy cotton. Then I went back to the hotel, with my mind made up.

I had expected the two recent arrivals, and Mike, but when I walked into the lobby they were all sitting there with a new guy.

'This is Trev,' said Dave.

'Right,' I said. Maybe I looked annoyed. I don't know why, maybe it was irrational on my part but I thought a six-footer with green eyes and hair the colour of carrots was going to prove a bit of a liability in Pakistan.

Trev gave me a dismissive nod. Surly bastard.

'What's your background?' I asked pleasantly.

'SBS and FFL,' he said. 'What's yours, darling?'

'That's none of your business,' I said. 'I'm paying you, so you don't need to know.'

He subsided in his chair muttering something about the day when he took orders off a woman. The others were inspecting their shoes.

'Dave, could we have a word?'

Dave followed me across the lobby.

'Where did you get him?'

'You said you wanted somebody that could handle a Zodiac. I've worked with him before. Sorry he's like this.'

'What's his excuse? PMT? I'm being very polite, Dave. You never even said you were bringing anybody.'

'I couldn't go into it on the phone. I did a deal. He's doing it for two fifty a day. And he is ex-SBS, I checked with a mate of mine.'

We went back to the others. Trevor was reclining with both arms stretched along the sofa back, staring at me as I crossed the lobby.

'Right. You guys must need a rest. We'll meet up at four in my room, OK?'

I sat behind the desk. The two easy chairs were taken by Trevor and Mike. Dave and Roger sat on the bed.

'I don't know how much you guys already know, so you can consider this a briefing as well as a planning meeting.' Trevor raised his eyes to the ceiling. 'This is the deal. The woman we want is called Laura, she's being held against her will by her husband in Islamabad. She hasn't got a passport –'

'No, she wouldn't have,' Trevor muttered under his breath.

'– but she can get one in India, so that's where we're gonna take her. This is her.' I passed around some wedding photographs. 'She's got a lot thinner since those were taken.'

Trevor took an uninterested glance and passed the pictures to Dave. I unfolded a map of Pakistan away from me across the desk and leant across to point with a pencil at markings which, from my awkward angle, were upside down.

'Here's Islamabad. There are flights down to Karachi every

day and we've been talking about getting her out by sea. On the other hand, there is a route across the mountains as far as Srinagar. You can see it there. Just.'

'How far's that?' Roger asked.

'About 130 kilometres.' Trevor made a snorting noise and crossed his arms. 'There's no active border post if you go round . . . *here*.'

'Just fucking snipers,' said Trevor.

'Yeah?' I looked at him.

'Yeah,' said Trevor, sniggering. 'It's not like Hadrian's fucking wall. Pakis vee Injuns, remember?'

'Well, thank you, Trevor. But that's the way we're going. I have decided that getting this girl out by sea is not an option.'

'How would you know?'

'Believe it or not, I have been in this country before. Mike and I have just spent three days checking out the harbour here. We –'

'So? What about the beaches? Look, darling.' He tapped the map. 'See those yellow strips near the blue space. Beaches.'

'Last time I looked they were full of French tourists.'

Trevor leaned back and swung both feet on to the desk. They crushed a corner of the map. 'What's the problem? You'll blend in nicely.'

'Take your trainers off the map, Trevor. Part of the problem is that there is a shooting war going on here in Karachi at the moment. If you'd been watching CNN in the last couple of hours, or even looked out of the window, you'd have noticed armed men in the streets. We are taking Laura over the mountains.'

'Brilliant.'

'You have a problem with that?'

'You dragged me out here to this shit-hole on a fourteen-hour flight just to walk some daft tart through a war zone?'

I sighed. Mike was looking at the ceiling, Roger was holding his head in his hands and Dave was looking at me apologetically.

'What is your room number?'

'210,' Trevor said. 'You won't get round me that way.'

Nobody laughed. I picked up the telephone.

'Hello. Could you get the bill ready for room 210, please. He's checking out.'

I got five £50 notes out of my bag and passed them across the desk. 'On your bike.'

He got up, kicking the desk. 'You know what it is with you, darling? Your head's so far up your arse you can't see daylight.'

I waited as he walked across the room.

'Trevor. You tell anybody about this job, you'll never work on the Circuit again.'

He slammed out of the room. I took a deep breath.

'Right, anybody else want out of this? Because if not, we're on a flight to Islamabad in the morning.'

And so we were. Dave, Roger, Mike and I fetched up at the Marriott hotel, one of the tallest buildings in Islamabad. It was a concrete pile with cod Islamic arches on the penthouse floor. I had learned from bitter experience, specifically rampant fleas, to stay only in upmarket hotels whenever I went to Pakistan or India.

Most of this city was four or five storeys high, built out of mud, with balconies and gaily painted advertisements in a script that was all dots and curves. Men of all ages ambled about in white *kurta*, baggy white trousers, and tweedy waist-coats with smart little round hats. Islamabad was slower, cooler and quieter than Karachi and I relaxed. From the window of my room I could see ten or twenty miles to the foothills of the Himalayas beneath a hazy blue sky.

'Don't get too fond of it,' I told myself. 'You're working.'

I was still inwardly triumphant about the abrupt disappear-ance of Trevor. I caught up with Mike at the reception desk downstairs.

'We want a Christian cabbie,' he was saying.

'You what?'

'Don't mess me about on this one, Jacquie. I know whereof I speak. I got badly done over by a Muslim taxi driver in Lahore.'

'Yeah, right.'

Anything for a happy ship. We split up. Dave set off to have a look at the mountain path, Roger went to recce the route to the airport in case the mountains proved impossible, and Mike and I waited for our cab. When it came there was a cross dangling behind the windscreen. The guy probably kept a supply in the glove compartment, I thought. Buddhas, Stars of David. The customer is always right.

'OK, Mike?'

'Right.'

We set off to the wealthier suburbs north of the city. The house where Laura was being kept was in a street lined with head-high painted mud walls with trees overhanging from inside. There was a wide double-sided iron gate. We got the driver to circle the block and come back very slowly. I looked through the black struts and saw a skinny creature in blue *shalwar kamiz*, her head wrapped in a shawl, standing on a path in front of a veranda. As the car passed she looked at us. She was fair-skinned. She was Laura. I thought our eyes met for a moment. Then she was gone.

In the days that followed, we watched the place. The husband, Mahmood, a tall handsome man with a moustache who wore baggy grey cotton Pakistani trousers and *kurta*, left at about nine in the morning and returned mid-afternoon. At eight or nine in the evening he left again, and stayed out for four or five hours. In his absence there was nobody about except Laura, the two servants of whom one was very old, and also a grandfather. The grandfather could have existed only in my mind. We never saw him, but Anne had told me that Mahmood once said there was a grandfather who lived in the house and never left his room. I was taking no chances.

'Any dogs?'

'No dogs.'

We were a working team now. Somehow we had all concluded that we were going to get the girl out and take her over the mountains to India. Roger and Dave started to buy water, matches, canned food and Bergens in order to plant supplies along the route. They recced the first few miles of the walk. The only obstacle seemed to be a manned fort a few miles out of Islamabad which, they promised, we would be able to hike around.

I just had to get the timing right. Timing was everything. One night, Mike and I quietly left the taxi in the dusk and started walking north. When we got to Laura's house it was dark. Mike gave me a leg up over the wall. I was wearing my black tunic and trousers, and with a black scarf wrapped around my face I glided silently between the trees in the garden. I came close to the house and began to sidle along its walls. Roger thought he had identified Laura's bedroom yesterday, and I hoped he was right, because by moonlight alone I couldn't see a thing. This was a muggy night and every window aperture with its shutters open looked like a black cave.

At the one which was supposed to be Laura's I spied a glimmer of light and peered over the sill. She was asleep on a single bunk inside. A tiny rush lamp flickered on the wall. I clambered into the room with inevitable scuffling noises, but she didn't wake up. I paused. There was not a sound in the house; no television or radio, no snoring. I crept forwards. She was lying on her side. I clamped my hand over her mouth and leant down. I saw a glint of white as her eyes jumped open in terror.

'Don't be frightened,' I hissed. 'Your mum sent me. When I take my hand away don't scream.'

I moved my hand and she twisted round to face me.

'Who are you?'

'I'm Jacquie. Your mum sent me. D'you want to leave here?'

'Yes.' She sat up suddenly. In the flickering light she looked eerily skeletal. 'Of course I do.'

'Hold on. You can't go now. Not tonight. Are you all right?'

'I'm covered in bruises. I'm four months gone, does she know?'

'Yes. Can you walk?'

'Of course.'

'Can you walk a long way?'

'Yes. I'll get dressed.'

'Not yet. Stay there. We've got to get you out without getting caught. I'm going now, but we're going to come back for you this week or next week. If an English guy turns up and says Jacquie sent him, do what he tells you, OK?'

'Ssh.'

She heard it before I did: a footfall in the corridor. She lay still on her bed. In a flash I was standing behind the door holding my breath. The latch was raised and the door opened inwards with a gentle sigh. I softly pulled the pistol out of my waistband. If whoever it was came in, I would be ready to clobber him with the weight of the gun in both hands. The door slowly shut again. For thirty seconds I held my breath as the person shuffled down the corridor.

'It was only Fayed,' she whispered. 'He's old, he worries about me. He can't do anything, he's only a servant.'

'I'm going,' I whispered back. 'Be ready to leave day or night.'

We had a few days in which to put everything in place. The main thing we didn't have was intelligence about the border we were to cross. I wanted to be sure that nobody would try and shoot us in the hills on the way to Srinagar. The following morning we arranged to meet for lunch in the hotel to assemble everything we knew and finalize the time when we would get Laura out.

At a quarter to one the phone rang.

'Is that Jacquie Davis?'

It was a male, English voice I did not know.

'They're on to you. Get out now.' The line went dead.

My mind raced. It had to be somebody from the consulate.

It would be the only way they could possibly speak to me. If that prat Trevor had said anything –

'If that prat Trevor said anything, I'm gonna strangle him with my bare hands.'

It was five minutes since the phone call and I was racing down the back stairs after Mike with maps, washing gear and a change of clothes. Everything else had been left. When we got out into the traffic Roger and Dave set off for the hillside.

Mike, waving at me from the cab rank, was already triumphant.

'Look, I got one.'

He slammed in beside the driver and I swung into the back seat. A crucifix swung merrily from the driving mirror. Mike gave him the address.

'What's your name?'

'Aziz.'

'OK, Aziz. Fast.'

We roared up to the northern suburbs.

'Slowly past that house. Very slowly. Stop.'

It was the same time of day as our first visit and Laura was out in the garden with one of the servants. Mahmood must be out. He had to be. The gates were old, about six feet high but rusty. I scrutinized their hinges, which were just bolts that slotted in from above but would probably hold. The central clasp though was feeble. It would bust open easily. The street was quiet. The yellow cab subsided hopelessly on its suspension.

'Aziz,' I said. 'Here is fifty dollars.'

A brown hand shot upwards and took the money.

'I want you,' I said, 'to ram those gates.'

Mike said, 'He doesn't understand. Aziz, drive very fast into the gates.' He smacked his right fist into his left palm.

'Those gates? They are shut.'

'They will open when you hit them.'

'My taxi will also open. Like a big fish.' His hands flew apart on the steering wheel and he gulped. 'My taxi. I saved for ten years.'

'We will buy you a new taxi.'

'More than fifty dollars.'

'One hundred dollars.'

The hand shot up again. The money was tucked into his shirt pocket. Inside the garden Laura walked slowly past, staring gloomily at the gravel path. Aziz reversed his cab.

'And when we all get back in,' I hissed, 'reverse like hell.'

'He doesn't understand. Don't worry, Aziz's not going to be practising three-point turns once he clocks what we're up to.'

If the gate didn't give way first time, she'd be bundled into the house and the doors bolted before we could try again. I was biting my lip in anxiety. Aziz held the jalopy on the clutch for a minute and then roared forward with his foot down. I saw Mike duck and I did the same as we hit the gate. It crashed open and we skidded on to the gravel. I leapt out and seized Laura. The servant grabbed her other arm. Mike headbutted him and I pushed Laura into the car. Mike leapt after us and hadn't got the door shut before Aziz had shot backwards at thirty miles an hour on to the street. We banged violently across the fallen gate. Aziz was gibbering. He turned the car and hurtled back towards town.

'Slow the fuck down!' screamed Mike. 'You're going the wrong way! We want the tourist vantage point.'

It was too late. Aziz, heading away from the hills, had torn right back into traffic. Turning a corner he braked hard. There in front of us was a classic Islamabad gyratory system. Every kind of light vehicle was trying to get round a cart which had collapsed spilling a load of melons across the road. As they were all trying to get past at once, they were all stuck. The pandemonium was intense, with horns blaring, people yelling and melons a foot in diameter bowling between hundreds of pairs of feet.

'We'll walk. I'll take Laura,' I shouted. 'Mike, if you can find another cab – I'll see you at the vantage point.'

We were out, and walking rapidly in the direction of the hills while Mike was still settling up with Aziz. I heard loud sirens from passing police cars on the main drag. We traced a path through the small market streets, our progress impeded by stallholders, small children and goods displayed on crowded pavements. We were both wearing *shalwar kamiz* but the rucksack I had slung over one shoulder made me conspicuous. I was sure that by now the servant Mike had decked in the garden must have contacted the police. There were no cabs in these back streets and if the misery on Laura's face was a good indicator, she couldn't go much further without starting to sob. Christ, I hoped she wasn't going to lumber us. I had finally walked into the main road and was trying to spot a free taxi when Mike and Aziz tore around the corner in search of us.

Aziz dropped us, smiling, at the foot of the tourist walking trail. I gave him another hundred dollars and told him to forget everything. He seemed very happy.

*

'What kept you?'

'Oh, this and that.'

Dave and Roger set off with us. Mike had already started to walk back down to Islamabad, its buildings and mosques jumbled higgledy-piggledy across the valley floor. He was going to return to London by air. Dave and Roger were both ex-SAS. We had maps, compasses, water and food. It was a nice day; the midday heat cooling down now, lots of butter-flies. Trudging the first mile up the hill path away from the city we could have been backpackers out for a day's trailwalking. Only it was four o'clock in the afternoon and we would have to walk all night, while it was cool. We would get no sleep until dawn.

'OK, Laura? Think you can make it?'

Dave was cheery. In fact Dave was a bloody scoutmaster, at this point.

'I have to,' Laura said. She looked determinedly up at the mountain. 'I've got to make it for the baby's sake.'

'Baby?'

'Laura is four months pregnant, Dave,' I muttered. So, I should have told you before. There's no need to look at me like that.

The first night was by far the worst. We were so tired, so freezing cold and so very aware that the city was still close. Until dusk we could see its lights in the sky behind us. When darkness fell, and there was only hazy moonlight to illuminate our route, one image kept flickering into my mind: the Esso tiger. I told myself I was overtired. This was true, as we had all been awake for far too long.

It was also true that it would be easy to get lost. Most of the time we were following stony tracks across scrubby ground.

Sometimes bushes and small trees reached above head height and it was like being on a jungle path. Roger or Dave took turns to scout forward, navigating by stars and compass, while the other one brought up the rear. Whoever was in front strode up to a quarter of a mile ahead at times, and had the hardest job. He had to find our way and at the same time stay alert for armed soldiers.

The fort lay quite near to the start of our route, low in the hills. I had seen a photograph taken in daylight: long mud walls around a barrack square. The place looked neglected but it was patrolled, and we had to make a five or six mile detour uphill to get round it.

We past it before midnight. The hours after were numbing. We rested for five minutes in every hour, drank water, rubbed our feet and slapped our arms about ourselves to keep warm. I heard a sob.

'I don't think I can do this,' Laura said.

She didn't have much choice.

I expected to sleep soundly during the first day because when we lay down in sleeping bags at dawn I felt exhausted. But concern kept me semi-awake. I dozed for twelve hours and when we got up for the second night's trekking, I felt as if I had only just lain down. The tiredness persisted. It wasn't a difficult walk; the higher we went, the cooler we were during the daylight hours and the easier we found it to make progress. Steep hillsides plunged on all sides. Far ahead, the peaks of the Panjal range stretched like a choppy sea to the horizon. Setting off late on the second afternoon we thought we could see K2 in the distance, snowcapped under an indigo sky. We were slowly climbing all the way, on firm ground with no big rivers to cross and no dangerous gradients. The stress came from having to stay silent and watch your feet, because small animals and the roots of trees had made deep depressions in the ground and if one of us broke or sprained an ankle, we would all be in bad trouble. For this reason we moved a lot faster during what remained of the day than we did at night.

It was about six o'clock, and I had just turned back to check on Laura two yards away, when a bullet hit a tree beside my head. Another gunshot followed at once. Laura's face froze. I grabbed her, hurled her to the ground behind a log and threw myself on top of her.

'Don't move.'

Close protection training is a reflex action. Dave, behind us, had hit the deck. Bullets were crashing either side of us. We had set off north-east, and were now travelling south-east. If these were Indians fighting Kashmiri rebels, then the Kashmiris must be the ones behind us. These thoughts shot incoherently through my mind as I stared at a rotten log a foot in front of my nose. I rolled off Laura.

'Keep still.'

Something shot out of the log and between the trees. I don't like snakes. I nearly jumped out of my skin. Another gunshot cracked into a tree. Things rustled in the dead vegetation around me. I would have given anything to get my body off the ground.

'There are snakes,' Laura whispered.

'Don't worry about them. Snakes can't blow your head off.'

I could see Roger wriggling rapidly on his stomach and elbows downhill towards us.

'They firing at us?' he gasped.

'Dunno. Think I should go and ask? Lend us a white hanky.'

'Very funny.'

'It's like that dickhead Trev said. Kashmiri rebels.'

Dave was crawling towards us uphill.

'We've got to head into that firing line.'

'We have?'

The firing stopped.

'West, Pakistan. East, India.'

Everything was quiet. None of us said anything. There was no wind. Everything, the birds, the beetles on the ground, perhaps even the snakes, seemed to be listening. We moved a short way on our stomachs, walked nervously, began again to stumble forwards through the darkness. We walked all night, silently. Somehow we passed through the firing line unscathed.

For the next two nights we found our way mostly in the dark. There was little time to talk and almost nothing to say, except how cold we were, how badly we wanted a shower, and how our feet hurt. Laura was wearing only sandals and she must have suffered. Sometimes she seemed overcome with despair; she just slowed, like a clock that needs winding, and lost all resistance. The guys tried to jolly her along, but it didn't work.

I told her, quietly and in private, that if she succumbed to years of brainwashing and started behaving like a dependent female, we were all screwed. She never complained once after that. She thanked us all for our help and kept moving, mile after mile. Unfortunately, this made me think I'd gone too far. I tramped on, worrying that if she got suspicious pains, she might be too stoical to say. If she started to miscarry here in the foothills of the Hindu Kush, the maternity unit would be Dave and Roger and me, a handy first aid kit, a camp fire and the five litres of bottled water we had left.

On the fourth day we were slowly waking up in the middle of the afternoon when we heard a single burst of random firing in the distance.

'Brilliant,' Dave said, sitting up and scratching his tangled hair. 'We're in the right place.'

'We are?'

'Yeah. That's shots in the air, you can tell. It's a wedding.'

'Oh. Shotgun wedding, I suppose.'

'Nah, that's what the locals do up here. It means we're near to Srinagar.'

The next morning, as light grew, we glimpsed a metalled road snaking between green terraces only a few miles away. We stumbled wearily up to Roger, sitting on a ridge.

'Made it.'

Dawn was rising behind the mountain range. There was a village of flat-roofed houses straggling up the valley. Five hundred feet below us, a bareheaded man strode a deliberate path behind a plough drawn by a bullock. The sound of its bell clanked through clear air.

'I just want to go to sleep.'

'Are you sure this is India?'

'Yes, Laura. We're about three miles from Srinagar. I've just seen two women in saris on that road through there. Don't worry. This is India, you're OK.'

In the village was a wooden *chai* house with a veranda round it, where farm workers sat eating bowls of rice with their fingers. They looked surprised at the sight of four dirty westerners striding down from the mountains. The owner flicked the ends of his turban self-importantly down his back and brought out a tray full of glasses of sweet mint tea. We told him we wanted to go to Srinagar.

'My cousin has taxi.'

'Good.'

'You go to airport at Srinagar?'

'Maybe. Has your cousin got a good taxi?' Silly question, really. God, I was tired.

'My cousin, his taxi is best in all India. Air-conditioned, takes all of you. He takes you to Delhi. You do not need air flight, my cousin very cheap, all four persons. His taxi is very big. You will see.' He was on the phone already. It was still before six in the morning but within ten minutes a new Toyota van came bouncing down the rutted village street towards us. The driver smiled amiably through the window. Negotiations followed. We settled a price. We piled in. Raj was the driver's name. We all said hello and settled at once to five or six hours of sleep. The air-conditioning breezed through the window, and there were no seats, but I curled up on my sleeping bag on the metal floor and shut my eyes. I was drifting off, as we pulled out on to the main road, when I heard Dave's voice near my ear.

'Have you noticed anything about Raj?' he hissed.

'Nice smile,' I said, without opening my eyes.

'One arm.'

'What?'

'He's only got one arm.'

I was too tired to sit up and look, but now I visualized Raj as he had appeared at the van window, and it was true, he had been wearing the train of his turban draped over the shoulder next to the window and hanging down. I thought about this for a while. Then I drifted in and out of sleep.

'Is it an automatic?'

'No. Shift.'

I fell asleep. From time to time I woke up; every time, we were still bowling along. We seemed to be going quite fast. We stopped, ate kebabs and nan, climbed back in again and lay dozing. When all the others were asleep I woke and sat up, coughing, amid clouds of smoke. The van reeked of cannabis. Raj was gleefully playing that game so popular everywhere in Asia: Chicken. Overheight, overloaded trucks with roo bars, their wooden sides painted with flowers and stories, festooned with fairy lights and pictures of grim-faced mullahs, would appear on the distant horizon, hurtling towards us in the middle of the road. Raj immediately put his foot down and charged straight at them until they gave way. The outcomes of previous Chicken games lay rusting on either side of the road.

Raj must have brought a supply of ready-rolled joints for the journey, because he was puffing happily on one of them while changing gear and steering with his one good hand.

We slowed down and stopped. I lay down again. Either I was dead tired or there had been something unhealthy about that kebab. A policeman leaned through the passenger window. He exchanged a few words with Raj and looked hopefully at me.

'You English? You got cigarettes?'

I fumbled in my Bergen and gave him twenty Bensons. He waved us on. Raj stepped on the gas.

'It's good you give him cigarettes,' he said. 'Or he stop me. In India, man with one arm is not allowed to drive.'

I call that downright unfair.

23

Anne flew out to New Delhi to be with Laura, and I flew back to England exhilarated with sheer relief. Thomas and I spent some time together in London. When he said I seemed calmer than last time, I told him I was pleased because I'd been able to rescue somebody. I was, of course; it had been the first big rescue I'd done without Ann and Buddy. But I kept thinking how badly it could have gone wrong if I hadn't kept the team together.

A few weeks later, another middle-aged woman was on the phone.

'It's confidential,' she said. 'Can I come to your office?'

She arrived looking flustered, wispy-haired and tearful. She dressed too young for her age and was overweight.

'It's been a month now.'

She showed me pictures of her second husband. She had done rather well financially out of her first marriage, having received a generous divorce settlement. But now she had fallen in love with this Filipino, they hadn't been married long, and she woke up one morning to find a note. He had been called away on business, it said; he would be back in a couple of weeks. She had noticed a few things missing. His passport. Silver, jewellery. Cash.

'But that's not important. I'm sure he's gone home to Manila. I've got to go and find out what's happened to him. His mother might be ill. He might have had an accident.'

'What's keeping you?'

'Oh, I couldn't go all that way on my own.'

Some people are so timid. She paid my daily rate, return flight and accommodation in Manila. We were there for a fortnight. I didn't find the husband. I found his three children and his wife, though.

Back from Manila with my sadder and wiser client, I flew to North Carolina to help Ann and Buddy out for a few weeks. *Rescue My Child* was selling well and they were overwhelmed by approaches from distraught mothers. They had a heart-breaking case on but were stuck without money to pay for the rescue. The Bangladesh rescue which Ann did had left them thousands of dollars out of pocket, and they were having to harden their hearts, but Sarah Ali's plight was more harrowing than most.

She was an American who had married a Yemeni, had two babies, and separated from him. The girl and boy were four and six years old when he snatched them from their school and took them to Yemen. The girl had a heart complaint and needed medication. Sarah was beside herself, but had no money to go over there, find her children and bring them back. The only way she could earn a living was as a singer and songwriter. She didn't make much. We all had faith that one day she would; she was a terrific singer. At the same time, we knew that terrific isn't all it takes. Somehow Sarah Ali could never get the right breaks.

She lived right over on the other side of America in Tacoma, Washington State, but came to North Carolina when she could and talked to Ann several times. She was deeply frustrated by the impossibility of making things happen.

And then there was Iceland.

I can't bring myself to write about Iceland. One day I will, but right now court cases are pending. We were hired by two divorced fathers who had children by the same Icelandic woman. They asked us to retrieve their children from Iceland where she had taken them, and it all went pear-shaped. Buddy spent a year in jail in Reykjavik and Lawrence and I, the two English participants, found ourselves unable to re-enter the UK in case we got extradited to Iceland as well. I didn't mind not going home, but Lawrence had just had a baby daughter. What hurt me most was the *Observer* newspaper. They printed an account of the whole affair which made me out to be a mercenary.

Once we were back in America, for weeks we talked about nothing except how to get Buddy back. Sarah came to see Ann and me at this time but I think she grew secretly disheartened. I could understand that. Buddy was, after all, a grown man and resilient. What Sarah wanted was her defenceless children.

She had one glimmer of hope: somebody else wanted our help in the Yemen, and could afford to get us there. So at least we would be able to recce the country. An Englishwoman called Jan Palmer had rung ISS from Birmingham. She had read Neil Livingstone's book, she said, and did Ann know about Nadia and Zana, the two English girls whose father had forced them into marriage in the Yemen?

Ann didn't. But in England, I had read lots of articles about Zana and Nadia. They had been ordinary Birmingham teenagers when their father offered to send them on holiday to his homeland. They jumped at the chance. Within weeks they had found themselves trapped in a remote village in the Mokbana mountains and married, against their will, to two local boys. Their father had sold them.

The story had been told in a book by Zana, the elder girl, who had finally got out. It was book sales that had made enough money for them to approach ISS to try and rescue Nadia. And the children. There were lots of children. Zana had left her baby son back in Yemen with Nadia, and Nadia had been producing a child every couple of years since she first got to the country. She now wore *shabbah*, spoke Arabic like a local and spent her days as a good wife should: grinding corn and toting water up from the valley. She seemed, in fact, settled. Zana was adamant that Nadia was desperate to get back to Birmingham but would not leave without her children.

We took down the details. They asked about cost; we estimated $20,000 up front to cover initial meetings and expenses. Jan didn't hesitate. Money was not a problem, she said. We met Jan and Miriam, the mother, in New York. Jan was a pleasant-faced woman in her thirties. She said she was a friend of Miriam's from Birmingham and had once been a journalist. Miriam was small, dark and tired-looking. I questioned Miriam, who had been married to a Yemeni for a couple of decades, about Yemen. She knew hardly anything other than what Zana had already said in public. (It makes you wonder what married couples talk about.) I sent a couple of guys up to north Yemen, where Nadia was living, to come up with some ideas. Meanwhile, I flew to Aden, on the south coast, on the pretext of being a travel journalist.

I didn't stay long. Staying in Aden, a noisy western-style city, was a lot like being in Saudi again, so there was hardly anything I could do. When I dressed in western clothes, I got my bottom pinched, and when I wore *shabbah*, I got fed up with lifting my long skirts over sticky heaps of chewed *qat* in the dust. Yemeni men seemed to spend half their time squatting in groups gossiping and chewing this stimulant and spitting great gobs of what looked like spinach.

Foreigners of both sexes were faced with the familiar problem: the inability to hire a car without a driver. The guys were staying in San'á, which is a beautiful ancient towering city in the north. They had themselves driven several hundred miles up towards the Saudi border, and took pictures, until one day their cameras were confiscated by officious military. The north of Yemen is mountainous, barren and sparsely populated. The few cultivated patches of vivid green, terraced land make the landscape look like a painting-by-numbers canvas that's been started and suddenly left. The village where Nadia lived was perched on top of a crag a few miles off the main road, up a dusty track which only four-wheel-drive vehicles could climb. I don't know what predators live out in those mountains, but the people build their dwellings like fortresses. Most of the mud-built, multi-storey village houses were clamped together in a kind of warren against the mountainside around a big dusty yard. There were only about twenty-five families there.

According to the two operatives I sent up there, the men of the village gathered together and prayed, as good Muslims do, every morning at sunrise. This was the only time during daylight hours when the men would be separated from their rifles. So if Nadia and her children were to be taken out of the village, the best time to do it would be first thing in the morning when the husbands and fathers were at prayer.

We couldn't get her out to the north or east. Thousands of miles of Saudi Arabia lay to the north, and Oman was south-east along the coast. There were checkpoints on the roads from the mountains south to Tai'zz and then to San'á and Aden. The Red Sea coast was not so very far away from her village, to the west of it, but there was no road there, and mountains to cross. There was no airport that Nadia and her children, who all had Yemeni nationality, would be allowed to leave from. Territorial waters were efficiently patrolled. The only possible way out was by rescue helicopter.

Lawrence was now back in England, so I felt pretty sure the Iceland crisis had blown over. I flew to London and drove up the M1 to Birmingham. Zana and Miriam lived in modest circumstances in spite of all the money from the book. It was heartbreakingly obvious that every spare penny they had was going into this last bid to get Nadia back. I had to tell them that the only way ISS, as a professional rescue organization, could return her to them would be to mount a small-scale military operation. Back-of-an-envelope calculations made me think it would cost well over £100,000.

They both wanted to go ahead. Miriam insisted that her French publisher would pay her a hundred grand advance. However, she was nervous about dealing with him. To hear this woman, you'd think she couldn't cross the road by herself. She would have to go to Paris, she said, and she didn't know the language and didn't like big hotels. She wanted somebody to go with her. In the end I sent a bodyguard and hired an interpreter for the meeting, but it wasn't necessary as the Frenchman spoke perfect money. According to Miriam, he said in clear English that he would pay her a £100,000 advance against future sales. If the rescue cost more, he would pay for it out of his own pocket.

The funds were in place, so I went ahead, sat down with the operatives who had been in Yemen and worked out a detailed plan. We looked at it from every angle and there were two options: flying in under Yemeni air force radar from Djibouti, or flying in from a ship off the Red Sea coast. The Djibouti plan meant a fuel problem, not to mention possible interception by the Yemenis. Djibouti was not a great place for chopper hire anyway. The only way round the problems was to buy a used helicopter, hire a pilot, ship them both up the Red Sea coast and set off on the twenty-minute flight inland from there. Once over the village, our team (including myself) would repel down a rope, hold the men at gunpoint and take the family back up into the helicopter one by one.

The plan was minute-sensitive. Nothing could go wrong, and the only way you can guard against anything going wrong is to plan and prepare. That was exactly what we couldn't do; there was no way of getting to know the village beforehand and Zana and Miriam had hardly any contact with Nadia. For all we knew, we might shin down our rope at five in the morning only to find her in the throes of yet another confinement. However, on balance, Ann and I thought the plan looked good and we discussed it with Zana and Miriam. They said we should go ahead. They wired money into the ISS account and we set the whole thing up. We put people on standby, started looking for a helicopter, and were checking suitable dates when – Sarah Ali came back into the frame.

Sarah had got tired of waiting. In Los Angeles she met a man called Logan Clarke, who said he was an ex-US Navy Seal, a Marine commando. He said if she could come up with $40,000 he would get her children back. She remortgaged her house and he approached a TV production company that made a show called *Hard Copy* and told them what he proposed to do. They lent him a camera. He, some operatives he'd hired and Sarah went to the Yemen.

I knew nothing of all this at the time. Sarah was the last person on my mind, busy as I was trying to hire ships, sort out personnel and find a pilot and a boat for Nadia's rescue. But I saw the *Hard Copy* programme later. Logan Clarke left the camera running, fly-on-the-wall style, in his hotel room somewhere in Yemen while he and the others discussed tactics. They were talking about getting the children off the coast in a Zodiac and he didn't seem to know one end of a Zodiac from another. The rescue went disastrously wrong.

All the men flew back to California and Sarah was left in Yemen to fend for herself. The first thing I knew about it was a frantic call from her sister. Within days Sarah phoned ISS from Oman, hundreds of miles east. Having been raped by a couple of locals, she had finished up in hospital where the doctors diagnosed bowel cancer. She was now going to have a colostomy before flying back.

At the same time, there was civil unrest in Yemen, and Miriam rang ISS to tell them to do no more for the moment as the situation was dangerous. Then it all went quiet. Years later, I saw a television programme in which Nadia insisted that she wanted to stay right where she was.

Logan Clarke began a career in television on the back of that *Hard Copy* programme. As for Sarah, her predicament touched the heart of at least one other person. Apparently a genuinely kind man, he sold his house and used the money to take her to Djibouti. There they hired a boat to sail across the channel between the continents. It is barely twenty-four miles wide at one point, and the sea was not rough, although the waters are patrolled. They were never seen again. According to the State Department, both Sarah and her companion are missing, presumed dead.

24

Nineteen ninety-three had not been a good year. Call me predictable, but I couldn't think of Iceland without a shudder. Now, when I was supposed to quit the Circuit the following summer, I knew I hadn't achieved all I wanted.

I needed time off to rest and think. My sisters went to Hawaii every year and I sometimes joined them; I loved the place. There was a strong Spiritualist tradition in the island, and I visited a medium there. He told me that I had been pretending to be other people for much too long. I should learn to look into myself. I should find out about the real Jacquie.

I didn't have a clue where to start. You look back, you see what happened, what you've learned, but there's no particular pattern to it. However, I decided to stay in Hawaii for a while. I could keep in touch with North Carolina by e-mail and fax.

I rented a house in Kailua, on the Oahu coast not far from Honolulu. It was a big low place, high on a hill, with a lawn surrounded by mango trees and banana palms. I swam, went scuba diving and woke up every morning to a view across the red roofs of neighbouring houses to the Pacific; it was the sort of place where you can take big decisions. Or in my case, avoid them.

When Thomas came to Hawaii early in 1994, he didn't point out that this would be the year of my retirement. We both knew I wasn't ready to discuss it. I was flying back and forth to the East Coast regularly, running ISS courses in close protection and evasive driving techniques. Child rescues were coming in all the time and I still had a lot of plans. We hadn't even talked about where we would live, if I quit. For his part, Thomas still loved the Caribbean and he wasn't ready to retire. My five-year-old promise to stop work hung between us, not quite confronted.

I had a neighbour called Tammy, a cheerful tanned woman married to a Marine sergeant and with a couple of small blond children. The US Marine Corps air base was just up the road and I knew her husband, Dale, and a lot of other Marines from the diving club. Tammy and I occasionally stopped to pass the time of day in the supermarket or on the beach. Whenever we talked, she seemed to be about to spend an evening at something called a Coda course. All her friends, who were other Marine wives, went to the Coda course as well. I asked what it was about and she said her husband was on Level Three and it was a support group. I was more bemused than ever but too busy to get involved. It was like my Spiritualism or Ann's born-again Christianity – one of those private things. And as usual, I had a plane to catch.

It was a shady estate of ranch-style houses in Florida. As I walked across the lawn to a big two-storeyed house in the trees, I got that sinking feeling. I had been handling meetings with bereaved relatives since I was eighteen years old and in uniform, but it is never easy. The man had sounded calm enough on the telephone, but the controlled ones are some-times the quickest to break down.

'Our daughter was killed in a car accident three months ago,' he had said. 'But our grandkids are still down there in Colombia.'

The door was opened by a composed, fair-haired matron in her sixties. She took me to meet her husband. We sat out of doors in the late afternoon watching sprinklers sway twinkling fountains of water on to the grass. The man was stooped, silent, as if defeated by the tragedy.

'The boy's eight and the girl's five,' his wife told me. 'They're all we've got of Carrie now.'

'But how come they're in Colombia?'

'They've bin raised by Carrie's ex-husband's family. They're wealthy people. The little girl was born down there.'

'So shouldn't they stay there with them?'

'Carrie left him when the girl was one year old. She went back to him last year and then she came away to us again. She said there was a bad business goin' on, with those kids.'

'What exactly?'

The woman laid her left hand on her knee and began picking at the fingernails with her right. She looked hesitantly at her husband. He leaned forward and said to me, as if the neighbours several hundred yards away might hear, 'Their grandpa was interfering with both of 'em. And their father's got a brother, he's a pest. Carrie had trouble with him.'

'You think they're molesting them?'

'I'm certain of it. I wanna get them back,' the old man said.

'Have you got photographs of the children?'

'That's the crazy thing. That family never sent Carrie one picture. She didn't have one with her when she . . .'

'Among her effects,' finished the woman quickly. 'There

wasn't a picture.' She took her husband's hand. 'The kids are all we've got left of Carrie.'

They spelled out their daughter's married name, Da Souza, and the family's address in Medellin. Buddy got it checked out and rang me.

'First the good news,' he said. 'These guys have got nothing on them for paedophile stuff.'

'Not that we know of.'

'Not that we know of, right. But we know a lot. We practically know what shoe size they take already. The Da Souzas are one of the families in the Medellin cartel.'

'Ah.'

'And Ann and I think it'd be cool for you to go in undercover, Jacquie.'

And these were my friends. However, Bud was right about the shoe size. Short of DNA mapping and old school reports, there wasn't much more that we needed to know about the kids' father. His name was Lambaro, he was five feet eleven and thirty-nine years old and he lived in an extended family with his parents and brothers and their children. The head honcho was his own father, the one the Florida grandfather thought was a child abuser. Old Da Souza had an excellent relationship with other members of the local cocaine cartel, with certain senior military men in government, with one or two judges, and undoubtedly with influential members of the police force. So if I fell flat on my face I wouldn't expect help from Victim Support.

We would figure out how to get the children out later. My first task was to get inside the house, report back on the general situation and take photographs of the children. As there were more than just the two children living in the house, without some means of identifying the right ones we could hardly start planning to get them out of the country. The grandparents were convinced that they'd be able to name them from the pictures I took.

'This is the most exciting thing,' the woman told me on the telephone. 'I'm so thrilled I'm going to see pictures of my grandchildren. You'll get them out of there, I know you will.'

'One step at a time,' I said.

I flew to Colombia from Heathrow, just in case anybody checked up on me. Medellin was a hilly city high up in the mountains and had a wild, frontier feel to it in spite of all the factories chucking smoke into the sky. Young men roamed the streets looking sultry, and the women wore tight, short-skirted Californian power suits and their black hair long. There was a good life here. In the afternoons people sat about at pavement cafés under shady trees, eating ices and gossiping to the constant racket of overheating traffic. All the men drove like maniacs, roaring up to corners in top gear, holding a fist on the klaxon if the lights were slow to change and yelling ribald comments out of car windows at the girls.

I got a taxi straight to the Hilton. It was one of the few western hotels in town and a DEA intelligence report said the Hilton bar was where Lambaro hung out. I had studied photographs of him and knew exactly when he should turn up and who was likely to be with him. On the night after my arrival I entered the bar and immediately caught sight of him drinking at a table in the corner with his cronies. I sat on a high stool at the bar and skimmed the pages of a magazine. Lambaro and his party were ordering trays of drink from the waiter. Soon most of the tables were occupied, largely by locals rather than hotel guests. I bought an aperitif and chatted quietly to the barman, asking him questions about the city.

At last Lambaro approached the bar and ordered a drink.

'You are English?'

'Yes.'

'What is it you are looking for?'

'A church, a swimming pool, a public park, a restaurant . . . You look confused. I am writing a book. I need to find these places.'

'Oh I see! You are writing a book. What kind of book?'

'It's a love story.'

'A love story! A love story that takes place in Medellin? I hope the hero is tall, dark and handsome.'

'He is.'

'You must let me show you these places. I know the town very well. I was born here.'

So kind, so close.

'You speak English very well. What do you do?'

'Ah, that is a secret.'

'No really, tell me.' I smiled and put my hand on his arm. He laughed.

'Why is Colombia famous?'

'Mmm . . . Coffee?'

He laughed again.

'Coffee. Of course. Anything else?'

'I can't think of anything.'

I had overplayed it. Nobody could be this dumb. I saw a flicker of suspicion, but he said, 'You are nice, you will come in my car tomorrow and I will show you everything you want to see.'

At eleven the following morning I was summoned to the lobby. Lambaro stood beaming in casual clothes.

'Come, we will go for a drive.'

Outside, two limousines had pulled up. Bodyguards had assembled around a heavy armour-plated Mercedes. One of them held the rear door open for me. I got in, the bodyguard got in after me and Lambaro was ushered in at the other side. Two men sat in front and we pulled away with two more bodyguards in the following limo. I was feeling the teeniest bit crowded. A message was being delivered, none too subtly. I chose to ignore it. I told myself that women who write Aga sagas set in South America probably get this sort of treatment all the time.

Lambaro was very friendly, showed me some lovely old churches and parks and took me for lunch at a pavement café. There was no mention of any wife, ex-wife or dead wife. As far as Lambaro was concerned, he had never been married; which rather put the mockers on asking him about his offspring. Would I have dinner with him tonight? he asked. I accepted. We were getting on rather well, I thought, given the pack of lies being peddled on both sides.

I was lying on my bed figuring out some literary excuse to get invited to his house when he rang at six o'clock.

'Tonight I would like to invite you to have dinner with my family,' he announced. 'I shall send the car in one hour.'

He certainly had lovely manners, did old Lambaro. And to be invited to meet the family, so soon! Perhaps I should entertain expectations. It was quite enough to turn a girl's head. In the shower I tried to imagine myself telling Thomas that I was giving him up in favour of marriage to one of the world's major cocaine suppliers. At least he would see the funny side. That, I decided, was the main thing wrong with Lambaro, apart from his conceit, his lies and his drug trafficking. No sense of humour.

The bullet-proof Merc swished out of town and up to the mountains. Everything was green and lush. The car wound upwards for twenty minutes along progressively narrower roads. We passed a high wall and turned through curlicued iron gates to the courtyard of a villa. Armed guards patrolled the boundary wall and waved the car through the gate.

Fountains played in the courtyard. Lambaro appeared, smiling, at the top of the steps that led to the front door.

'Jacquie, my dear. It is so kind of you to come.'

A short fat glowering bandido in expensive threads had appeared behind him.

'You must meet my father.'

Da Souza was over sixty, one of those guys with rough edges who is always going to be a short fat bandido even if you dress him out of Savile Row. But he got a lot of respect. Everyone, especially the crowd of small dark children who now tumbled out to meet me, deferred to him, and the armed guards were practically wetting themselves. His wife was a handsome woman of about sixty, very elegant, with a high-bridged Spanish nose and perfectly plucked eyebrows. She wore her hair in a tight bun and smiled a lot. She had no English; none of the older women did, I was to discover.

On a terrace overlooking the swimming pool high on the mountainside, cousins and brothers and sisters had gathered for drinks. The children ran about between grown-ups, happy in their own world. I wished I spoke Spanish, because I would have liked to have found out whose kids these were and work out the right ones by a process of elimination, but it could wait. I was kept busy answering questions. It was mostly the men who asked me about the book I was writing. By the time we went in to dinner, I was starving, but I had pretty much formulated the plot of a saleable Mills and Boon.

The children were despatched to some other part of the house before dinner. The rest of us ate a delicious meal at a long table in a panelled dining-room. Afterwards, in classic macho style, the men stayed to smoke cigars and the women repaired to the terrace where some of them actually picked up tapestry. A senior army officer arrived at about eleven o'clock, emerging from the house with his peaked cap in hand to pay his respects to Madame, Lambaro's mother.

It was a lovely place. I could look across the pool to the jungly edges of the property and the lights of Medellin on the hillsides below, and I could smile and nod, but that was about it. Without Spanish, I could not contribute a great deal to this gathering. At eleven-thirty I returned to the city. Lambaro, ushering me into the bullet-proof motor with gentlemanly courtesy and a tender kiss on my hand, assured me that he would call the next day.

The next day he rang me at the Hilton. He was devastated, today he was entirely occupied with business. But I must spend the weekend at the house, he insisted. The pool would be at my disposal. The car would arrive after lunch tomorrow.

When Saturday afternoon came I was shown to a bedroom overlooking the entrance. I put a swimming costume on under my wrap, and went out to the terrace with a little camera in my pocket. All the children were splashing about in the blue water below or running on the surrounding grass.

There were seven or eight of them, and the eldest was about ten. Behind them, beneath the blue sky, the city lay steaming in a heat haze. I saw the guards watching me and suspected they might think this was no place for holiday snaps.

I swam for half an hour and exchanged smiles and nods with the charming ladies at the pool. I learned the names of the children; none of them were the names I had been given in America, but that didn't necessarily signify. The guards seemed to have lost interest so I risked a few photographs while their backs were turned. There was a small boy and girl nearer the house, so I moved behind them as if to get the scenery in the background. Out of the corner of my eye I saw a manservant scuttle indoors.

'Jacquie, how are you?' Lambaro appeared smoothly at my side. 'I hope you are enjoying yourself. I should be spending more time with you.'

'Oh, but you're so busy.'

'Unfortunately, yes. So much work.' I tried to envisage what international drug supremos did all day and came up with something out of a Second World War film involving maps and deployment of resources. He gazed at me with rapt attention and pushed my hair away from my face. 'But I promise you that this evening you shall have the whole time with me. After dinner tonight, we will spend a little time together, I think.' He kissed my shoulder. Then he kissed my other shoulder. 'Until this evening, Jacquie.'

I should coco. Half an hour later I made my exit to the bedroom. I stashed the film in my handbag, took my make-up off with lots of grease, and lay down with a magazine. Time for dinner. I didn't move.

At last there was a knock on the door.

'*Señorita*?'

An elderly servant poked her concerned face around the door. I groaned. I turned over. I pointed at my stomach.

Five minutes later, up he came.

'Jacquie, my dear, do you need a doctor?'

'Oh.'

I closed my eyes. An hour passed. A doctor arrived. He prodded my stomach.

'Oh. Oh.'

'Did you drink water?'

'Yes. In a café this morning.'

'Gastroenteritis.'

Soup arrived. I left it to get cold, swilled it around my mouth, stuck my fingers down my throat and threw up in the lavatory. I didn't bother to pull the chain.

Lambaro returned.

'Lambaro, I am sick. I must go back to the hotel.'

He insisted that I stay overnight. He ran a finger tenderly along the nape of my neck. He bent over me in concern. I groaned, turned towards him and breathed a soupy gust in his direction. His head was suddenly withdrawn.

I left in the morning for the hotel and was on the first flight out on Monday.

The photographs were developed in Miami. They were pretty definitive pictures, given the stress I had been under when I took them; if there was any resemblance to Carrie, it would show up. I spent a whole afternoon with the grandparents and those photographs, but it was no good. They could not be sure which of the children were hers. I left a couple of very sad old people behind at that house.

*

'Colombia?' Thomas's voice crackled on the phone. 'Are you crazy?'

'It was fine. I was only there for a few days.'

'Jacquie, your luck can't last for ever. Remember what you said. The time has come.'

'Yes.'

'So?'

'You mean the five years are over. I know, Thomas. I'm thinking about it. I'm tying up loose ends.'

'And you're staying in Hawaii while you tie them up.'

'Just for a few months.'

'You said that before. And now I turn my back for two minutes and you're in Colombia. You have to learn to say no. You can't keep going off on these mad jobs just because people ask you. One day you will be in trouble.'

He was working towards his own retirement with no faith that I'd ever give up the Circuit. At first, I hadn't trusted him. Now, he didn't trust me.

'What's Level Three?'

I was in Kailua, ambling up the beach road with Tammy.

'It's like, when you've had an alcohol problem or drugs, it's like the Marines say – this is your last chance. If this doesn't work, pal, you're out of the service. It's a residential course for six weeks. First they do detox, then they go on a twelve-step AA program. You know the big pink hospital on the hill?'

'Uh-huh.'

'Dale was up there.'

I wasn't all that surprised her husband had a problem. One of the younger Marines had hinted at it.

'So he drinks?'

'He's got a coke habit.'

I was shocked. I had always been told that cocaine addiction was nature's way of telling you you had too much money. I had seen a lot of drug abuse when I was part of the security team that clamped down on 'Heaven', a club in the West End of London. We were talking about a Marines sergeant here, for God's sake, married with children, who lived on the beach and went diving.

'How can he afford it?'

'He can't. We can't, Jacquie. In any sense.'

One of the marines had invited me to a party that night, as it happened. I don't know what I expected. Maybe it wasn't going to be the policeman's ball. Maybe people would get pissed and fall over. Make fools of themselves. Fight, even, though I hoped not.

You could say I was totally unprepared.

I walked in to a riotous crowd and within minutes I'd been offered a line of cocaine. Marijuana was being smoked wherever I looked. I got a drink, talked to a few people and hated what I was seeing. Most of the Marines here had wives, young women they had already introduced me to at the beach, and nearly all of them were slobbering over a flashy girl or another man.

The Marine who'd invited me was giggling in a corner with a friend of his. I pushed a path through the room and grabbed his arm. He was a good-looking corporal in his twenties.

'What's going on here?'

'What?'

He saw the disgust on my face and took me out on the veranda. His friend followed.

'What's the matter?'

'How can you guys behave like this?'

'Am I getting the right message here . . . ? Jacquie, you have a problem with this party?'

'You're all fucking yourselves up. All these drugs.'

'We're adult. We can handle it.'

'People get addicted to that stuff.'

His friend put his arm round my waist.

'None of us are addicts, honey.' He grinned at me. 'We've been medically discharged from addiction. That's official.'

I was bewildered. The Marine corporal looked uneasy.

'Maybe this isn't the right place for you, Jacquie. Some of us are just, like, letting go. We've come outta Level Three. If you know what that is. Can I take you home?'

'No, thanks. I'll make my own way.'

I went back inside the house. I wanted the loo, and struggled across a couple of rooms full of people and up some stairs. The door at the top usually led into the bathroom. I opened it. On a bed, Tammy's husband, Dale, shut his eyes and moaned. He was getting sucked off by a young Marine I knew.

I turned and got out.

'They treat us as well,' Tammy said.

'They treat the wives?'

'Sure. Women keep making the same mistakes, you know. Some of us have been married to abusers before. So on the Coda course we find out what makes us keep going back for more, and change it. Coda stands for co-dependency.'

'What's that?'

'Come to a meeting and find out.'

I'd got nothing better to do and frankly I was fascinated. Did Tammy or her friends have the first idea what sleazebags their husbands really were? As I locked the house door that evening it crossed my mind that maybe I should stay indoors with a good book. I was humiliating these women, going to their therapy group to spectate. It was hard not to feel superior. My own marriage had been awful, but I had known no better in those days and I hadn't repeated my mistake.

They met at a big house about three miles away. When I got there, eight women were about to sit down on chairs in a semicircle in the garden. I knew most of them already; they all had kids and I'd met them at barbecues or the beach or with their husbands, diving. The facilitator of the group asked them all in turn how the week had gone and they told her.

'Joe was, like, he's going to take the boy up to his buddy's for an hour before we go down to the beach.'

'So, what would have happened before?'

'Little Joe and me would have been stuck home all day while he stayed up there drinking. He'd'a come home, we'd'a had a fight. You know . . .'

'So what happened this time?'

'I was, like, this is what happens when we go down this road, and how it made me real hurt inside just thinking about it. And Little Joe wanted to do something else. And I came up with alternatives. A whole other plan for the day. I kept on like that.'

'And?'

'He was kinda surprised that I was talking. Like before, I'd react to him. It was, like, because we both knew I was gonna get hurt, he could get to play wife-beater. This time I was

294

laying it on the line. I was saying, we both know I could get hurt, the kid could get hurt, and we none of us want that. The road starts here. So let's go in a different direction.'

'But he still wanted a drink with his buddies.'

'Sure he did. But he's working on that too. Like before, he felt like I'm Joe, I'm a drinker. Now I'm treating him different, I'm helping him to get a different identity.'

I was surprised, the way they picked out small incidents to illuminate something. They were a lot more self-aware than it had ever occurred to me to be. They were people who were trying to get control of out-of-control situations.

One of them was at the group for the first time. She complained a lot. Her husband was always out or asleep, he spent all their money on heroin, she had to do everything because without her the family would fall apart. Her complaints sounded pretty reasonable to me. She was right. What else could she do?

'It doesn't matter how hard I try, I can't do the right thing.' She started to cry. 'He just, like, blames me for everything.'

The facilitator and the others in the group started asking her about her marriage. He had been a smackhead since his earliest years in the Marines. Why had she married him?

'I thought he'd change.'

'Why?'

'I guess I thought I could show a shining example.' She gave a timid laugh. Nobody had been interested in her for years, nobody had listened, and now here were eight or nine people who wanted to know exactly what was going on. 'I thought, if I was good, like, if I cleaned house and cooked like his mom and looked nice and never slipped up, he would appreciate me.'

'You mean, he'd feel sorry for being bad to you.'

'Yeah, I guess.'

'He'd see you as a martyr and be real contrite. "I bin so bad, I got a saint here and I owe her." That stuff.'

'Yeah. In the back of my mind that was what I thought.'

'Your daddy expect all that from you?'

'Sure, my dad's got real high expectations. He used to beat us if we didn't do what he wanted. It never did us any harm.'

The others laughed and she looked surprised for a minute. I didn't get it either, at first.

'What do you think, Jacquie?'

'Erm . . . I . . .'

'What about *you*?'

It was perfect timing. It was what I had been looking for: some kind of explanation. Why did I need to work so hard? Why was I so desperate to be strong and independent? Why did I always mistake help for condescension? Why did I always see myself as a rescuer? Why could I not play any part other than Saint George? Over the weeks that followed I went to every co-dependency meeting. I listened to the others and found in their accounts a lot in common with my own patterns of behaviour. I understood why I had been trying so hard to please.

I didn't have to try and impress other people. I didn't have to risk my life at the drop of a hat. 'You're no good to me dead,' Thomas had said. He was right. What I had to do was find out what Jacquie wanted.

25

I couldn't stop work straight away. I went back to England
and began to wind my business up. My reputation was shot
to pieces since the *Observer* article, so I didn't exactly expect
people off the Circuit to be beating a path to my door. At
Christmas, I told Thomas I would definitely come to him in
the spring. Yet somehow by the end of February I still had
too much on to just drop everything.

'Jacquie, you said this before. I'm ready. I'm just waiting
for you to say you are ready, too.'

Thomas was on the phone from the Caribbean. In my
mind's eye I saw the serious way he looked when he said this
sort of thing.

'But not just yet. I've gotta –'

'You know, I am beginning to think you have a problem.
You sound like an addict.'

'How can you say that?'

'It's true. You get a high from being on the Circuit. That's
what you're going to miss.'

'Oh, for God's sake. I don't need this.'

I was furious. I thought I knew myself pretty damn well
since my psychological co-dependency had become crystal
clear. The last thing I needed was amateur psychoanalysis
from my boyfriend. The arrogance of it. I happened to be
away working for six weeks after that and we didn't speak.

At Easter, just as I was desperate to break the silence between us, he wrote me a sweet letter of invitation to an annual gala dinner in Hamburg.

We made it up. He was wonderfully kind, he was romantic, he gave me a lovely wristwatch and I knew then that we both cared about each other so much that we had to be together for good. I must be the one to make the effort. Only by now I had taken on so many little bits of work that things were starting to snowball again. If I stopped now I would be letting people down.

We talked a lot, the whole weekend in Hamburg. I told him everything that had become clear to me since the co-dependency course and how I was seriously trying to extricate myself from commitments. We came to an agreement. I set myself a serious deadline. By the end of September, I would quit. I promised him that after September I would never take another job on the Circuit, and I meant it.

It was July, this would be one of my last assignments, and I needed some sunshine, so I was quite pleased when I had to follow my target to the Spanish coast near Marbella. He was my client's husband, and I had been watching him for weeks.

Madeleine was an elegant woman in her early fifties. Her husband had an interesting job and travelled all over Europe, while she shopped and lunched and got her hair done. They owned a big house in Hampstead and an apartment in Spain. They were, by all conventional standards, very successful.

'He's having an affair, I just know it,' she said. 'He's been different ever since we went to Spain after Christmas. I think he met somebody down there. He hardly ever came back to the apartment, he was always out. And it's the same story now. He's got appointments in the evenings, he has to spend all these weeks away. I just want to know who it is, that's all.'

'Have you asked him?'

'Yes. He said what you'd expect a man to say. I was being neurotic and it must be the change of life. We've been together for thirty years.'

I began to follow him around London. He was grey-haired, red-faced, chubby, short and rather anxious-looking, with two chins. You wouldn't notice him in a crowd. I was sure he must have wonderful qualities but, sadly, I couldn't see anyone falling in love with him. He was probably a regular little dynamo at work, but apart from one or two descents into a dubious basement bar near his office, where he had a quiet drink and left, he led a social life of extreme timidity. I never saw him talk to any women. He was so predictable, he even drove out to Heathrow when he said he was going abroad.

Once there, though, he didn't fly to Milan for a week as he had told Madeleine; he got on a plane to Malaga. So maybe she had been right. Maybe he did have a girlfriend in Spain.

'He's going away again in a fortnight,' Madeleine told me. 'He says it's Frankfurt, but wherever it is, I want you to follow him.'

I checked up. He had bought another return flight to Malaga, and was going to stay there a week. She gave me the phone number of the English people who owned the apartment next door to theirs. I rang them and arranged to rent their flat for the week the husband was there. Now all

I needed was a companion. I would feel a lot less conspicuous if two of us went, and Emma, a friend of mine, had just got her divorce through. She was feeling low and jumped at the chance of a week in the sun.

It was a pretty little town on a headland, with a gritty beach and rocks to sunbathe on, and a friendly promenade of bars and shops. The apartment building was more like a spreading Spanish house, festooned with ivies and pelargonia and having balconies all round. You could lie out on the balcony in dark glasses and a sunhat and pretend not to listen to what was going on next door. I spent the entire first morning out there. The couple on the other side were at it like rabbits before breakfast, which was fascinating but unimportant. From the errant husband's flat, not a sound. If he had a woman in there, she was either asleep, dumb or she'd got a headache. But perhaps he was waiting for her to arrive.

All that day, which was a Friday, I watched him. He ambled off to the shops at about ten and bought some groceries; then he ambled back. Emma, who was enjoying herself and, I suspected, working through some of her own issues around infidelity in husbands, watched him at the mini-market and said she couldn't tell whether he was buying enough stuff for two people for two days or one person for four. I was none the wiser. I heard him coming into the flat and nobody greeted him.

By the end of the morning I was pretty sure he was on his own. Maybe he was having some sort of business crisis, I thought. Maybe he wanted to get away from creditors or flog the business and follow the Path of Enlightenment or something, and didn't want to share his troubles with his wife. This was probably a wild goose chase with no woman in the story at all.

He sat on the beach most of the afternoon, with a book.

At six o'clock he was back in the apartment and I heard the shower running. At seven-thirty he left, with me and Emma a hundred yards behind him. He walked purposefully down to the seafront, past the tourists drinking at tables in the dusk, and into one of the bars. This was more like it. I was sure he was going to meet somebody; he wasn't smartly dressed or leaving a pungent trail of aftershave, it was just the way he seemed to know exactly where he was going.

When we came into the place five minutes later, he was sitting at a table with his book and a drink. On his own. A paunchy English holidaymaker of fifty in a pale yellow polo shirt and grey slacks, minding his own business on the Costa. He could have robbed a bank in the next five minutes, and if you'd put out that description there would have been dozens like him brought in straight away.

'Hello, girls, what can I do you for?'

I was sure I had seen the barman somewhere before. He was conspicuously tall, about forty, with receding hair worn long at the back like a seventies footballer, and dressed (Spanish theme, innit) in a black embroidered waistcoat and a white shirt with full, bloused sleeves. We sat at the bar, so that I could keep an eye on the front door, and looked around. It was quiet so early in the evening; just me and Emma, the target, and a few other tourists starting to drift into the one big dimly lit room with a stage at one end and a dais for a band over to the side.

We asked for a couple of glasses of sangria.

'Down for the week, are you?'

'Yes, it's nice here, isn't it? D'you live here all year round?'

'I do, indeed. You nurses, are you?'

'Yes, how did you know?'

'We get a lot of nurses.'

It was the waistcoat that rang the bell at last. Its silver embroidery looked just like the coat of arms on the board outside HMP Brixton. Years ago, one of my policeman friends in Marbella had pointed this barman out as the driver of a getaway vehicle in a famous robbery. Well, at least he had put his ill-gotten gains to good use. He was very friendly, the life and soul, and in the next hour the bar began to fill up nicely. I could no longer see the target but he hadn't left and nobody had joined him until five minutes ago. I got up to go to the loo.

His chair was empty, though the rest of his table was occupied by a noisy group from the north of England, and I decided he must have gone to the Gents. I went back to the bar.

'Can you see him?' I murmured to Emma. 'Did he go out?'

'No, I've been watching the door.'

The barman looked across at our long faces.

'The cabaret's coming up now,' he said, encouragingly. He leant over to take my glass. 'You'll die, honest. Can I get you another?'

I was considering a Campari and soda when a sudden Twang! boomed from a speaker above my head. I nearly fell off my stool. I swivelled around open-mouthed. Lights had gone up on stage, illuminating a false marble column and a black backdrop. As I watched, fascinated, an immensely tall, glamorous transvestite, robed from head to toe in a lemon satin flamenco frock, all diving décolletage and a black polka dot frou-frou on the fishtail skirt, swayed on to the stage, seized the mike and began to mime a loud and passionate song. I tore my eyes away and scanned the crowd.

'D'you think we've lost him?'

'I can't see him anywhere.'

Emma had been struggling through the audience, trying not to look as if she was looking for him. I decided to finish my drink before I went walkabout to see if I could find the target further along the prom. I couldn't leave now; the singer was terrific. He wore a curly black wig like Joan Collins and looked half blind from sheer weight of mascara. Stomping his heels and clacking his maraccas, he swanned off stage blowing kisses and tossing paper roses. Beneath the applause and catcalls the record changed.

Out of the wings bounded a second figure: a shorter and altogether tubbier one, in a black halter-neck swimsuit with white straps and fringes and an outsized conical bra clamped firmly on top. As Madonna teetered on her stilettos, tossed back her wild blond hair and pouted her scarlet lips, I recognized the two chins.

'Like a VIRGIN –' she bellowed.

Speech almost deserted me.

'Em, it's 'im.'

I nearly fell off my stool. I dug Emma in the ribs.

'What? Where?'

She was peering at the front door.

'It's HIM!'

'On the very FIRST DATE –'

Emma got the giggles and spluttered sangria down her nose. A woman from Scarborough was laughing so much she looked in need of medical attention. My target was the sensation of the evening.

'Who are they?' I gasped at the barman. 'Do they work together?'

He flicked a limp wrist.

'*Well*, love. They're good friends.'

I went back the following night and took holiday snaps of the whole act. My target bawled a lovely 'Una Paloma Blanca' in bursting crimson flamenco with three tiers of frills and matching crimson lipstick. His upper arms were mottled fake bronze and the things that man couldn't do with an ostrich feather fan weren't worth doing. Oh, I did enjoy myself.

Breaking the news to the client was going to be a delicate task. I would have to keep a straight face, for a start. She rang me the night I got back.

'Did you see her?'

'Yes, I saw her. I think we'd better meet. I've got some photographs.'

'Wonderful. Shall we have tea? I'll be in Piccadilly tomorrow. Let's go to the Ritz.'

'Er . . . let's not. Perhaps somewhere a little less public?'

We met at Brown's Hotel. It is very quiet, very discreet and well upholstered, so if she burst into tears the sound of her sobs would be absorbed by wall-to-wall soft furnishings.

'Did you bring the pictures?'

'I did.'

I reached for my handbag.

'What's she like?'

'Very tall. Dark. Spanish.'

I took the Kodak pack from my bag and pulled out the

shot of the slender flamenco singer in the yellow satin dress.

'Oh my God,' she said. She looked dumbfounded. 'I never thought it'd be anybody like this. I can't compete.'

'It gets worse,' I said. I laid the shot of Madonna on the table.

She froze. She was leaning forward, and I couldn't see her face, but she did not move a muscle for about twenty seconds. Then she burst into hysterical giggles.

'I'm so sorry,' I said, poker-faced.

It didn't seem entirely the appropriate comment to make. Her shoulders were heaving, her eyes were streaming and she was lying back in her chair.

'It's such a relief,' she said, and exploded again. Women from the Shires were looking at us very oddly. I had to keep passing her tissues to wipe her eyes with.

'Why is it a relief?'

'I was thinking of sacking the maid,' she gasped. 'My underwear keeps disappearing.'

I often wonder what she did about it. I rather think they're still married. Anyway, I went home with a smile on my face.

Later that evening I got a phone call from Aruba, in the Dutch Antilles. It was the chief officer of Thomas's ship. I knew something was wrong.

'Now sit down. Calm down, Jacquie.'

Thomas had had a heart attack.

'Is he all right? I'm coming. Tell him I'm coming.'

'No, stop. There's no need for that. It is a mild attack only. He will be taken back to Europe before you have arranged a flight. You would have to fly to Caracas – just stay where you are.'

305

I spoke to the chief officer several times the next day and the day after. Thomas was in hospital, Thomas was fine. He'd be med-evacced home probably tomorrow. In the middle of a phone call to a friend I heard myself saying, 'This is the beginning of the end. If they take his ship away, he'll be lost.'

The chief officer kept saying Thomas was about to be flown back to Hamburg. It would take me a day to get there, as there was no airport on Aruba. But this was going on too long. I couldn't sleep, I was helpless. I got the telephone number of the hospital and rang up. I had to speak in Dutch to the ward sister.

'How is he?'

'Comfortable.'

'Please tell him I love him.'

'I can't tell him anything. He's unconscious. He can't hear.'

'But that's not a mild heart attack!' I said in English. And then, 'I'm flying out to see him.'

'No. He will arrive in Hamburg tomorrow.' She went away and came back with the flight number. At last I had something to do. I booked a flight to Hamburg that would arrive an hour before his.

I watched the arrivals board. He had landed, thank goodness. I would see him. I needed to see him, he needed me, we had to be together through this. I willed him to be strong. I strode up and down.

I was being paged. I heard my name on the Tannoy. Something was wrong. Two men from the shipping line were waiting at Information.

'We are very sorry –'

Thomas had had a second heart attack, literally on the tarmac. They had not been able to save him.

Some things you can't change, no matter how much psychological insight you think you have. Like the way you deal with death. I switch into organizational mode. I deal with the funeral arrangements and the will and the grieving relations and the flowers, the wake and the memories, and I have to tell myself I will carry on for the sake of other people.

At first, this was no different. His children and his first wife came to Hamburg. We grieved together. I brought his mother from Düsseldorf for the funeral. Not long afterwards, I took her back to live in East Berlin. She had lost her husband years ago, and now her only son; she had never been to the West until after the Wall came down, and there was nothing for her here now.

The second wife wanted Thomas's cabin cruiser. She had no right to it, as they had divorced with a full and final settlement, but she insisted. She announced that she intended to contest the will. Thomas's daughter was upset.

'Don't let her have it, Jacquie. Dad wouldn't want her to.'

I thought about this. I thought about the ugliness of a court case and the cruel behaviour of this woman and I said, 'We'll sink it.'

I drove to Vlissingen with Thomas's daughter and we pulled the plug. When we drove away we knew that over the next few hours the vessel would slowly subside to rest on the bottom of the marina.

Thomas was never coming back. He would not be there in September, we would never share the house in France, we would never sail the blue Caribbean together. Alone, a few weeks later, I took his ashes out into the Baltic and scattered them to the sound of 'The carnival is over'. That was when I realized that Thomas's death was different, after all.

In him, I had found what I wanted at last; and I had been too slow to see it. I had been too selfish: I had wanted to stay on the Circuit.

Everybody I have ever loved has now died. Without Thomas, there was no point in carrying on. If only I had understood that sooner.

Perhaps somebody was trying to tell me something. You can't have it all.

READ MORE IN PENGUIN

READ MORE IN PENGUIN

BIOGRAPHY AND AUTOBIOGRAPHY

Freedom from Fear Aung San Suu Kyi

Aung San Suu Kyi, human-rights activist and leader of Burma's National League for Democracy, was detained in 1989 by SLORC, the ruling military junta. In July 1995 she was liberated from six years' house arrest. *Freedom From Fear* contains speeches, letters and interviews, as well as forewords by Archbishop Desmond Tutu and Václav Havel and gives a voice to Burma's 'woman of destiny'.

Lucie Duff Gordon Katherine Frank

'What stays in the mind is a portrait of an exceptional woman, funny, wry, occasionally flamboyant, always generous-spirited, and firmly rooted in the social history of her day' – *The Times Literary Supplement*

Cleared for Take-Off Dirk Bogarde

'It begins with his experiences in the Second World War as an interpreter of reconnaissance photographs . . . His awareness of the horrors as well as the dottiness of war is essential to the tone of this affecting and strangely beautiful book' – *Daily Telegraph*

Mrs Jordan's Profession Claire Tomalin

The story of Dora Jordan and her relationship with the Duke of Clarence, later King William IV. 'Meticulous biography at its creative best' – *Observer.* 'A fascinating and affecting story, one in which the mutually attractive, mutually suspicious, equally glittering worlds of court and theatre meet, and one which vividly illustrates the social codes of pre-Victorian Britain' – *Sunday Times*

In Harm's Way Martin Bell

'A coruscating account of the dangerous work of a war correspondent, replete with tales of Bell dodging, and in one case not dodging, bullets across the globe in order to bring us our nightly news' – *Independent*